"IF WE CONCENTRATE ON ACCEPT-
ING OURSELVES, CHANGE WILL
HAPPEN. IT WILL TAKE CARE
OF ITSELF. SELF-ACCEPTANCE
IS SO HARD TO GET YOU CAN'T
DO IT A DAY AT A TIME. I'VE
FOUND THAT I NEED TO RUN MY
LIFE FIVE MINUTES AT A TIME."

Words like these have helped to
put many people on the road to
self-fulfillment. Dr. Lair's
ability to "tell it like it is"
reaches us on a very personal
level. In his own down-to-earth
language, Lair discusses such
ideas as:

Why we are so afraid of ourselves

Letting go as a life goal

Love—from your deepest heart

Discovering your sexuality

Touching people

"I AIN'T MUCH, BABY—BUT I'M ALL I'VE GOT."

BY

JESS LAIR, Ph.D.

FAWCETT CREST • NEW YORK

"I AIN'T MUCH BABY—BUT I'M ALL I'VE GOT."

THIS BOOK CONTAINS THE COMPLETE TEXT OF
THE ORIGINAL HARDCOVER EDITION.

Published by Fawcett Crest Books, a unit of CBS Publications, the Consumer Publishing Division of CBS Inc., by arrangement with Doubleday and Company, Inc.

ISBN: 0-449-23585-8

Printed in the United States of America

38   37   36   35   34   33   32. 31   30   **29**

DEDICATION

My name is Lair from the German lehrer—teacher—and while I am the man in the front of the room and the name on the front of the book, you who are my students and friends and loved ones are the teachers and the author. The miracle is that so much of so many of you are here. Each time I reread this book I feel your presences and I am deeply moved by your speaking again across the span of days, weeks, years—even from the grave itself. The honor and joy for me is in having been with you. And in having such a family, friends and students who were ready and waiting to love me. But first, last and always, this book is dedicated to my wife, Jackie, who so lovingly opened my eyes to most of these things and who so gently helps me down many of these paths.

CONTENTS

"I AIN'T MUCH,
BABY—BUT I'M
ALL I'VE GOT."

ONE

This Is All I Know

The ideas in this book reflect a search that I began when I was thirty-five years old. I had an advertising agency in Minneapolis. I also did some marketing consultant work; I told businessmen how to make out plans for their business, and in some cases, executives how to plan their lives. And I had the world's greatest plan for my own life. I was going to work ten to fifteen more years at a business I hated and detested. But I was going to work a lot harder and faster so I could make a lot of money and I could retire. I had that plan all written up and one day at lunch I showed it to my financial consultant and adviser.

He looked at the plan and made some suggestions on it, but I felt funny about the whole thing. And on the way back to the office, all of a sudden I had this very strange feeling. I think what happened was my heart said to my head, "Now look, if you are crazy enough to throw your whole life down a rat hole, chasing something that you don't believe in, that's fine. You can throw your whole life away for money and material gains. But this Norwegian heart, it ain't going to go along with you."

I had a heart attack on the way up the elevator. I staggered to my office and slumped forward on my desk until the worst of the pain went away. I got hold of a doctor in the building across the street and foolishly told him I felt well enough to walk over.

So I walked over. He laid me out flat on an examining table and found I was right in the middle of a heart attack. He called an ambulance, they put me on a stretcher and hauled me to the hospital.

As I lay there in that hospital bed, I thought to myself, "Boy, some way you've gone a long, long way down the wrong path through a whole, long series of rotten sick, destructive choices. You've gone into things that you've got no sense in being in. There is almost nothing left in your life of what you really are." And the resolution that I made, in one of those lucid moments when one is intensely calm, was *from this time on I am never again going to do something that I don't deeply believe in.* And that decision, made under that kind of pressure, has stuck with me pretty much ever since.

I went home from my heart attack. I sold my business. We had a big, five bedroom colonial in the richest suburb in the United States and I had given my wife a sports car for Christmas. We had a liquor bill that was higher in some months than what we now spend for groceries. We gave up all of that. And if I hadn't had the wife I had, I could never have made such a drastic change.

My wife and I and our five kids, two to twelve, moved to an old farmhouse that rented for $60 a month. The only way the heat got to the upstairs bedrooms was through a hole in the living room ceiling. The kids slept in sleeping bags because the cold upstairs would freeze water. We rented a couple of horses so we could have a little fun and I went back to college.

By moving to the farm, we had enough money to help get me through graduate school. The first year I earned a Master's Degree at the University of Minnesota. I found I enjoyed school so I stayed on and got a doctorate in psychology in the next two years. During these two years, I started teaching writing at the St. Paul campus and enjoyed that. When I finished my Ph.D., I stayed on two years at the university, but I kept wanting to move to Montana, so as soon as we could we did. My grandparents had pioneered in Montana and I had always wanted to live there.

But all during that time, I can see now, I was constantly looking for the principles of change. How do you take your life, when you've got it all bent out of shape, and make it into something halfway decent? And the thing I started looking for hard was the kind of ideas that would help get this life of mine back into some kind of shape, to help reverse some of the wrong trends in my life.

Socrates said, "know thyself." But what is striking to me as I look back on this process that started seven and a half years ago now, is that there are some new ideas around today to help me change and to help you change. There are some things in psychology now that really work. And most importantly, there is a lot of common sense psychology in us and all around us that we just need to open our eyes to.

I have seen people who had sunk to the rottenest, lowest levels man can possibly imagine, such as alcoholics lost in skid row. Some of them were so shaky they had to send a runner out for their wine. They were even afraid to go out in the street. They were so afraid of all people. And if the runner didn't come back with their wine, they had to figure out a way to get another buck and a half together so they could get somebody else to go out.

Every once in awhile a man in that kind of trouble who had hit bottom would look at his life and say to himself, "I'm going to grow. Because if I don't, I'm going to die." And he sees, "In my egotism and in my self-centeredness, I have put myself here. I was escaping all responsibility for my actions."

By hitting bottom and being hit as hard as he was by life, he is forced to concede, "Nobody else is to blame for this. None of the people I blamed are around me any more. I'm to blame for this. I caused this." And when he sees that, he is on his way. People like that can really turn their lives around.

I have walked into groups of people like these at Emotions Anonymous and Alcoholics Anonymous where the acceptance they had of me was like the warmth coming from a stove. (Emotions Anonymous and Alcoholics Anonymous are organizations for the emotionally troubled and alcoholics. They also have open meetings anyone can attend.) You could feel it. Absolutely, positively feel it. I'm not talking about some nebulous psychological notion. I'm talking about something I have experienced and that others have experienced and that is commonplace. You, and anyone else, could walk into one of those open meetings and you would feel the same acceptance that I have felt.

These people in Alcoholics Anonymous and Emotions Anonymous have found and are using the same basic ideas being explored by some psychologists today. The core idea can be expressed simply as an acceptance of yourself. Related to that is acceptance of others. This notion of acceptance works tremendously well.

I used to think that these ideas worked only because alcoholics and neurotics were in such extremely critical situations. It was life or death. And I thought, "How are you going to hit everyone on the head with a heart attack, or with alcoholism or with neuroticism so that they can turn their lives around, too?" But recently I have found I was wrong about this, and that not-so-troubled people can use these ideas to improve the quality of their lives.

My initial experience of ten years ago reflected some of my searching. I have found that college students are quite ready and able to take hold of their lives and make some changes so they reverse some of their self-destructive trends. They find they can grow a little in a day, instead of die a little, so they are the more beautiful people which each sees potentially within. As I watched my students grow, I thought, "Sure, but that's because college students are more open. They are more open-minded, not hardened like we adults."

A change in my thinking came when I spoke for three days to nursing supervisors from five states and got an even better response. I thought, "Well, that's kind of strange." Then I thought about it and it really wasn't. The older you get, the more experience in living you have. And the clearer the end result of some of these destructive tendencies becomes.

When you are younger, you can't see the implications of saying, "To heck with taking care of me, baby, I'm going to get that money, man. I've got to have that money to calm my nerves down. My need for money overwhelms me and I'll do anything for it." So you start down that path and at first you don't see any consequences of your decision. But when you've been around for thirty or forty years and seen more of the results of your mistakes, you can say, "There really isn't, in material things, what I thought was going to be there."

Then I realized these are ideas that both young people and old people and all the ages in between already believe in and can handle. You don't need to be sick and down and out to see the urgency and the necessity of them.

That, of course, is what we're concerned about right now. What is our potential for really living? What can we do? How and why should we find a different way of living our lives?

I see now that we've got the opportunity at any stage of our lives to take a hand in the things that happen to us. I started out in my life with some choices, and I kept branching off in different destructive directions. Had I exercised the kind of restraint I found at thirty-five when I was twenty-five, my life could have been, I think, different. But forty-five, fifty-five or ninety-five isn't too late to start.

I recently talked to sixty businessmen about this set of ideas. I got a better response from them than I got from a class of younger people. That's because some of you younger people, for reasons we will discuss later, have limits on the amount of courage that you have, you have limits on the amount of strength that you have. So many of my younger students find my ideas very frightening. And even though I say to them, "Hey, you don't need to *do* anything with the ideas I offer—you just need to understand them. That's all that I'll ask of you." Nevertheless, some can't stand even to listen.

Partly, it is because we are all frightened at what we will find in ourselves. The best example I have seen of this was a mother in my class who was really worried about what she might find deep down. She asked me, "What if I find I'm a sex maniac?" I didn't have a very good answer for her at the time, but now I have.

Since the question, I have seen hundreds of people reach deep within themselves. And always what they found has been a relief and a joy—both to the person himself and to those with him or her at the time. Anyone who dares to reach deep within themselves, finds something very wonderful. I have seen it happen so often that it is a commonplace to me now. Everyone who is willing to try finds a power and a glory and majesty within them that is just breathtaking.

One of my students expressed his thrill at seeing this in others and himself by saying, "Isn't it wonderful that I can be a real me and know how great that is. And also know that if someone doesn't respond to me, it's not the deep me that's wrong. It's just that I wasn't able to go deep enough into myself."

So the power, glory and majesty of you is waiting for you.

That sounds bold of me to say. But the mere fact you have this book and have been able to stand it so far suggests it's true for you too.

We are going to be confronted with one huge problem here and that is that your whole tradition of learning from books and classes has been so word-oriented. The problem with words is that they are very slippery things. And the thing we are trying to learn here is not words—we are trying to learn living. How can you talk about love? How can you talk about a father hugging a child with words? Would you rather have a hug—or would you rather have someone say, "I'd like to hug you?" Talking about something isn't the same as doing it.

Well, this is the problem: Words are tricky. And in this book, everything I say to you is wrong. It misses the whole mark. This book is not Truth. Because our finite minds cannot know Truth. We can only try to come as close as possible. And the closest I can come to truth is not in words but in the feeling behind them. So as you read, you must read between the lines because that's as close to Truth as you and I get. And you must see the inconsistencies and not let them bother you because we are talking about an infinitely complex life from a limited, finite view. When you catch me with two inconsistent ideas, the Truth is probably somewhere in between.

The ideal kind of teaching is that which goes on outside the classroom where it is all show and tell and no words. It is almost all teaching by example. Most of the young kids at Bridger Bowl in Bozeman, Montana, are good skiers. Most of them learned to ski by watching other kids skiing—and by just doing. They can't tell you how to ski "because you just do it," says some little kid as he goes whizzing down the hill. He is learning without words interposing.

In this book, you and I will have to overcome that problem. We're going to have to use words. But we must never make the mistake of confusing the words and the knowledge of the words with anything that is really important. The only thing, the only important objective of this book is *to be different*. If we are not going to be different, we are just using the words to fool ourselves.

Now it's very simple for me to teach you a whole lot of new words, a whole lot of new phrases, new explanations and new ways of looking at things. That is very simple. But it is very hard for you to overcome this schooling and bookish tendency so you can see that what we are talking about is a different way of being.

Let me give you an example. One of my summer school students was dean of students in a Midwestern college. When he would come home from class his two little girls would run to him but he was busy and said, "No, run along. I can't play with you. Daddy's got to study." And so they pestered him all afternoon and all evening as long as he was trying to work.

When he heard me talk about all the physical love the Zulus give their children, he said to himself, "Hey, they need some loving." So when he came home and his little girls came to him, he would sit down, pick them up on his knees and hold them. He asked them, "What have you been doing today and how has the day been going for you?" And they would tell him. But after a little while, they would get their fill. They would run off and play and he could go and study all night long without interruption because they were happy and he was happy. He had given his little girls what they needed. He had filled their cups that day.

In class one day he said, "You know, I've always had this big shell build up around me as the big Dean of Students. I can see now that last year I was kicking students out of college just by the numbers. They would walk in the door, I'd look at their records and say, 'you're out,' just like a computer."

So in the fall, he went back to the college and he called in his dean of men, dean of women and dean of student activities. He sat them down and told them his story. He said, "Look, I've been acting like a Prussian general here. It's dumb. I've been trying to live in a false case, and I'm going to get out of it and try to be a human being—me." Well, you can imagine the astonishment on the faces of those fellow staff members as the old Prussian turned soft-heart.

Later he wrote to me and said, "Jess, there is an unbelievable difference here. We've only got half the kids on probation this year that we had last year. The whole student body feels differently because four or five of the staff who were crucially concerned with the student body changed our way of working with them."

Well, this kind of thing is what we're after here. For this book to have an effect on your life, you must not read the words, you must get the spirit of the ideas.

An English major was reading the earlier, shorter version of this book. She had separated from her husband and a friend had recommended the book to her. She told me, "I was antagonistic when I started reading. I found two or three grammatical mistakes in the first few pages. Then I realized that wasn't how I was supposed to be reading this book. And I had tears in my eyes by the time I got to the fourth chapter." She claimed that these ideas helped her get back with her husband again.

Speaking at a religious retreat, a Search, I told the group they must not listen to my words. They must listen between the lines the way you read a love letter. And afterwards, when the people were summing up what they got out of what I said, a Vietnam veteran said, "Jess, when you said 'listen between the lines,' it really struck me. I had been reading Erich Fromm and trying to practice his ideas. But as you talked I could see that I was just practicing those ideas on other people and I wasn't getting the spirit of them. I wasn't getting them inside me."

So as you read this book, don't fall into the word trap. Don't rush to tell someone what you've read or argue with some small point. Try to make these ideas come more alive in your life. If you don't or can't do that, you're missing something. These are ideas that have changed people's lives.

What are some of the discoveries I have made? I found I needed people because I needed the love they could give me. I found that love was something I did. I found that the way I showed people my need and love for them was to tell how it was with me in my deepest heart. I came to feel that was the most loving thing I could do for anyone—tell them how it was with me and share my imperfections with them. When I did this, most people came back at me with what was deep within them. This was love coming to me. And the more I had coming to me, the more I had to give away. And this helped me see deeper within myself, accept myself and tell more about how it was with me. All this came out of an acceptance of myself as I was. I had to throw away as much of the fake as possible and recognize all my feelings and all my actions as me. So I was able to see and accept—: I ain't much, baby—but I'm all I've got.

There are a small group of ideas that seem to me crucial: acceptance, emotional honesty, trust, believing in others, handling our fears, learning to love and work. I was talking to my students about trusting people, and Sherry sat in the front row and fought me. She said, "You can't trust anybody—people are no good. The minute you do something for them, they'll get you." She said, "I worked with my lab partner on a project and he went and turned it in and said it was all his, and he got an A and I got a C. Just shows you can't trust people."

Well, this was about the eighth week of the quarter and it was the first time that I had taught these ideas completely. For some reason I was kind of patient with her. I said, "If that's your experience with life, well, okay, but I just don't see it that way." Later she said, "I went home that day and I started to think and all of a sudden while watching 'Get Smart' on TV, a little light bulb clicked on. I realized what this 'nut' was doing. Educating students to accept people without fears of hurting yourself.

"All this time, I was accepting the bad part of people, leaving the good part to the selected few—me and my friends. Since people are both good and bad, you cannot accept just a part of them or rather a part of their behavior; you must accept them as they are—good *and* bad. If I accept Johnny the troublemaker, I accept both his bad and good qualities. I might not like his bad qualities but I have to accept him in all matters.

"Here the 'nut' had turned into a genius. Wait a minute. I might be wrong. I decided I must have proof of his theory.

"The grouchy old widow neighbor of mine was going to be fifty-five on Sunday. What the heck, I can make cakes, why not make her a birthday cake and see what reaction I get from her. Maybe I don't really understand her. I know, I'll bake a cake and let my husband take it down to her—that way if she barks too loud I won't get hurt. Stop! You stupid fool you—I must understand the reason why I decided to make this act of graciousness. Be yourself and put all your effort into it. If she doesn't appreciate it—then I must have done something wrong in presenting it to her.

"Sunday afternoon I took the cake down to her; I knocked on the door. I was feeling sorry for myself. Just a minute, you're supposed to give her this cake and no matter how she barks—try and make her day pleasant.

"She opened the door and barked, 'Well . . . what do you want?'

"As I handed the cake to her, I simply said, 'Happy Birthday.'

"Her face turned white while she said softly, 'Please come in.' I had never been in her apartment before. On every table and on every wall, she had pictures of her husband, and they showed some of the activities they used to share.

"As she was cutting the cake, tears came to her eyes. She said, 'You know, Sherry, you look quite a bit like my daughter.'

" 'I didn't realize you had children.'

" 'Oh, yes. I had four—one girl and three boys. My husband and three boys were killed in an accident. My daughter and I survived, but she scarred her face badly. I've never forgiven myself, since then. I had insisted that we take a trip back East; it was in Michigan where the accident happened.'

"What could I say? Here I was, involved in self-pity up to my neck. She had self-pity, too, but for more reasons than I could count. All I had done was give her a chance to talk with me (not just at me).

"So in one quarter, one man taught me to apply teaching not only in the school room, but also in my own life. Carl Rogers was right when he said, 'When I accept myself as I am, I change, and when I accept others as they are, they change.' Listening to other people talk on the subject they choose is accepting them and their ideas. It may take years to learn to be the best listener, but at least I'm starting. Listening to your students or other people, you'll find where they are. Where they are is where you begin to teach.

"I now want to teach. The fear I had is gone. It may come back for a brief stay, but it won't be a crutch. By accepting myself and others, I can see how Freud said, '. . . to love and to work are the only two things in this world.' I will even push it farther . . . 'to work is to love.' Teaching won't be a job, but life itself.

"Every person has a different method of teaching. Mine will come as the students come. My methods will change as my students change.

"In brief, your process is a process of teaching life. The major part of life is acceptance of others, and yourself."

"THANK YOU FOR TEACHING ME TO LIVE"

Well, I didn't teach Sherry to live. I was just working on that same problem myself and she happened to listen in. Like an ear to a keyhole. That's kind of what you are doing in this book. You're going to have your ear to the keyhole while I try to learn a little bit more about this business of living that I started on ten years ago in a hospital bed, where if I hadn't changed I would have died.

Now there are many ways of dying. Most of them involve dying on your feet like I was doing. I see my young teaching students sitting in class, and almost every one of them are violently opposed to dress codes. Yet I predict that ten years from now half of them may vote for a dress code in their schools. That's how far away they are going to get from where they are today because of an accumulation of little wrong turns and dying to life. I've seen that you can die at a very early age.

I had worked these ideas out primarily for teachers. To my mind, the sadness of teaching is this: All of our teachers, good and bad, know what a good teacher is and should do—but only about half of our teachers can do it. That means that only half of my students, only every other one of them, is going to be able to come close to their "ideal."

I see now that teaching is like all other human relationships. In fact, I think teaching and nursing are two of the most intense human relationships outside of the family. My business now is trying to change the odds for my teachers and nurses so everyone has a chance to be the teacher or nurse or the person he or she wants to be. But I know from bitter experience that there is a limit to how much changing each of us can do. This is a slow process and it takes patience. In fact, patience is one of the most crucial aspects of it. We can't revolutionize ourselves tomorrow morning. It took me a long time to get all screwed up. So I need to give myself plenty of time to change to some new, better way.

I told my students how hard it is for me to accept myself. The first time one student heard this, he realized he had given up on himself. He had been turned down by six out of seven schools for advanced study in physical therapy. He hadn't even checked into the seventh school because it was far away and he was sure he would be turned down. He went back to his room, sent a letter requesting an interview to the seventh school and was eventually accepted—all because he first accepted himself.

I told a class how poor I was at accepting people. Another nurse realized that she wasn't accepting them either. When they tried to talk to her she would say she was interested, but she was backing out the door. Now when someone wants to talk she sits down, even if for just a few minutes, and really listens.

I told a mother that I punished my kids partly because punishing them satisfied me. She went home and was horrified to discover that her kids were good on her good days and bad on her bad days; punishing the kids came mostly from within herself. This realization was enough to help her overcome most of the problem.

I told my students how hard it is for me to tell people I love them. One girl came to realize she was building a wall between herself and her parents, and made the first move to tear it down.

I told my students how hard it is for me to be real—to tell what is in my deepest heart. But I told them that when I am able to be halfway real with people, they usually respond by being real in return. One student thought that was a good idea, so he screwed up courage to try it on the grouch in the neighborhood. He knocked at his door and announced he had stopped by for a visit. The grouch turned out to be a nice guy from New York who was just not used to the more open ways of the West.

I told my students that we all need more love in our lives— that we need more things going for us. One student went home and thought about this. When her boyfriend came that evening, he asked her what she wanted to do. She had been keeping him at arm's length with a constant diet of organized activities on dates. She said, "Let's just ride around and talk." So they did and before the evening was over they both realized they had so much in common they wanted to be married.

Extreme examples? No, commonplace happenings. The way one student said it when he finished our time together was: "Thank you for teaching me what I wanted to know."

So these are some of the things that have kept me from the closeness with other people that I need and that is so terribly vital to all of us. In this material world, we've got everything that is possible for a nation to have; we've got five times, or ten times, or a hundred times as much material prosperity as anybody else in the world. Yet if anyone wants to argue that it's the material things that make you happy, they've got trouble. In fact, that's one of the reasons, I think, why younger people today are so sensitive to the shortcomings of material prosperity. They're saying, "Hey, there's a whole big life beyond having a house and a car. And I want a part of that."

But the bar to you and me participating in that life is we have to participate in it as we really are. We can't fake. I must deal with the world as I am and as it is. And this way I can get the love and tenderness and joy into my life that I want to.

I sat in on Emotions Anonymous when I was first starting this process and said, "I wish I had more close personal friends." The minute I said it, I realized I didn't really wish that. I didn't want close personal friends because they'd be too close to me and I couldn't stand the self awareness a close relationship would force on me. And I realized I wouldn't want to be a friend of mine. A friend of mine was somebody I took off the shelf, played with for five minutes, and then put back on the shelf and said, "Wait a year or two—or five years until I'm ready to come back and want to be a friend of yours again." What a dumb way to be.

So I said okay. I was ready to face the music and admit that a friend means really being a friend and you can't have more than two or three close friends, or you have fallen into that same trap. When I moved to Montana a few years ago, I did it differently. I've got a few close, personal friends now. I didn't have them before because I didn't really want them. I didn't dare risk the self-disclosure and self-awareness that was in close relationships. These are the kinds of changes that we're going to be working on.

Change in people is psychology. So this is a book about psychology. But don't let that scare you. This book is aimed at helping you control and change your life. It is also aimed at helping you control and change the people around you. These ideas are useful and valuable to all kinds of people in ordinary and in critical situations. They can be useful—or vital—to you. But you must constantly realize that a mere understanding of ourselves and others is not the only goal. My goal (and I hope you consider it for yours) is to find understanding that can help you and me actually change our lives into more beautiful ones—five minutes at a time.

TWO

Why Are We So Afraid
of Ourselves?

Now, why are we so funny? Why do we run away from the love and affection we desperately need? I used to think it was like a psychological manifestation of original sin, that we were all doomed to live this queer, odd life. Why am I so strange? Why am I so needing of love and affection? Why am I so insecure? Why am I so concerned about: Who am I? What am I? Where am I?

Like all the big problems in life, this has been covered in Peanuts. The dog Snoopy is lying on top of his dog house in a very dark night and he's asking himself: "Who am I? Will I come to a happy death?" He is having one of those terrible times in the night and he's so despondent and depressed. When the sun finally comes up, Snoopy goes to sleep and the kids walk by and say: "Isn't it wonderful to be a dog? You can just sleep all the time." Snoopy opens an eye and says, "No, only when the sun is up."

So, again, why am I this way? As I say, I thought it was nature, part of man's lot. To some extent perhaps it is. But I heard a story recently that put a lot of things into place for me.

I was the first speaker at Montana's state Newman Convention. I stayed to listen to the second speaker and found he had an amazing story to tell.

The speaker was Reverend Carrol Ellertson who was a missionary to the Zulus in South Africa. He told of one of the most miraculous stories I've heard of in my life. I've heard of the wonderful child rearing practices of the early American Indians, but Reverend Ellertson's description of the native Zulu culture was the most beautiful thing I have ever heard described.

When you were born a Zulu, you were nursed at your mother's breast and carried on your mother's back with your bare skin against her warm, bare skin for two solid years. You were given more physical contact and more physical love and affection than probably any but a handful of children in American culture get.

Here, because of sexual taboos and other reasons, we've gone backwards. We are moved away from breast-feeding and with it a lot of advantages for both the child and the mother and the reciprocal relationships that exist here. But the Zulu child had more than that going for him.

When his two years were up and a new baby came along, it was time for him to be put down on the ground. Often his cup was still not filled with physical love. But he had lots of kids in his village to love him. Because their cups had been filled, they didn't hate little kids and weren't mean to them and angry at them.

When this little Zulu child cried because he needed to be carried and held, one of the older children picked him up and held him and carried him around. You've all noticed this in pictures of African settlements. So there was a continuation of physical love and affection from both boys and girls as well as from the mother.

Then there was another thing going for this Zulu child. The child did not have just a mamma, but it also had a bunch of mamoos, who were all of the mother's sisters and other women who loved this child because *they* had been loved as kids.

They were not screaming, "My God, I didn't get the love that I needed. How am I going to make supper out of an empty cupboard? How am I going to love you, you dumb kid? You're screaming at me for love and, hell, I haven't got anything to give you. I'm so dying to be held and loved and stroked and caressed that I cannot stand it. And yet I'm supposed to give to you something that I never got anywhere near enough of. I don't know how to give it."

Instead, these were people like those great people you see in our society who have been loved, and so they love.

The small Zulu also didn't have just one daddy. He had the dadoos, his father's brothers and other male adults who talked to him about hunting, showed him how to make a little bow and arrow and all of this kind of stuff. They spent time with him and they "joyed in his presence," as someone once defined love. So on into adult life there was for both the boys and the girls this abundance of love and affection and attention and tenderness.

Now that is a radically different situation than the one in which most of us were raised. It accounts for a great many things that I see as crucial problems. One of the things that was communicated to Zulu girls sounds very strange to us—yet it shouldn't. Each of their girls were told, "You are very beautiful. You are very beautiful because you were uniquely created by our God. You are an Aleluthi. And everyone knows that all the children in the Aleluthi family have always been very beautiful."

You see how hard this is for us to understand. The minute we hear somebody being told they are beautiful we have to back away. We think, "Well, compared to what? Only one can be beautiful." But not the Zulus.

They grow up knowing that beauty doesn't have anything to do with their hairdos or their clothes or their face or their figure. But it's got to do with the fact that they are uniquely created by God and so are beautiful. Isn't that some idea! We Puritans know that that's nothing to believe. The only beautiful people are those who are God-fearing people and do as the good book says and get all kinds of rewards right now. Anybody who has got a wart on their face, why they must have done something spiteful to God because he was looking down and gave them that wart on their face, everybody knows that. We are God-fearing people in this country, nice friendly little Puritans. Baloney. We've got Christianity twisted around so far you couldn't recognize it, and they're talking about the kind of Christianity that you can find in that Friendly BIBLE where there's just the kind, loving stuff.

Now it's a sadness that our sense of beauty is so twisted. But it's not as deep a sadness as that still deeper thing—the lack of love. Because that strikes at you and causes some other very, very terrible problems. I think, and I have seen all kinds of evidence of this, that each of us has a deep and terrible hunger for love. And particularly, because we didn't ever seem to get as much love as we needed from our parents and from the particular kind of society we were raised in, we look back to our childhood frantically and despairingly. And we keep hoping for the affection that we didn't get enough of. And I see all kinds of people, fifty and sixty and seventy years old, looking to their parents and still frantically seeking love and affection.

Our cup has to be filled up or at least be reasonably full so that we can walk away from our parents. But in our society this so often doesn't happen. We're inclined to protest, "Oh yes it did! There was a lot of love and affection around our house. There really was." Well, tell me about some. "Oh, we did a lot of things together." Okay. That's better than nothing. But what does that mean in terms of how many times you were held, how many times you were kissed, how many times you were told that you were loved. How few times were you told or given the feeling, "I despise you." How few times were you told or given the feeling, "You are no good. You are not to be trusted. You are worthless." How few times were you given the feeling, "Why did you ever come into this family, you're the worst thing that ever happened to this family."

These are not figments of my imagination. These are not exaggerations. My students have told me all these things about their family lives. One said, "You know, I've never been trusted in my entire life. And my most common memory of my childhood is being told 'I despise you.'" When you grow up in a situation like that, you're going to have awfully little in your cup.

I know that person probably got many loving things from their parents and the other crucial adults around them. But for my student the reality of today was their feeling. And that feeling was that they were not loved but were despised.

And the trouble with so much of the love that we got as children was that it was a conditional kind of love. "I will love you *if* you get good grades. I will love you *if* you wear your hair a certain way or a certain length. I will love you *if* your friends are the right kind of people. I will love you *if* you marry well." Not I love you *because* you are my child. I love you *because* this is the way God made you. And because it is conditional love there is no way that we can ever really measure up enough. And we feel tremendously unworthy. So we cave in and do what our parents want.

This constant caving in and bowing to our past and to our parents and to our homes is particularly difficult for us because it persists on into our adult life so long and so tremendously. And it tends to warp our behavior in one of two ways. One way is to see our lack of love. So we slavishly twist our lives into any weird kind of configuration that we think will finally please those parents and that society. We turn our lives upside down and inside out in a frantic attempt to please somebody else—especially to deliver what we think our parents wanted from us. There's no room in there for pleasing ourselves and this gives rise to that kind of conformity in our lives where it's just like we were stamped out by cookie cutters. Because we're trying to please some nebulous "others" and most of those "others" have got stereotyped conceptions of what the world should be, or we think they do, and we try to live up to them.

Or we can react another way. We can violently rebel against everything our parents and society have told us to do and say, "I don't want you. I don't need you." We turn our lives upside down. And we do everything exactly opposite of what these people want us to do. We grow long beards and we smoke pot and we have our dresses shorter than anyone else's. And we do everything that will bug other people and make them hate us. But there, too, we are locked in—just as tight as we are the other way.

Just look at our non-conformists. One of my freshmen said about the Minneapolis campus, "The non-conformists look so much alike that I can't tell them apart." What kind of non-conformity is that? What kind of doing-your-own-thing is it when doing your own thing means doing and saying and looking exactly like everybody else? This isn't any kind of freedom. It is mere rebellion—locked-in behavior.

Now you must understand that I'm not criticizing my parents, they did the best job they possibly could. In fact, looking back on the things that they did for me, I can't figure out how they managed it. In some cases they made a whole lot of meals out of empty cupboards. They gave me a whole lot of love and affection and tenderness when it must have been very, very difficult for them to do so.

My mother was terribly burned in a fire when I was about a year and a half old and she was pregnant with my brother who is two years younger than me. Her shoulders, one arm and all her hair were burned, and her face was completely disfigured. She was at Mayo's for skin grafts off and on for two years. And there was a terrible physical pressure on her plus the pressure caused by her appearance, and the financial pressure on my father, and the separation from his wife for that long period of time. All of these things came right in the midst of a depression when there was just no money at all. These had terrible effects on them. Nevertheless, they were able to surmount and survive most of them themselves and give my brother and me many very happy times in our lives.

The society that I grew up in was a small town. There were some wonderful people in that town. I can still remember walking downtown on a summer day. And you know how long a summer day is when you're thirteen or fourteen—it's about a year long, each of those hot days. And you're looking for something to do. You walk into Hub Ole Johnson's clothing store and he's just sitting there willing to talk to you about duck hunting or deer hunting or guns. And this is a wonderful thing—kind of a miracle in a way. So there were a few adults who were like Zulu dadoos. Ralph Black took some of his time and used it to start my brother and me pheasant hunting. Yes, I got some wonderful things. But I didn't get what Reverend Ellertson described. And I haven't met anybody else who did either.

No, this isn't any criticism of our society—or our parents. A lot of times they dished out lots more love than they had been given. But if we're going to do anything about our need for love, we need to see it very, very clearly for just what it is. That way we can make our peace with our parents and with our past. And we can walk away from our need rather than endlessly conforming or endlessly rebelling.

Our job is to use the intelligence that we have to avoid the continuation of this chain down into our children's lives. We must say to ourselves, "Okay, I can get from some place else in the world all kinds of love and affection and joy and tenderness that I can pass on to my children, and into my family and break this chain with me as much as possible."

Part of this peace that we need to make with our past requires compassion. Because no matter how bad a parent someone has told me about, all I need to do is say, "What were *their* father and mother like?" The minute I ask the question that person's eyes kind of widen. And the minute you put it that way—it helps. You see your own parents so much more clearly. You can walk away free. Not locked in rebellion nor locked in conformity.

Now, there are occasionally some people who have received this kind of unconditional love and affection and tenderness. Duke Ellington was being interviewed on the "Mike Douglas Show." Douglas asked him about those early hard days that all musicians have had. Duke Ellington said, "I didn't have any." And Mike Douglas was aghast. "What do you mean? Didn't you starve? Didn't you suffer?"

Ellington said, "No. I started right out doing what I most liked to do, working with music. I had faith in myself and it was easy." And he added, "When I was a little boy, I was loved so much and held so much. I don't think my feet hit the ground until I was seven years old."

But that's not a comment you're going to hear on every street corner. Because of the tremendous love and affection Ellington had, he had none of the usual questions. None of this "Who am I?" "What am I?" "Where am I?" He knew he was a musician and he was Duke Ellington, and he went to work writing music and right away it was good.

In my experience the more a person has received the kinds of things the Zulus received the better able they are to answer: Who am I, What am I, Where am I.

"I'm Jess Lair, I'm a teacher at Bozeman, Montana." "And where are you going?" "I don't know. Wherever I'll be tomorrow—that's where I'm going." And the thing I'm saying is, you ask this Zulu boy or girl who they are and they say, "My name is so and so of such and such a tribe." And that's who they are.

So the Zulu story and the physical and other love involved has tremendous implications, and number one is our freedom from our parents and our freedom from our past. This determines the amount of moving room we have in our life. I recognize that this is difficult to apply to ourselves.

You and I are hesitant to say, "Oh man, I'm really warped and twisted by my past. I'm really just locked in by conforming to the past (which is the most common thing) in a foolish and vain attempt to please. Or I'm rebelling against the past."

I can't very easily see myself doing either of these two things. But it's easy for me to look at ten people next to me and see how all ten of them in their behavior show many of these signs. Well, then, once I've done that, my friend, the next and logical step is to look at the eleventh guy, me. I have to say, "Wait a minute now, if I see signs of this in ten people, what does that say about the eleventh one?"

Okay, so we need to make our peace with our past, so we can walk away free. Now, this is the other sad part of this situation. Are we going to get any more love and affection from our parents than what we got? No. Do we need more affection in our life? You're damned right we do. How are we going to get it? We've got two choices.

We can go around like we are—I can go around faking, you know. "Oh, hey, here's a big hot shot, the big professor, the big fancy deal." Who's going to give that mess, that big faker, any love, affection, joy and tenderness? Nobody. Everybody's going to be back peddling. You can't get away fast enough when somebody's faking it to you. Okay, what's the alternative?

I can do as I mentioned and that is punch some holes in this fancy silo I have built around myself and say, "Hey here's the real Jess Lair. He's got lots of problems, the same kind of problems you have. And the same kind of problems everybody else in the whole world has. And specifically he's wrestling with getting his life back on the track after having it knocked off for a long while. And trying to live five minutes at a time as a way of avoiding some of his mistakes."

But there's one big problem here. What I'm saying is be real to people and in return they'll be real back with you and being real is love.

But we find it so hard to be real. I think it is because we are so afraid of what we would find deep inside if we dared to look, and I think the reason we feel this way goes back to when we were a little bitty kid, about a year old, before we had any language, we were not loved enough. So we had two choices. But we had no language then so it was a very difficult choice for us to handle. And it's a very difficult thing to imagine what goes on in a little baby's mind without language.

This little kid looks at this huge overpowering world around him and these two people that he's around so much. They're in effect, communicating to him through their feelings to drop dead. He can choose between two things: something's wrong with them, or, there's something wrong with me. Now which way did you go on that question? Here's little me. Am I going to look up at those big giants and say something's wrong with them—the all-powerful ones? They can open doors and do all kinds of things. No, it must be that there's something wrong with me. I was rejected as the pot that was misshapen.

Well, the funny thing is, most everybody feels some of this same inadequacy because they felt they were unlovable. So most everybody feels the same way, but we don't have any good way of communicating with each other about our real feelings. And we often keep those feelings so hidden from ourselves, we don't even know they are there.

We've got a whole nation full of people who to one extent or another feel that in some way, shape or form, their particular pot was not as pleasing to the maker and to those big people around them as it could have been. And in some of our cases, and most notably mine, the feeling is, "What a slob I am. Well, I'm going to have to put up a fancy front. I'm going to have to make a ton of money and have a big fancy job and a fancy career to show people I'm really some beans."

The funny thing is the lack of love works against the person. His feeling that he wasn't loved because he was unlovable makes him turn against himself. He runs and hides himself from the world which is the worst thing he could do. It cuts him off from the love and affection and joy in his life that he really needs.

He doesn't see the problem clearly. He wasn't loved because those older people didn't have any more capacity to love. Instead, he sees himself, because of his lack of love, as being unlovable because there's something wrong with him. Because of his feeling that there's something wrong with him, he doesn't dare reveal himself as he really is to people. So unless he gets his head straightened out he won't ever get any love and affection—all the rest of his life.

He lives a life that is a tight, artificial construction. And then all of a sudden when he's forty-five years old, he walks down into the basement, takes a rifle and blows his brains out. The people around him thought his was a beautiful life, but that's what so many say about suicides.

By the way, I've got bad news for you—not only is suicide the second highest cause of death among college students but suicide is the college-educated person's disease. And that's not surprising, because if you've got this sickness that says I'm no good, a college education and all the careers, prestige and income that go along with it is one of the best ego patches you can stick up in front of this inferiority you see. But suicide shouldn't be surprising. When you see that there's nothing inside you and that nothing's ever going to get inside you, you just despair. In that moment of despair you may end your life with a bullet or start dying from an ulcer or heart attack or what have you.

That's what happened to me when I was thirty-five despite a wife and children whose love I was blind to. I was letting so little love and affection come in. And I needed so much. I was getting all kinds of money, all kinds of recognition, all kinds of prestige, all kinds of big, fancy deals. But not near enough of the things that I really needed.

This is why I see the Zulu story as particularly crucial. Most of us weren't given enough love as children. If we had had our cup filled up, we could have walked away free. And secondly, because our cup wasn't filled up, the very self-esteem that we need to go to work with and use to fill up our cup, we don't have—in fact we have the opposite. So that this is why the Zulu story is so crucial to me. And this is why I fight self-awareness the way I do, because I have to take a good hard look at some of these sad things that are me or you.

What I'm talking about isn't just an old people's problem. I find young people have just as much trouble really loving each other and their little children as us older ones do. It's not hard to talk about loving but it's terribly hard to do.

One student was the kind of girl who dressed exquisitely. But when a gal in Bozeman, Montana, is running around in the kind of clothes Saks Fifth Avenue patrons would envy, this says that she's got a fantastic need to put on a certain front. Because, in Montana, you have to work hard to find clothes that look that good. Before she buys a dress she's got to look at a hundred of them I'm sure. Each morning, when she gets up, she's got to go through some real gyrations to make sure each one of those things she puts on fit together into the kind of costume that just knocks your eyes out.

In her class were a couple of guys who in terms of outward appearance could perhaps best be characterized as rummies. But in the course of a few hours in our small discussion section, it became very clear that these two "rummies" had real hearts. And they had for this girl the most precious thing there is in the world which is some acceptance of her just the way she was and some love and affection for her. And they were happy to be with her because of what she was, not because of her face or the clothes she had on that morning.

She was in a terrible bind. She felt, "Gee, these guys are tremendous. They've got something great for me." But then she would look closer at their appearance. And I was saying to her, "The problem you and I have is that we look at these two rummies and they really bother us because to us everything has got to be perfect. All the rifles have got to be Weatherbys. All the cars have got to be Cadillacs. All the jewels have got to be from Winston's. All our friends have to be the beautiful people—or we feel shoddy and second-rate."

And I said, "Yet we look outside and see that the real, honest people of the world, the ones we're really going to have to be with, are the people that we tend to see, in one way, shape or form as the rummies of the world. And this is what is just killing us." And she just gave a scream and started to cry. Because this thing strikes that hard. This fake front that I build up and that some of you occasionally might build up is that overwhelming.

We must see that the love and affection and joy and tenderness that we need to fill our partially filled cups is waiting for us. There is only one person standing in the way between us receiving that or not. And that's us.

In a paper this girl wrote, she said: "People are puppets of society. They pull each other's strings. We do what others want us to. Why don't we try to pull our own strings? Why even consider it? In doing so, we might and probably would not cave in to society. We would be ourselves for once."

This is just a reflection of our hesitancy to act on what we really feel. And we don't dare let our feelings out. We know that we need to get some recognition by other people of what our feelings are. And we need to get some recognition from other people that they feel the same way too. Then we don't feel, "I am the only screwy one in this whole world. I am the only one that was ever put down by these two giants for being defective." When we see it's the same way with others as with us, this gives us tremendous comfort for ourselves. This helps us to say, "I ain't much, baby—but I'm all I've got."

When we see everybody else is in this same boat with us pretty much, this is a real encouraging thing. We say, "Okay, this is all I've got, but this is all anybody else has got, too. So I'll take on the world with what I've got." Sure Duke Ellington has got a lot more to fight the world with than me, but he isn't going to fight me anyway because he doesn't want to.

A young grad student who had read my book said, "Dear Jess (I feel I can call you that)—I read your book. I don't care much for the way it is written but I like your ideas. I have felt the same way but I feel so lonely and ashamed." Well, the terrible sadness about that letter is that this graduate student is surrounded by hundreds of people who feel all the same things he and I feel. But he has never dared open up enough of himself to those around him to find out they feel exactly as he does.

This is what my students see in our group discussions. Everybody feels just like they do. So it's dumb to feel alone and ashamed with your ideas when nearly everybody feels as you do. But until you open up, you can't find that out. So this is why I see so much need for us to fully recognize this terrible and overwhelming need we have for love, affection, tenderness and joy in our lives.

And we all need to understand that each of us were uniquely created. For each of us, our beauty lies in our uniqueness and not in trying to be something that we aren't, but in trying to be what we are and seeing our uniqueness takes a lifetime, in my experience. We can't make any long-term plans beyond just living five minutes at a time and seeing what our hand turns to naturally. And it will show us what we are and that is something very beautiful.

In a *Life* article, Barbra Streisand observed, "When I catch a person in repose and they are completely relaxed and just themselves, then they are so beautiful." I think you have all seen this. We don't think of people at those times as something fantastic because there are no skyrockets going off but there is such an ease and smoothness and calm beauty there.

I have to add, there's another side to the Zulu story now, and it shows us how to produce delinquent children—or other types of alienated young people, and sadly, it's simple. The Union of South Africa, as part of its apartheid policies, has a rule that only the Zulu men can leave their village to go to town and work in the factories. A man has to work in the city at the same job for eight years before he is allowed to bring his wife to town to live with him.

As you can imagine this breaks up the family unit which is the center of all Zulu culture. Then, when you bring your wife to town, she too has to work to support a family. A man makes $80 a month and the food costs are similar to those in this country. So both the father and the mother have to work. As a result of this policy, the children are raised without the benefit of the Zulu village culture. In the city there are no parents and adults with time to care for the children. These children are now growing up. They weren't nursed and carried by their mothers for two years. They didn't have a dozen mamoos and dadoos. They weren't given love, affection and the feeling they were unique and important.

So these kids just roam the streets and they exhibit all the behavior our delinquents exhibit. We know how to produce delinquents. And we see that the problem goes deeper than just parents but involves all the other adults who could help a child grow up but don't have time.

What's the answer to solving the problem of the delinquents? I don't know. It's kind of late now. But I know one of the things it isn't, and that's to scream at the delinquents. The people we should be screaming at are all the people who played a part in producing the delinquents. And who is that? Me, for one.

Like when one of my students came to me recently. He was run down by a bunch of student cowboys who cut off his long hair. This made him feel terrible and he needed sympathy at the particular moment. You may say, "Well, he didn't deserve it." Nevertheless, he needed it and I didn't give it to him. He got something less than that.

You say, "Well, that's a slow process, to love them out of being rebellious." Yes, it is slow but it was an awfully slow process to create the problem, too. It takes our society eighteen years to create a problem, so how come we're going to just solve the problem with jails or courts or something in just a few years.

It's just like me with the long-standing physical problems and neglect that led to my heart trouble. It took ten to fifteen years to create the problem. I'm not going to solve those things tomorrow morning. I have to realize that if it took fifteen years to develop a problem, it will take fifteen to twenty-five years to alleviate it. I see young guys of twenty-five to thirty out running on the track. They have been out of shape for five years yet they are determined to get back in top shape in five days.

This is the same short sightedness we show when we look at the alienated ones. We want to solve the problem immediately because it is an offensive problem to us. I'm as offended and distressed as you are, but I think we need to show troubled young people the same patience you and I ask for when we are trying to change our lives and find new ways of living.

What about the opposite extreme? The people who rebel with violence? Can you reach them with love or understanding? Well, society certainly needs to protect itself to some extent from them. But I think that society must also recognize the source of the violence.

For example, say I'm your supervisor and I make your life miserable by constantly humiliating you every chance I get. I push you in every kind of way. You keep taking it. And you take it and take it. Finally, one day you'll very likely blow your lid unless you have superhuman restraint. You're going to do a number of things in reaction to my oppression. You're going to do a number of rather irrational things as well as some very rational ones. And this is what I see as a very useful explanation of a lot of the violence.

I think violence often comes from the same source that would make me violent in the situation I just described. I would pop my supervisor in the nose, curse him and his parents to the ninth generation and quit my job. Well, quitting the job is the rational answer, but the other responses are irrational and for them I can legitimately be thrown in jail. But we've got a judge in Bozeman who would probably handle me this way:

He would say, "I'm throwing you in jail. You shouldn't have done this. I can see some of why you did it. But you can't take the law into your own hands." He would say that, and that's the kind of justice I respect because it shows an awareness of my feelings as well as my actions. I don't excuse the violence but I can understand it.

One of my women students had this reaction to the Zulu story. She said, "Do you suppose that the reason girls don't walk proud is because they are really afraid to. They are afraid because of what people will say if they do notice them, and they don't want to be hurt by people's comments? I was really impressed by what you said because it is true and I had never really realized it or noticed it."

Yes, some people will be offended by it. But it will do a lot more for you and the rest of the world than the small cost involved. You see? I am an affront to some people because I am me. Okay, that is the price you pay. The thing you have to realize though is part of the reason you are an affront to them is because you are doing what they would like to do and want to do. I think that is one of the reasons we kill great people like Ghandi, King and the Kennedys.

To me the Zulu story says in a vivid way that what we really need is love, tenderness, joy, beauty, feeling in our life. And this book is focused on how we can get more love into our life by helping us improve our relationships with all of the people around us. We can't sit and cry and blame society and our past. That kind of self-pity is a sickness. One of my nineteen-year-old freshman students wrote, "For what I am today, shame on my parents. But if I stay that way, shame on me."

What we need to do is draw on the strengths and intelligence we have and use it to reshape our lives. Since society is simply a composite of millions of choices, as we change the choices we make, our society will be changed, too.

THREE

Love—From Your Deepest Heart

Two years ago, I told my students to be congruent—to bring out what they were inside. It's an idea developed by Carl Rogers. But I had trouble explaining it and so my students had trouble using it. They kept asking me what congruence was. So I switched to another of Rogers' words and talked about being real. But both here and in congruence, a lot of times being real meant letting out the anger at the other person. And while the anger was real enough I noticed a strange thing in our discussions of these ideas in small groups.

What my people needed to get out most of all wasn't their anger—it went deeper than that. They wanted to voice those deep things that had been bothering them for years. And none of those real deep things were anger. They were troubles— some of them pretty big.

I think a turning point came during the middle of fall quarter a while ago. My class met in a large group of 150 twice a week and then broke down into five smaller groups of about thirty one hour a week. We sat around a big open centered table and everyone had signs in front of them with their names on. The groups were as leaderless as I could make them in the sense that my only role was to tell my own story —and let the group go where it wanted to.

The Friday morning discussion section had been together for an hour a week for four weeks. On the fifth Friday morning a married woman in the class started things off by telling

41

us that she was illegitimate and had been given by her mother to her grandparents to raise when she was five. She wondered if her mother had done this because she loved her or because she wanted to save her marriage to a man she had subsequently married. She had never talked to her mother about this and was wondering if she should or could. She was in tears as she talked.

A married guy in class responded to her and said he was illegitimate too, and that he was able to talk to his mother about it.

Another student said he wasn't illegitimate but his older brother was, and he had just found this out from his older brother but he had been sworn to secrecy about this, and it bothered him because he wanted to talk to his mother about it.

At this, a young gal said that it really struck her to hear these three stories because her son was illegitimate and she found herself taking out her anger at the father on the son.

Then a tiny gal said that she could see how some of them felt because she had given up an illegitimate baby for adoption when she was sixteen.

Now, usually the troubles we have hidden away inside aren't quite that spectacular—especially the ones that people will trust others enough to admit to even in the very trusting climate of these groups. But I was struck by what that first woman's bravery did for about twenty-five people. Her story —and the others—communicated something very powerful to all the members of that group. I think what that was, was love. It wasn't married love and it wasn't perfect love. But I think the only word for it was love.

So I think love is when we tell what's in our deepest hearts. I think that is the most loving thing we can do for someone. Then, if they choose, they can tell us back what is in their deepest hearts. That is love coming back to us. That's why we need other people, because they are the only ones who can give us the love we need.

There is a potential confusion here. We shy away from the word love because in the married form it connotes sex and in the religious or popular form it connotes a vagueness and a fakery that we hate. When I first started talking this way someone said to use the word like instead of love. I didn't want to.

One day a student turned in a sentence written on a card. It

said, "I like you *because.* I love you *although.*" And these two
sentences say the distinction between the two words so well. I
like you *because* we have the same tastes in clothes or literature or music or politics. But I love you *although* we don't
have the same tastes in clothes, literature, music or politics. I
love you because you are a "child of God and an inheritor of
the Kingdom of Heaven." And deep down, you are full of the
power and glory and majesty that is uniquely yours—and I
am waiting for you to release it. Just like the Zulus.

So this is what I saw in that group. As those five people
opened their hearts to the other twenty, the twenty opened
their hearts to the five. Now the twenty had the same kinds of
problems as the five. Some of them later admitted to the
group or to me privately what those problems were. But there
was a special bond developed between the members of that
group. And each of the twenty-five went away with something
that I have found can last a lifetime. That's the warm glow
deep down that contact with a loving person can produce.

Now, when I tell students, businessmen, nuns or nurses that
love is what is in their deepest hearts, I don't get any more
questions. They know what I mean. And they know what
they have to do. They know I'm not talking about their anger
because while their anger may go deep, it isn't in their deepest
heart. All that is there is their humanity—the humanity
they've been so frightened of and have hidden so long.

I know we can't go this deep into ourselves every day. So
we need a way to talk about what we do each day, and so far
the best word I can find for that is emotional honesty. But
again it's emotional honesty that often sidesteps our anger. I
see much of our anger as being rooted in our fears. And our
fears come out of our sense of aloneness and separateness
from others. So as we get at what's in our deepest heart and
get love back, it quiets our fears and aloneness and the anger
just drops away. I've seen this so often in A.A. and Emotions
Anonymous. The long-time members who have worked the
program for years are sweet people. There is no anger in
them. You can call them any kind of name and they won't get
mad. They used to fight and quarrel constantly but there is no
more anger in their lives.

Emotional honesty or being real, as I see it, is simply a rigorous honesty about ourselves and our feelings. So, being the
real, deep-as-possible, deep-as-appropriate us is love. When I
tell a fellow teacher about some mistake I make in teaching,

that is a loving thing, too. And my students and I find that the deeper we go into our hearts, the more likely we are to get a loving response back.

Now there is something about telling you, "Hey, be emotionally honest. Be real," that may make you quibble. Some of you may even say, "What is being real? I don't know how to be real." Or, "I am already being very, very real." But there is one sure-fire answer for this. Being real is the opposite of faking it, and all of you know when you are faking it. At least in my experience, we all do.

For example, you can walk into a crowded room and all of a sudden feel very, very uncomfortable. You will very likely start talking about the fancy possessions that you have, the degrees that you earned, all of the honors that your parents and relatives and friends to the ninth generation possess. That's faking it, friends.

It isn't that these things aren't true. It isn't that they aren't appropriate to be talked about occasionally. But I don't think it is any accident that in certain situations I string out all of these fake things like little beads on a necklace. It's because I am frightened. So I know when I am faking it. I think we all do. And the opposite of that faking, I say to the person who keeps bugging me about what is real, the opposite of that is being real.

Okay, can I really be real? No, not very real. I don't know who Jess is that well so I can't really be real. But the funny thing here is that just trying to be real helps me be real enough so this is just one awful big improvement over what I had before. And there are two indications as to when you are being real in my experience. When you are really being real to somebody, they are inclined to be real back. And, of course, if they aren't real back, you tend to stop and it doesn't continue. Also, when you are really being real to someone and they are being real back, that litttle fire starts deep down inside. And this warm feeling is, to me, a sure sign that something very precious and important is going on between two people.

Now—a lot of time people come to me and say, "Hey, Jess, I am really being real. I am just standing here being as real as I can be. I have always been so lucky that I have been able to be so real, so like me just as I am." And I frequently find myself saying, "Well, your tummy warm?" "No." "Mine ain't either." You know? And they look at me kind of funny.

Sometimes they will say, "Hey, man, you are building a wall against me. You are building a wall against me, and I can't get through." Maybe I am. I have built some walls against some people in my time. But in some cases I don't think that is so. I think a lot of the walls we see in the world are of our own building.

Originally, I was going to call this book "Real Is Love" because I don't know of anything that I have ever seen that is more loving that one person can do for another than to tell that other person how it is *really* with them in their deepest heart. To give, in a sense, a part of yourself.

To my mind this is the answer to this problem of love in a society where one guy has one wife. The kind of love that I am talking about has nothing to do with physical intimacy. Someone may say to me, "Hey, Jess, this is how it is with me." Hopefully, I will reciprocate in some small measure and say, "Yes, and this is how it is with me." I sometimes think that there is more love in that situation than there is in many marriages.

One of my students last quarter was writing about her relationships with her boy friend. She said that when they had started to go together last spring quarter, neither of the two were virgins. They had sexual relations right from the beginning. She said, "You know, looking back, we had some crucial things between us that we weren't facing very well. So we used sex as a cover-up. It was a nice way to divert our attention from some rather serious problems between us."

So during the quarter, she told the boy friend, "School's out —chum. No more. We are going to go about the process of getting acquainted with each other before we start jumping into bed with each other again." And she did. "But," she said, "it was easier for me because I knew what I was trying to do. I was trying to help him as much as I could by being as real as I possibly could. It was harder for him because he didn't know as much about what was going on. He didn't have the class to help him. And he felt I was rejecting him by cutting off intercourse, but we are making it go and things are going along a lot better now."

There is so much thinking of love as physical intimacy. Yet physical intimacy, when that's all there is, isn't worth any more than the small sum it costs in any city. Those of you who chose to get into bed with each other think something big has happened. Well, something very small has happened. And if you don't believe that, you swingers, just go out and try being blazingly real with someone this afternoon or this evening. It is a lot tougher to do than it is to jump into bed with someone. A lot tougher. But, fortunately, a lot more satisfying and rewarding. You may say, "Hey, man, that shows you're really over the hill, old dad." Well, maybe. Maybe. But I have lots of warm, vivid memories. And I am just not quite that far gone. I don't ask you to take my word for it. I ask you to go out and prove it to your own satisfaction.

So that's why I think "Real is Love." And if real is love and love is what we need, then we had better learn how to be real.

What's stopping us? Well, one of the biggest problems is the one I mentioned in Chapter Two—that we think we are not worthy. We think we are the faulty pot. We think no one could stand us if they really knew us. It's like this little gal said in her paper last quarter. "My main problem is that I cannot accept myself. When I was a small child, my mother told me that she hated my guts. From this experience I cannot accept the idea that anyone could possibly love me since my own mother did not. I will probably always have this problem unless I can get help or help myself.

"There is a guy in Great Falls that is truly in love with me. I know it. But I will do everything possible to try and disprove his love for me. I treat him like dirt and I am very sarcastic with him most of the time. I do these things because I love him so very much and yet I cannot bring myself to show it because I don't want to get hurt. I can even realize what I am doing to him but I still do these unjust things." Okay, that is an extreme case of the kind of self-hate so many of us have.

Take the analogy of the farmer who had just a few seeds of wheat. What does he do with his few seeds? Well, the first thing he had better do is plant them as quickly as he can at the most opportune time. He has five wheat seeds and he plants them in five different places. And he takes awful good care of those five grains of wheat. Say three of them sprout because at first he's not very good at picking places to plant his wheat. But pretty soon, at one hundred grains of wheat on each head, he has three hundred grains of wheat. And he plants these and pretty soon he has bushels of wheat. But he had better plant and handle those first seeds very carefully.

That is how it is worth loving. We've got very limited resources at first. So the answer is, rather than start with the hard-to-love people, we had better love the easy ones. When we love the easy ones we improve the chances we will be loved back. Then we use some of the favorable experiences that will occur to give us the courage, to give us the energy, to give us the understanding to do a better job next time. The experience that my students have had in this has been quite good.

"Last year I felt terribly inferior," admitted one student, "especially around one particular person in one of my classes. This year we are good friends, because I have learned to accept her. I could be real with her after I had put aside my fear of people and lack of self-acceptance. I have learned that taking life on five minutes at a time is one of the hardest things I have ever done. But I am much happier for it.

"This minute-to-minute caring has brought me some of the greatest experiences that I have had since coming to Bozeman. I derive happiness from the people and things around me. Sometimes the depression is still there, but not nearly so severe. Nor for so long of a time as it once was. Now I know what it is like to feel the warmth of love for people. It is a glow that burns deep from within. Two or three months ago I knew no feeling that could compare with this. Now I see faces and know there is a unique person behind them. I feel a joy in knowing that I, too, am a unique individual. Two or three months ago I doubted my worth as a person."

Another gal lost her boy friend. He was killed in an accident. She stopped in to see me. Later, she said in her paper, "My first true contact with your views did not occur within the class. It occurred when I visited your office shortly after my return after Tom's death. This tragedy has indeed upset my life but at the same time it hardened my own mistaken beliefs. Direct confrontation with your unshakable viewpoint caused my once strong attitude to tremble. Offering no sharp criticism, you, piece by piece, destroyed my misguided security. Leaving your office with the words, 'Just think it over,' ringing in my ears I spent many restless hours. With only dead ends behind me, I decided to review my past.

"I found that I indeed have a problem. Your famous story about the farmer and his few precious grains of wheat is quite applicable. My seeds were indeed few and because of their rarity they were hoarded. When through the loss of Tom, they were lost, I was left with nothing only because I lacked the courage and the foresight to plant and plan for future crops.

"My next statement may sound corny, but I began to see

the light. Your system and mine now is sort of a borrow-return base. Give to those around you and they in return will give back a greater reward. Like money drawing interest from a bank, it grows only when invested. Now that I saw that your plan just might work I was anxious but frightened to give it a try. Since so far my crops had been complete failures, I had little reserve with which to begin again.

"Now my story gets funny. One day last week, a particularly beautiful one, I was walking along quite lost in my own thoughts. As I gazed up, I looked into the most beautiful blue eyes I have ever seen. Never being a terrible flirt, I am still amazed at what occurred next. I turned to this complete stranger and said, 'Hi, isn't it wonderful out.' Trying to remember the look on this handsome stranger's face, I can only recall shyness. He walked on a few steps, then turned and walked back to where I was still standing. Quietly and with a chuckle he asked me for a date. We had yet to exchange names. I must admit that your class fails to prepare students for such results.

"I was so surprised and shook that I cannot to this day remember what I said to the poor guy. But somehow I escaped to my room hoping never to see him again. Then just as suddenly as it had come, my embarrassment disappeared. I felt great and alive for the first time in ever so long. I suddenly found that the world is full of lonely people like myself just waiting for a sign of interest and love. I have also found that it is just as much fun to give as to receive. I am not saying that I know all the answers but I have solved the hardest problem, discovering the inner-person within each of us just begging to give and receive love, not just from a few select persons, but from every living and breathing soul."

These people are like you and me. And the sadness is not only that is this terribly hard to do, but it is terribly hard to admit to ourselves that we don't even try. One of the exercises that I use and that I will give to you right now to demonstrate this to yourself is to go tell five people that you love them.

I don't mean to tell the next five people you meet on the street that you love them. I mean to tell five people where this is appropriate. I am sure some of you are in the good situation of having used these words where they apply frequently so it isn't much of a problem. But more frequently there are parents, husbands, wives, close friends to whom the words "I love you" would have been appropriate a long time ago. But yet they have never been said. And this is why you frequently get such drastic results when you do this assignment.

One of the most common responses to these words when they have been long delayed is that the person will cry. One girl said, "When you gave me that exercise, I thought of my parents and the trouble I had with them. So I called my mother and dad and told them that I loved them." They said, "What's wrong?" I said, "Nothing," and they started to cry.

A nurse called an old nursing supervisor of hers out in Washington long distance one night. She and this woman had had some trouble when this woman was her supervisor originally but, nevertheless, this woman had also been very helpful to this girl. And she had a real, deep feeling for her still, despite the difficulties they had together. She said, "Hey, I love you." It was about five minutes before the woman on the other end of the line could stop crying and start talking again. A mother in my class wrote me a card. She said, "I told my son I loved him. He cried. He's eighteen." But why?

Well the answer is: We think we *feel*, we think we are *alive*. Obviously this is the natural thing to think and one of the best ways to avoid the fact that we aren't doing a very good job is this. But then we will get some sudden shock and realize, "Hey, we aren't doing what we thought we were doing." Some of you are going to come up to people where the words "I love you" are very appropriate. But you are going to choke on these words a number of times. To your horror, you are going to realize, "I am just not quite living the swinging life that I thought I was." You see?

What will happen if we won't face our emotions honestly? I have seen the bad result in myself and people around me. In an attempt to get some love and affection and tenderness and yet hesitant and frightened to reveal themselves to the world, they turn and start building the fanciest, greatest kind of wall they can imagine. And they use every kind of symbol to build something.

You can use power or an attempt for social position. You can use clothes. I often see women who are meticulously made up, where everything about them is just so. Hair, clothes, everything. There isn't a single hair out of position. That says trouble to me. That does not say beauty to me. It says here is someone who is so overwhelmed with appearance that she cannot let one single strand of hair be out of place or she will feel just like she is naked.

There are lots of other ways of running away from the world. Oddly enough, one of the ways of running away would seem to put you in most direct contact with the world. You see this in people in what could be called the helping professions like counseling, teaching and nursing. Some of these people, unfortunately, are seeking escape and are using their ostensible close and intimate contact with the world to run away from it.

Usually they don't last in their professions very long or they switch to a more impersonal spot in their profession because it is a hard fake to maintain. But these people don't have any more capacity to really listen to anybody than to go to the moon. And I think, "Oh boy, what about that poor little kid that came into their office for some help. Or, what about the poor patient who gets her for a nurse?" Yes, there are many ways of running away from the world. There is only one way of facing into it.

Now, perhaps you are inclined to say, "Jess, you are making too big a thing out of this. I really have got something going for me, and I don't want to sit around and listen to you say I haven't." If it is great for you, wonderful! But I find this hard to accept. In my experience people who are deeply loving people are one in a thousand. Or at least no more than one in a hundred. Now if fifty people in a class of one hundred want to tell me, "I am that one in a hundred," I will listen, but I'm not convinced.

This is not something that is very easy or very common; if it were, our lives would be drastically different than they are.

Now here is the second assignment I will give you. This isn't theory. It works. Do this if you want to have more meaningful, closer relationships with others. All you need to do is with five people speak of what you feel in your deepest heart. Speak of these difficulties you have of accepting yourself. Speak of your fears and your worries.

And you know what the other person is going to do? What would you imagine? "Feel sorry for you?" No, they won't feel sorry for you. Most of the five will want to be closer to you and they will reciprocate with the same thing. They will recognize their kinship with you. And they'll feel calm because they will see that you and they are in the same boat.

Almost everytime I've mentioned the mistakes I've made as a teacher I find that people have come back at me and said, "Oh, boy, I've made those mistakes, too. And so I'm glad to hear that you've had that kind of problem." You can see they have been afraid of admitting their problems because they thought they were the only ones who had them and if someone found out they might get fired. Now, I'll give you the opposite kind of experiment where you fake it. It's an assignment that I hope you won't do on purpose. But if you're like me, you find yourself doing it despite your hatred of it. It's where you put some more bricks in place in the silo you're building around yourself. Pictures of the smiling father, the smiling mother, the smiling nun, the smiling teacher or the smiling nurse are painted on the silo, and it's all fake.

We will put a couple more bricks in place. Real fancy, glazed bricks. So what you do, if you're a nun, is to go up and tell another nun, "I was so worried last night. I felt bad. I was talking to Mother Superior about what I had done that day, and she told me what a fantastically dedicated nurse I really was. You know, she said she had never seen a nurse as dedicated as I was. And it just embarrassed me so to have Sister tell me these things. I just felt so bad."

Try this and you'll find people can't get away from you fast enough.

Or you can say, "Gee, my problem is just terrible. I paid my income tax the other day and I had to take four thousand dollars out of savings because I made so much more money last year than I expected." That will really get people. You know, they hope you are lying but they are afraid you aren't. I tried this on a guy once as a joke but he believed me. We will always believe the best about the other guy but not about ourselves. And people will run away from you in droves. I guarantee it.

Here are some other ideas. Complain about how poor the airconditioning system is in your new Cadillac. Or how bad vandalism problems are at your second home in the country.

I remember a conversation like this between two women in Houston. These women were loudly complaining to each other about the terrible problems they were having keeping their swimming pools cleaned out. Now this happened nearly twenty years ago when you had to be pretty rich to have a swimming pool. And I'll bet these two gals really loved each other's company.

So you see the sickness in that kind of faking—yet how easy it is to do. I've been sitting around with groups of people where everyone was close and having a good time telling stories and laughing. And I've seen myself or someone else say some faking thing and bust the group up like a bunch of flushed quail. They couldn't get away fast enough.

Now you try these experiments.

A nursing supervisor once asked me, "Aren't what we might think of as common people better at being real than people with more responsible positions?" In my experience about half of the people with big jobs didn't get them in the nicest ways. Some of us have clawed our way to the top rather than floating to the top like cream, some of us are in positions of authority because it was damned important to us to have responsibility and get the money and prestige as patches for our little egos. So a lot of the people we passed by on our way up the ladder are far better at being real and telling people how they really feel about themselves than we are. Of course, this doesn't apply to you or me. It's just an idea others should consider.

Now when you try this, you will see how hard it is and how rare in all our lives. But when you succeed in being real and someone is real in return you will see how good you feel and you will see how rare that is, too. And you will see how different our lives would be if all of us were much more the person we really are deep down.

Okay. Now, to tell five people that you love them isn't easy to do. But its lots harder to show five people that you love them by telling them how it is with you in your deepest heart. I know people who have never done that to anyone—or just one or two people. When you do go out and be real to five people, you are going to have one, two, three, four or maybe five be real back to you. And perhaps in one of those cases you are going to get that little glow there in your tummy. And then you get up tomorrow morning and you remember that and your tummy feels kind of nice and warm. You've got some reserve, see.

You've got something to go with, to help you be a little bit more real, and to help you go a little deeper into yourself. And the thing that you can find, if you choose, is here, ready, waiting and available to you: You can come more alive to life. Just as crucial, you can avoid something that scares me to death, and that is you can avoid dying to life.

You are either open to life or you ain't. And the way to stay open to life is to get some love and affection and joy and tenderness into your hearts so you can really look at your life and live it five minutes at a time.

Otherwise you are like a person who starts on a trip and he paints his car windows black. And he starts from Minnesota and drives west and you ask him what the scenery is like about a thousand miles later. "Oh," they say, "it is flat country with a lot of trees and grass and many lakes." And you know they are driving through say Miles City, Montana or the mountains. And you say, "Hey, why don't you just open your window and take a look outside. It ain't like that out there." But they don't know that. They've got the windows painted over. They are dead to life as it is around them.

You can come alive to life by getting some nourishment for your heart so that it doesn't shrivel up and want to die. And you do that by going out and being as real as you can and getting as close to what's in your deepest heart as you can. That helps you be real more often and helps you be more real next time. You can't live your whole life twenty-four hours a day that way. But do it five minutes at a time and sneak a few five minutes in today of being real and getting those rewards. And then sneak in a few more five minutes tomorrow of being real and get those rewards. You will find a drastic change in your life.

So when I talk about being real, I mean we should take away a piece of our mask and show the fears and worries we have, not our angers. The result is that we actually change the world we live in by the way we act. It isn't that some people are real and others unreal. I find that the more real I am, the more real people there are around me. So being real helps us have richer, deeper relationships with the people around us.

Another way of looking at this is with Berne's idea of game-free conversation. He tells in his book about the patient of his who started being real. The things she saw were really there, and she was really there. She was in an art gallery and a man standing beside her said, "I like Gauguin." She said, "I like you, too." So they went out and had a drink and he was a nice guy.

It's hard to be real. It's frightening. We are all good at faking so faking to five people is easy. But being real to five people is very, very hard. I think part of the problem is that being real makes us vulnerable to the other person and that scares us. I also think there is a more crucial reason why telling what is in our deepest heart is so hard for us. It is directly related to acceptance of ourselves. To be real, we must first halfway accept ourselves so that we can see what we really are.

We are finite human beings so we aren't capable of being very real—we can just try to approximate it more and more as we go on. But we also have a terribly egotistical view of how great we are, and we can easily be horrified at the great gap between what we see as we work at being real and our exalted view of ourselves. It's like that song, "Is that all there is? . . . to a fire, to a circus, to love." Yes that's all there is to love. But it beats hell out of what we have when we are faking it.

A good example of this is the many people who did all the work for a Ph.D. except their thesis. Most Ph.D. aspirants are aware of their ignorance. They know they don't know. So it isn't hard for them to write a thesis. They know their thesis has lots of holes in it, they know where those holes are, and they know it's going to take a lifetime of study to learn the things needed to plug some of those holes.

But there is another type of Ph.D. candidate. He has such an exalted self-conception (which I think arises out of his deep fears and a sense of inferiority) that he can't admit to himself that he doesn't know. So when he sits down to write his thesis, he sees something less than exalted words coming from his pen. At this point he has two alternatives. He can accept this and say, "Okay, that's me," and keep on writing. Or, he can refuse to accept his words and not write any more.

The same thing happens when we try to be real. We can try it and we may even feel the other person being more real back, but we can say to ourselves, "I don't like this. Life must be more than this. There must be something better for me." And maybe this is true for that person. Maybe something else will come along that is better. Or maybe that person's role in life is to feel that they are standing at the candy store window of life with their nose pressed against the glass.

I find I can accept these problems and limitations of being real. I know that I'm not very real compared to what I might like to be. I know how slippery and tricky I am when it comes to fooling around. And I know how frustrating it is that each of us is trapped in our own skin like people in metal shells who can only tap in crude code to each other. I can accept all these things. I see them as the finite nature of the human condition. Most of all, I've seen this problem is not as big a one as it might seem to be at first.

Sally, a teacher friend of mine, responded to the dilemma I just discussed with this story. She had seen it done to illustrate approaching a limit in mathematics. The teacher puts two people on opposite sides of the room. He has them move halfway toward each other. Then halfway again. By always cutting the distance in half, they will never touch—in theory. But as a practical matter they can be very, very close to each other.

I see being real the same way. We can't ever get so we are completely real. But we can gradually learn to be real enough so that our lives change drastically. This is another way of looking at acceptance that really helps me. In the last three years it has changed the whole character of my life.

Will it work for you? The only way to find out is to try it. Be real about yourself to a number of people. Some of them will probably be real back. You should feel something different because of it. So it's worth a try.

But there is one important caution. This is a long way from "Telling it like it is, baby." When we hear this, we are tempted to tell about the things around and outside us. But we can't ever know about those other things and other people. We can't go outside our skin and inside their skin. So the only thing we can be real about is ourselves. This is all we can ever know. So it is enough to try to be real about ourselves and avoid being distracted by what seem to be other people's problems.

One of my students put the problem of being real this way. He said, "I've never allowed much of myself into a relationship because I felt that any show of emotion would allow people to see my humanness. I always wanted people to think I was a physical-mental-super-God, not to be confused with a lesser term—human being. When I approached someone I wanted them to think, 'Here comes God.' When I arrived, 'Here is God!' When I left, 'There goes God.' Boy was I dumb. And I'll bet they knew it.

"I had such a fear of my weaknesses showing that I couldn't be Gary. No. I was a combination of John Kennedy, Jim Brown, Omar Sharif, Paul Anderson and John Wayne —I just looked a lot like Gary.

"My girl knew I was somewhere beneath my phoniness and

she thought this class would help me. It has. I'm going to tell her I love her."

The best summary of these ideas came from a girl who heard me speak at a religious Search. Each person must sum up in writing each speaker's message. Here's what she said:

"I look around at the beauty of the world. It is beautiful—a smile, a tear, a raindrop, a sunset. I look into myself for the beauty of my world. Am I woman enough to see my imperfections? What's more, accept them? The beauty of being human is being imperfect *like* my sisters and brothers and this communicated to them is loving them—accepting them. What does it do for me? From a love sincerely enacted I will get a sincere love in response. That's what the world needs now—more love."

The daughter of one of my fellow faculty members read my book. Her father brought me a poem she had written for me about being real. So I wrote a poem back to her:

People needing other people
Is just four little words
Of a big song.
But there is only one people.
That's me—and I need you.
But the sad funny thing is
How each of us run away
From our needing people.
Even using a song about it
To run away.
But it hurts so much—at first.
And then it feels so good to find
That real is love.
And so love is waiting for us
Twenty times a day
Behind all the funny faces.
We just need to take down our fake face
And let the beauty, power and glory out.
We can love so often and so well
That the minutes fly and the days are long.
For love is real and real is love.

FOUR

Accepting Yourself—
Five Minutes at a Time

What I want to talk to you about next is acceptance. It's been around a long time—the idea of it, anyway. Everybody says it's common sense. But I find it's pretty uncommon and it's more talked about than done.

The idea of acceptance has been around two thousand years. It's the heart of Alcoholics Anonymous and Emotions Anonymous. The best expression that I've seen of the idea is by Carl Rogers. He says, "The curious paradox is that when I accept myself just as I am, then I can change." Now there's a whole lot of things in that one sentence.

The first part says: The paradox is that when I accept myself as I am. That means that you take yourself, I take myself, just exactly the way we find ourselves. I don't fudge on anything, and I see all kinds of things that I would like to fudge on. I see many facets and aspects of myself that don't agree with my conception of what I should be. Nor do they agree with society's conception, as near as I can see it, of what I am supposed to be. So I find it very troublesome to accept myself as I am.

But the "curious paradox" refers to the second part of the sentence. When I accept myself as I am, then I can change. The sentence is saying that you change by *not* concentrating on change, and not defining what it's going to be. The power of positive thinking is just the exact opposite. If I want to be what I want to be, I just decide what I want to be and then I be it. Whereas this thing says the exact opposite. It says that I take myself just exactly as I am. I forget about change. Accept it all, just as it is. And you are just screaming at me, "No, no I can't! I've got this and that quality and I can't accept it all." But that's what this idea is about. It's looking at ourselves and accepting it all. And only then do we change.

The next question, of course, is what do we change into? And here again there's a big difference between the power of positive thinking and acceptance. Positive thinking suggests that all of us know very clearly and very well what we should be. And what we should do. And what we are. But in my experience, that is not true.

We do not know what we should be. We do not know what we should do. And we do not know what we are very well. And the answer, it seems to me, is that what we are is kind of like an unfolding of some mysterious thing. The excitement of life is partly waiting to see who it is and what it is that we are. And in my experience we cannot see to the heart of ourselves. We cannot see the path that is best for us.

So that the way we change, in my experience, is that we change and become more like that unique and ideal person that lies within us. But the odd thing is that we can't control that change.

And if you say, "Aw, Jess, you're all wrong. I see this millionaire and that millionaire. And they sat down when they were seven-year-olds and decided the life of a millionaire was the life for them." Yes, there are exceptions to what I am saying. But they don't impress me very much. Because if you want to make the material accomplishments that are typically set as goals your final measure in life—fine. But I'm not satisfied with that because there are too many shortcomings to that kind of a goal in life. The people I admire are the people who find themselves rather surprised at seeing what they are doing, at what their life's work has become. I think this is best exemplified by the people who really respect themselves. They start out doing what they like to do. And then just follow that. They end up sometimes by accomplishing great things. But accomplishment as such is not interesting to me. I'm as interested in the person who just started out following what he likes and who isn't any big beans outside his own little community. He's just a person who's happy with himself.

I see, in our society, this concept of greatness is a terrible distraction and a terrible difficulty to all of us. It makes us constantly question ourselves in the things that we are trying to do in pursuit of this greatness. We say to ourselves, "If I'm so smart, how come I ain't rich?" Well it's a ridiculous question.

I could just as well ask, "If I'm so smart, how come I can't sing in the Metropolitan Opera?" That's just as ridiculous. But it's a challenge that's continually thrown back at us by society and particularly, by the part of the society that wants to stress fantastic material accomplishments. The question, appropriately is, "If I am so smart, then is my life proceeding along about as well as it can?" And this is the question that we had better be able to answer "yes" to. If I'm so smart, am I using that smartness as hard as I can to handle my life and manage it as well as I can, and hopefully the answer to that is "yes."

The question of greatness, the question of accomplishments, material and otherwise, is a side issue. In a way you can say that's kind of in the stars. Some small group of people happen to be in the right place at the right time, riding on the right wave until they stand high. But that's beside the point. The central point is whether each of us are *standing* or not. Are we accepting ourselves just the way we are, working with ourselves just the way we are, or not? That's how change comes.

A good example is Martin Luther King. You say, "He got shot, didn't he?" Yes, he did. But he was trying to do what he believed in as well as an imperfect human can. How long a life is, is of little consequence. What counts is what we do with the days we have. Do we move toward what we are by seeking it? Or do we deny what we are by refusing to accept it?

There were black ministers. But the black ministers in Montgomery, Alabama, had a special opportunity. And one of them happened to have the particular set of talents necessary in that situation.

Now again, it's sad that we say "Phooey! I can't accept myself just exactly the way I am. This and that and that characteristic has got to change. For example, I am way too inhibited. I want to be a swinger. I don't like this inhibited side of myself." Well the funny thing is that when we look at ourselves that way, we frustrate the process by which we grow.

And again, it has been my experience that we're not capable of saying along which lines we should go. Our power lies in areas that we know not of. And the way we have access to the power and glory and uniqueness in us is to avoid making any bargains with life and with ourselves. "Okay. This is me at this moment. And I will accept it all as well as I possibly can." So that's how Rogers' sentence goes. But it is an awful big task.

We talked about being real, but to be real, you need acceptance. All you can be at any given moment is what is there. That's all that's real. I can't say, "Hey, being real to me is putting on this kind of act or that kind of act."

Now, a common question is, "If I can change and be different than I am, how come I don't run the risk of being phony?" Now you see what I'm saying really is that we can't change by concentrating on change. If we concentrate on accepting ourselves, then the change will happen. It will take care of itself. And it will go along lines that we don't know of and are incapable of planning. Someone else said, "Okay, fine, you say be real. Be myself. Where do I start?" And this is where we start.

Now I haven't talked too much in these few chapters about the specific application of these ideas to different occupations. In my experience I don't need to talk a lot about applications because what we're talking about is the processes and business of living. And very few of you have any difficulty understanding that you can't be better at nursing, teaching, or whatever, than you can be at living. You can't be a better businessman, husband, wife, brother, sister, roommate, son or daughter—than you can be at living. Everything we do is all bound together. And, to my mind, the strength of those ideas is that they lie at the heart of real change in our whole life rather than at fussing around at this part or at that part.

There's some research, for example, on teaching which suggests that *both* the good teacher and the poor teacher know what a good teacher is and does. It's just that the poor teacher can't do it. I find that the people who have difficulty, whether it be in business, teaching, nursing, are pretty much the people who are running away from themselves. They're using their occupation and all their other activities outside their occupation as means of running away from their lives. And there are an awful lot of ways to run away from yourself. And there's only one way not to run away from yourself.

Now, what I'm talking about is probably the hardest thing

there is to do. But it is also tremendously valuable to you. If you would give me five minutes for the whole book, that five minutes would be on acceptance of yourself—as you are.

I'll add another thing that I discovered fairly recently about acceptance. Self-acceptance is so hard to get you can't do it a day at a time. I've found that I need to run my life five minutes at a time. And I find that most of the mistakes that I make come from violating this notion of living just five minutes at a time. I find I must look at myself and look at what I'm turning my hand to and say, "Hey, Jess, is that you?" And if I ask that question, I find that automatically and always, there is a little voice that will answer and say "yes" or "no." Not ringing loud and clear, but clear enough that I can hear it. And the voice hasn't always got a yes or a no. Sometimes it's, "I think it's more yes than no." And it's about as certain as we can get in this uncertain world.

But I find that by using this idea of taking care of the minutes, the hours are full. And the days take care of themselves. The funny thing I've noticed though is that the days go fast now. But because the days are full, the years are full and they go slow.

There are kinds of feelings and ideas that need acceptance. It's almost impossible to describe the play of feelings and thoughts and questions that flow over your mind in the course of a whole day. But when you start looking at your life five minutes at a time, you are acutely aware of these things. And I would suggest, as your exercise for the day, that you just try to say, "In this next five minutes, I'm going to take a good look and really watch myself and really try to be me just as I am and accept just exactly what I see."

A while ago I was reading in the *Farm Quarterly* about outstanding farmers and ranchers. One story was about the man who developed silver platinum mink. He's the man who organized Emba—the mutation mink breeders association. Another story told of a man out in California who owns about five thousand acres of California land where it costs two or three thousand dollars an acre.

As I read those stories, I kept getting sicker and sicker and sicker. And I thought, "Oh, Jess, you dummy. You know you're not making anything of your life and all these fat cats are moving by you at a high rate of speed and leaving you. You're just eating dust, boy. You better get to work. Put aside all these cobwebby, crazy notions of yours and do something that really counts. Something that really makes an impression on the world.

"In the academic world, there are a lot of ways you can make a real impression in the world. You can go out and do a lot of articles on the appropriate subjects. And you can get government grants. You can set up an awful storm. Within five years, you can be a real big wheel in academic life."

And the sadness, particularly in my case, is because I used to be a public relations man, I could do this much more adeptly than most because I'm extremely skilled at managing all these kinds of contrivances and I know how to concentrate my efforts in certain areas to get the maximum push with the minimum amount of time. So these were some of my five minute periods that night.

I looked at these men's successes and then said, "Okay, Jess, calm yourself down. Are you doing what you're supposed to do? Yah. Are you trying to do the best you can? Yah. Is it going to make you famous and a lot of money? No. Okay, so what?" And the answer is again, so what? I'm not going to make fame and money my rule because I don't like what I see in the lives of people who live by that rule. I've got to have enough to eat, but beyond that, you don't need an awful lot.

One of the powerful effects of this acceptance of self is the way our ability to communicate with others changes. Once we start putting our own house in order, we have a much better heart toward others. And in my experience, I've never seen a case of a person who really has a good heart toward another who wasn't able to communicate that at least at 90 per cent effectiveness—and that's good enough. I doubt that you've ever been with a good-hearted person where you've had a serious misunderstanding with them. If there are small areas of misunderstanding, your good-heartedness toward each other will help you clear them up.

But if you have a bad heart toward somebody or some group of people, there is no way in the world you can communicate with them so they will like it—just no way. I don't care how you fake it. No matter how skillful a liar you are, the fake will show through. So in my view, this acceptance of self is crucial to our life goal—and it is also crucial to communicating with others.

A lot of students say, "Hey, I'm not very good at accepting myself." And the answer is of course not. The answer is you get a lot better. It's like learning to ride a bicycle. Practice helps.

Somebody else asks, "Can you get so you're perfect at accepting yourself?" And the answer is, "No, you can't." As near as I see it, it's like peeling an onion. You get off one layer of acceptance of feelings and thoughts and ideas and problems, and then all you've got left is another layer underneath. You keep on working on that all your life, seeing new paths for yourself, new areas that need acceptance. I think, in a way, that when you get to the center of the onion, it's a bad sign. That means you're ready to die. Because you know all and you see all. But none of us are ever going to get to that point, so there's no reason to worry about it.

But this is what I think living is about. I don't see living having to do with any special goal or end. It seems to me living has to do with just that—living. It's a process. We are either living and using those things that are around us to work with today, or we're not. Now, unfortunately, most of us are not. Most of us are like kids waiting for Christmas.

I'll never forget the first quarter that I was teaching. My students had left home in late September saying, "Oh boy, I'm sure glad to get away from those folks and our old house. Boy, I'm going away and be free. I'll kick up my heels and have a lot of fun." And then just before Thanksgiving, there was a change. My students started thinking about Mom and pumpkin pie. All of the fights that they had had, started to dwindle and they were just anxious to get home. And they got home for a day or two and found it was not quite as dreamlike as they had looked forward to. They came back but then again, my students soon started thinking Christmas. And they had this magical notion of Christmas. "Only twenty more days 'til Christmas." "Only seventeen more days 'til Christmas" were the cards they wrote each day for the class. And then a little gal, I think oddly enough her home town was Wisdom or Wise River, said on a card. "Don't wish your life away. Christmas will come in its own time." And of course that is what we're doing.

We're continually planning and looking ahead to tomorrow, next week, next year, when we get out of college, when we get married, when we get a job, when we're this, when we're that. And we *walk right on by* so many of the things that are in our life today. We don't even see them. Because there's a power and a glory and a majesty in this life and in us. I've seen all kinds of evidences to support the fact that there is. And it's here—right now. Right this minute—just as you are right now. But you won't see it at all if you run yourself down. You will, if you take yourself the way you are right now.

Now you say, "Hey, man, that sounds great, but that ain't enough for me. You mean I've got to take this mess that's sitting here right now the way it is. That's all there is?" Well, yah, that's all there is. But it's just one awful lot. And it's just a tremendous amount more than there was before. Because what you've got right now is something. What you had before when you were looking ahead to next week is nothing. That's death. That's being dead on your feet. That's throwing life away. It's like one of my students said, "When I get up in the morning, it's still tomorrow." Here's a person who's in the habit of looking ahead so much that nothing ever happens in today. It's always tomorrow.

I was explaining these ideas to a friend of mine, Bill Gove, down in Florida, and he said, "Hey, Jess, what you're saying to me is, I ain't much, baby—but I'm all I got." And that's right.

It's like David on the way out to face Goliath. All he had was that sling shot and five smooth stones. Okay, like David, you've got two choices. Are you going to run and hide in a deep cave? (And there ain't any cave big enough and deep enough to hide in.) Or are you going to walk out there, wind up and give your stone a flip.

Now it takes courage and I recognize this. So did the poet Van Doren, who said, "It takes courage to be happy." Where do you get your courage? Most of it was given you by someone. It sounds a little bit like the guy who comes in and talks to you about how you can make money on the stock market. He leaves out one big important consideration. To make money on the stock market, you've got to have some money. I've never liked the guy who did that to me.

But here, I don't see any choice in doing this and I think there are some answers to it. But I do recognize that I and some of you are exceptionally low on the kind of courage that it takes to do this. And why? This is where the Zulu story comes in again. As near as I can see, we weren't given that courage by the adults around us in the crucial stages of our lives. I was very lucky, I had a number of adults who believed in me deeply and warmly and what courage I have, I got from them.

A lot of people say, "Jess, it's great how you can do the

things you do." And most of the time, when they are talking about something good, they're talking about something that comes out of that courage that was given me and it's nothing that I deserve to take any credit for.

Maybe someone has a short supply of courage. Well, I've got no right to jump all over them. I've had students who say, "Never in my entire lifetime do I remember either a parent or another adult who trusted me or who believed in me." Okay, where is that person going to get his or her courage? Part of the answer is that right out of these ideas themselves comes the help. But it's an awful lot tougher if you don't bring much of a bank account with you in terms of some kind of fundamental courage, some kind of ability to be somewhat optimistic, somewhat hopeful about life.

An ad for the Peace Corps had this test. Look at this glass of water which is filled up halfway. Describe the glass of water. You can describe it as half empty or half full. And if you describe it as half empty, it tells me something about your fear and fright of the world around you.

This acceptance of yourself is a troubling thing. Most of the rest of our talk will be about acceptance in key areas of our life. I'll give you a lot more examples of specific acceptances, because it's about the only tool that I've found effective as I try to let my life run itself a little more sensibly than I did before. It lets you be a little more alive to live.

Now there's a second level of acceptance. One of the ways that I change is that I can accept others more as they are. When I am open to my feelings about myself, I see that I alternate quickly between moods. In one moment, I'm so impatient for money and financial success, I'm ready to rob any bank that's left unguarded for an instant. At the next moment, I'm pounding on one of my kids because I'm mad at the world. And the next moment I am something else. When I've got a string of these real bad moments, I am relieved by anything that I can take hope in.

Okay, I have to look at that mess, and say, "That's me? That's Jess Lair? Yah, that's me. Okay." Now—once I've done that for a while, how in the world am I going to look at you and some one specific thing you're doing and be outraged at it? And not accept you the way you are? There's no way. Once I see that all of the feelings and problems of the world are in me in one way, shape or form, how am I going to get mad at them in you. And I haven't got a lot of energy left over to throw rocks at you. So those are the two levels of this paradox.

Now when I accept myself as I am, I free myself from all my preconceived notions of who and what I'm supposed to be. And when I accept you as you are, I do one of the most precious and valuable things for you that has ever been done and can ever be done for you.

I think you can all look back and see a few people who have taken you just the way you were. No deals, no bargains. They take you because you are you. They take you as you are, unconditionally, no ifs, ands, or buts. Not, "I will accept you if you will stop doing this." Nor, "I will accept you if you cut your hair." Nor, "I will accept you if you shave your beard." Nor, "I will accept you if you do all these other things, if you wear your skirts longer or shorter or whatever the case." All these deals.

To achieve a better potential when you put down this book, you must still face the same old world. But the world is a different place than it was when you picked it up—if you will do your part. The reason is this: When we accept ourself as we are, one of the ways that we change is that we are calmer. And we stop bugging people. And the minute we do that, we don't get bugged back near as much. You see that's Lair's first law—Bug and thou shalt be bugged in return. So the world *will* be different because you'll be causing less problems.

Also acceptance of the other person communicates itself to them magically and he becomes not a different person but a different person to us. Like I said, each person has got two sides to him, a head and a tail. And each of us are painfully aware that we've got two sides, and if somebody wants to see our bad side, they can see it awful fast. Not very many people seem to want to see our good side. But when we really try to accept ourselves as we are, so that we can show that good side, it's there, available to people. And when we accept the people around us as they are, we see a lot more of the heads of them and less of the tails of them. In those two senses, we can change the world substantially.

Now there's one additional way we can change the world. And that is that once we have a clearer sense of who it is and what it is we really are, we drop away from a lot of people who are misery and trouble to us. It's not that there's something wrong with them, but those aren't the right people for us. As we drop away from those people, our life again can be different. I know after I had my heart attack, one of the things I looked at was some of the people I called my friends and thought were my friends. A lot of them weren't really; we were just kind of mutual enemies. And the minute that we each went our own separate ways, we were both happier because of it.

I'm sure one of the ways you see this is in your friends of high school days, or particularly after you get away from them. Some of those people you look at and say, "Oh, how could I have stood that person?" They were friends of convenience. We needed each other and clung together as to a life raft in the middle of the ocean. But there was no real friendship.

We also need to stay away from situations that are troublesome for us and find situations that are pleasant and supporting to us. This may mean changing jobs, where you live, interests, many things. Look at all the situations you are in each day and ask yourself, "Are they really right for me?"

So there are quite a few ways, you see, that we can change our lives around. This is, of course, if we want to. If we do these things. I'm talking to you about the ideas that I've found crucial to me in getting my life into better shape. So we're not just beating our gums here about some hypothetical, abstract kind of thing. We're talking about something real, something tangible.

Now—one common response to something like this is, "Aren't you going to get an inferiority complex from looking at yourself the way you really are? Gee, I ain't much, baby— but I'm all I got." Well you stop at the "ain't much" part and you might think this is an inferiority complex. In my belief, the experience is just the opposite. The inferiority complex is the guy who is running away in stark terror from what he is and trying to smoke screen it with all kinds of fancy talk and fancy doing and fancy things. So the best antidote to an inferiority complex is this whole idea. Because it says, "Yah, I'm not much, but that's all I got."

As a woman student expressed it, "I have been thinking how simple it is for people when they decide what they must do. A lot of time you go trying to fight, like Don Quixote, the windmills. But when you do decide, it is really quite simple. I believe that is each person's greatness, to be able to decide. How foolish it is to go on and not decide."

Recently, a nun asked me what really made me change.

Was it the people who believed in me? Or was it the crisis of my heart attack? Or what?

I think it was the crisis. Also, I was ready to change. I had lived out the results of that destructive line of behaving and I could see that it led nowhere. Just to being dead on my feet.

I think that is one of the things that is happening in this country. As we carry technological development further and further, our young people are saying to you and me, "Look, this doesn't make sense. This fantastic preoccupation with money and other resources going into more and more accomplishments is dumb."

Going to the moon isn't all that important when you compare it to some of our problems like the fact we can't talk to one another. If I had a show of hands in my class on how many are happy with the richness and quality of their lives and their relationships with other people, very few would say they were. Yet most of them are reasonably satisfied with the material side of their life. Sure they would like newer cars. But they would rather work on some of these ideas to improve the non-material side of their life.

You may ask, "Don't I have to understand people so I can carry on this feeling of acceptance?" Yes, you need to understand people. But most of all you need to understand yourself. I think when I see what I am and what I am capable of becoming, then there is no reason for me not accepting another person. The more I exalt myself, the more difficulty I have accepting others. I don't see it as a matter of understanding them. I can't understand exactly why he is doing specific things the way he is doing them, but I can have at least a general understanding. And there's all the resource material in the world right inside of me for all that knowledge to come from.

A man who will probably have very few problems because of all those he has seen in himself wrote me this letter:

"This is my way of saying thank you. Let me explain.

"Someone sent me your book, but I promptly put it in my file and forgot it.

"In September, I had to quit my job. I was strung out, my work was getting to me. I had money problems and my wife and I were having a bad time.

"I committed myself to the state mental hospital and spent three months there. You talk about a lost person with no job, no wife, no money. Man, the world came to an end.

"I was discharged in December and went to stay with my mother. The next Sunday I went to church. The minister quoted from your book. I don't remember the quote but it rang a bell that I had the book.

"Well, to make a long story short, I have read and reread it every day. *Accept myself*—the words seemed to jump from the pages. This I've never done, now to start.

"Your thoughts and ideas in the book have given me a new lease on life. I am trying to put some of your ideas to work. Although things haven't made a great change as yet, I do feel something inside of me that wants to grow."

A nurse said this:

"Facts and definitions are not what I need. That's not what my family, or my friends or my patients need. We all need *ME*. A *real, live* me. Okay, so how do I get to be real? You say know yourself for what you are—and then accept it. But I don't even accept the parts of myself I admit to. How can I accept the rest of the ugly mess?

"Well, you gave us a hint. Try a little of yourself out on others. If they come back with a little of themselves, then how can the part I showed be so bad?

"Hey, if they like part of the real me, wouldn't they just possibly like the rest? Like you said, the people who are real back give me enough to start uncovering more of the painful things.

"I haven't done enough work on accepting myself. It is painful. And I don't expect to ever finish. But I'm started."

So this is a problem for realness. The best way to describe what it is that we're in pursuit of is the description that Michelangelo gave of how he sculptured the statue "David." Somebody said, "How did you get David?" He said, "I took a block of granite, and I chipped away everything that was not David."

And this is, as I see it, the process of living. We're trying to get rid of those things that aren't us. We're looking at ourselves each day, five minutes at a time and saying, "Hey, Jess, is that you?" And every once in a while, I'll say "no." And pretty soon that particular thing will drop away. And that means we're getting closer to what lies beneath.

Now, in a way, the analogy isn't correct because the what we are isn't any fixed, immovable thing like a granite statue lying underneath there to be discovered. It is changing in itself. But the way we get at this process, this thing that is inside us, this more unique self that is us, is by this process of discarding the things that aren't us. And what we have left is us.

By working on it five minutes at a time, anybody can do it.

FIVE

To Change—
Go Beyond the Classroom

In the first four chapters I have laid down the major ideas that will be more completely developed in the rest of the book. But before we go on to those ideas we need to talk about a terrible problem that blocks change and reduces the possibility for change in our life. That problem comes from all the sins that have been committed against you and me in the name of education. As a result, the minute we approach education or books we turn off all our critical faculties and either slavishly submit to anything that is done to us in education's name or we blindly reject everything to do with it. Since this is a book on changing your life, you need to avoid the two dangers mentioned above and see that this book is about changes in your life and needs your careful and active participation.

Learning is vital to your life. Almost everything you do throughout your day you learned. If you didn't have the learning capacity you have, you couldn't live as you do. And you have a confidence in your ability to learn outside the school situation that is important. But it kills me to see the way people lose all their confidence and independence when they get next to schools or books. It happens even to very mature and successful people who return to school. There is some real, practical, everyday learning available to you from books and schools. But to get that learning, you need to be hard-headed and trust in your own ability to direct your learning and not abandon your responsibility to your learning.

This book won't work for you if you reject everything linked with formal education. But it also won't work for you if you slavishly accept everything in the name of education and miss the point that this book is about changes in your way of living. Not just changes in your way of thinking.

It is a mistake to think that real education has the goal of doing something within a narrow, classroom situation with absolutely no relevance to your life outside the classroom.

But people have been subjected to this process so long that they have started to fall into the notion that education has to hurt to be good—like medicine. And people are in a position now where they run their lives in terms of education on two paths. You learn like a demon everywhere outside your formal educational life. You learn how to drive a car. You learn how to kiss a girl. You learn where the post office is. You learn how to make a bank receipt. You're learning every day of your life. It's the kind of learning that occurs naturally, and it's learning where you expect immediate significant results—or changes in your behavior.

A good example is ski lessons. You go up on the ski hill and you take ski lessons. And you expect to learn to ski. You don't care about the anatomy of the knee joint or the physics of the ski turn. You want to be able to get down the hill, look halfway stylish and not kill yourself.

So you have, outside the school situation, these very pragmatic, sound, sensible, wonderful rules about your learning. You take ski lessons for how long? You take them until you can ski well enough. Well enough for who? Well enough for yourself, that's who. And then you quit taking ski lessons. Are you worried about a grade in your ski class? Not a bit. Do you want ski lessons to be as unpleasant as possible? No, if you're a girl, you hope you'll get a good-looking ski instructor who is single and who has a rich father and who is going to think you're terrific. That is what you're hoping for.

But what happens when you pick up a book to study or walk into a classroom? You say, "Okay, I am prepared to suffer." It's just like medicine in the old days. Your grandmother took some medicine and it tasted just awful. That gave her a real good feeling. Because it tasted so bad, she was sure she would get well by tomorrow morning.

The basic goal I see for all education or learning comes

from a statement Carl Rogers made. He said approximately this: "I'm interested only in learning that leads to significant changes in your behavior."

The danger with a book like this, which can be read in three to ten hours, lies in overlooking the object of the book —and of all learning—which is significant changes in your life. We make a mistake when we take a learning process that is normally and of necessity spread over a long time, and try to compress it way too much. We alternate ski lessons and practice sessions. Same way here. You can take all these ideas out at once and turn your whole life upside down and suffer —and fail miserably. Or you can take an idea out, see how it fits and then take the next idea and repeat the process. Then maybe go back and look at the first idea again.

I've found a dozen or more books that have made a real change in my life. They are all listed at the end of this book. In most cases I'm still absorbing lessons in them. In a few cases, I've learned the lessons so well that every paragraph of the book is familiar to me. I'm still trying to do these things better, but I know what I'm trying to do and why.

We must respect the rhythm and pace of learning. We learn to ski better over the summertime, too, because I find each winter that I have worked out some little problem that was there the previous spring.

The problem is education is also like stew. Time helps it. When stew is heated the fourth time all the different flavors have worked their way through all the ingredients. Well, learning needs this too. This is especially true for the hard kind of learning we are talking about here, which involves examining and changing your whole pattern of life because this is real hard gut learning. This isn't just reading. It isn't like learning the multiplication tables. It is literally learning to live.

We are talking about ideas that have revolutionized other people's lives. And they can revolutionize your whole life, too. So you need time to think, time to reflect, and time to compare one thing with another. This new learning is not going to be any nice neat package. When we get things down to a nice neat package, we usually find the real big learning is lost to us. Because life is a complex of inconsistencies and the whole thing is, in a way, a mystery.

Why is education so fouled up? I think one of the biggest

reasons is this tremendous tendency to grade everybody. All one can measure are some little pieces of information that aren't very well related to significant changes in your present and future behavior.

The grading fallacy is particularly harmful to the purposes of learning because it separates you as learners from your teacher and this shouldn't be. The ideal in education from kindergarten through college and into all life is that we are a community of scholars. In this case the community consists of only two people, you and me. We are both learning. Each of us has a set of experiences which are different from the other person's. We are both going along the path of learning together helping each other. And while you can't communicate your learning and experiences directly to me, you have many stand-ins among my students who help approximate what your responses and contributions might be.

Evaluation does have a place in learning, but it needs to be kept free from judgments. For example, if I am taking ski lessons from you, I want to be able to say, "Watch me make a couple of turns and tell me how to turn better." I know I can make the turns, but the point is I want to make them better.

You may say to me, "Hey, let me tell you about my experience I had at trying to apply your idea of accepting yourself. See if you have any ideas about things I might do different."

So we can have evaluation. But we need to avoid in evaluation this drastic sense of hierarchy. I try to avoid this when I teach. I'm asking for evaluation from my students as much as they are asking for evaluation from me. During the course and at the end, I ask my students to tell me what things they thought were effective and what things they thought weren't. I need the counsel of the people in my community of scholars. There is no such thing as "the lowest learner."

The more we see each other as fellow learners, fellow members of the community of scholars, the more the grading function disappears as unnecessary. Each of us are learning as if we were a many-stranded cable, and we are learning on each of our thousand different strands.

It is foolish to say, "Where are you?" Or, "Where am I in this process?" "Am I further ahead than you?" Such questions are ridiculous—and harmful. Because in some lines you are ahead of me and in others I may be ahead. But in a way, I don't even understand such an idea as ahead, or above, when it comes to learning which is really living. Am I living a richer life than you? Boy, I doubt that. Are we both trying to live and grow—instead of dying on our feet? I sure hope so.

This is where the community of scholars idea plays such a crucial role in education. It helps us to see the need to help each other. But to operate that way, the teacher must get rid of his own need to please himself and his own ego by putting himself above people and making himself high and his student low. This is an inflation of his ego at the expense of the learning process, and most important of all—at the expense of the confidence of the student in his own learning.

Another way our schooling has overwhelmed so many of us is in our language. The English teachers and the status seekers have tried to take away our tongue—our language—and too often they have succeeded well enough that we can't speak as truly as we should.

A few days into this quarter, one of my students came up and wanted to drop the class. She was very puzzled and our conversation went about like this:

"You're a doctor, aren't you?" "Yes, I am."

"Then why do you speak so poorly? Do you do it in the hope your students will like you better?"

"No, I do it because I'm a lot better user of the language than you are."

"But," she said, "I'll be teaching third grade and if I talked like you do, my students would learn bad habits."

"Honey," I said, "you don't need to worry about that. If you go into that class and talk in that stilted way of yours, they won't pay any attention to you."

I told her the story about Mark Twain, the greatest user of our language who ever lived. His wife found the profanity he used in his speeches a problem for her. So as she was tying his tie before a dinner speech, she uttered a long string of his bad words. Twain just looked at her and smiled.

"Libby," he said, "you've got the words, but you ain't got the music."

And that's the problem with the terrible fear we bring to talking and writing. That fear screws up all the things we say. We worry about correctness. There ain't no such thing. This language is a living thing and the way you and I use it is the way she is.

Bergen Evans, the great linguist, says that we don't hold up a mouse and ask if it's a correct mouse. Same with any word and any use. When you and I are ready to use a word, it means we've heard it enough so that it's the best word to use. Granted, the English teachers won't catch up with us for fifty years, but that's their problem. By the time they adopt what you and I are saying today, we will be a long ways down the road.

Fear in the use of yours and my language hurts so bad because it communicates itself to the people around us. I had a good friend who was a graduate student of mine. We had a deep feeling for each other. But when he talked to me, it was always in complete sentences. From his eyes and his face, I could guess at his feelings, but how much better it would have been if he could have forgotten his fear and spoken from his heart. But that fear is so deep that it will be years before his language loosens up.

All you and I need to do is throw away our fear of our English teacher and listen to the people around us. We can soon be far better speakers and writers.

I can't be in all places at all times listening to all conversations, but I can get a pretty good idea about it by listening to the conversations of the people around me. I really don't care too much what they are saying in New York or New Orleans because my problems center around how they say it here in Montana and Idaho and Washington and Oregon. And I can get a real good fix on that.

But because of a fear the English teachers of the country have tenderly bestowed on us, we're scared stiff of our damn language. We don't have any confidence in our ability to use the tongue. We actually use the language like masters, but we don't see that and know that and understand that. And this is a big problem in communicating with each other.

Once you can get over some of the fear of your language, you can do it. I wrote my Master's thesis and my Ph.D. thesis in first draft and then handed them to the typist for final typing. Someone commented that both of them read like novels. And to an extent, they did, because I had the courage to write very simply and very clearly. And I was willing to accept the problem that to do so meant that each idea I put down stands just as it is for the whole world to see in all its nakedness. The idea isn't clothed and embellished with great big, beautiful words in the hope that people wouldn't quite see it or quite understand the shallowness of the idea. It is very naked and simple. What ideas I put there, any one of you could read and understand completely. And from understanding it, you could see the ideas that weren't there. Now this is a very dangerous and, as I say, naked feeling. But you've got to be willing to suffer this.

Because I was willing to pay that price and had a reasonable confidence in my ideas, I could do it. I knew my ideas weren't overpowering. But I have learned through bitter experience that it is much safer to take a chance on the meagerness of my ideas than it is to clothe them in a lot of excess words and big words and confuse people. I get into a hell of a lot more troubles by confusing people than I do by sticking my own little ideas down in clear form.

So that's the idea I used in writing my Ph.D. thesis and lo and behold, I just had to change two or three things in it. Not that it was so smart, it was just a small thing like all such works. But it was clear.

Now how does this apply to your writing and speaking? When you are writing, put down just exactly what you want to say. Real simple. Like you're writing a personal letter to your Aunt Grace. And it will do just fine. If what you end up with isn't fancy, it's because what you've got to say isn't fancy. It's plain. If you can't tolerate that plainness, think up some ideas that make it really smashing and then put them in. But make it clear.

And in our speech we need to aim for direct, vivid, colorful language. That way we can get the music into our speech —the music Mark Twain loved.

So to hell with Miss Scholtz, the old grammar teacher. If she wants a dead language, let her molder in the dust. You and I will take this language we love and need and move her down the road a ways. And, we will be able to tell each other our feelings—with real feelings.

So in guiding your own learning and in speaking of your feelings your confidence is crucial to you. Anything I do that detracts from that confidence is harmful. Anything that I do that scares you or overwhelms you or makes you dependent on me in any way is bad. Only you can be the captain of your ship. Only you can direct your growth. Only you can choose the lines that your growth can take so it truly reflects your uniqueness—and adds to the strength you need to keep on growing.

SIX

Controlling Behavior

I have said that this book is about psychology. Unfortunately, you are inclined to think of psychology as just talking about human behavior. But it isn't—not at all. Psychology is the control, prediction and explanation of behavior. But the trouble I have found with so much psychology is that the particular explanations of behavior offered won't stand up to the test of controlling or predicting behavior. And my point is that if an explanation doesn't lead to control or to prediction, it isn't a psychology that's useful to you.

You've always controlled behavior so you have always been a psychologist. The point of the book is to make you a better one.

I think Rogers indicates a way. If you tell someone how you feel about yourself, he will reciprocate in kind. I have done this. Most of the time, the response is as predicted. Through the control of my behavior, I am controlling others' behavior. And I have faked it with people and got faking responses right back.

Now, there is a problem in controlling behavior. It seems to conflict with the idea that each person should become the person each is uniquely capable of becoming. Is it bad for me to control your behavior? Should I come up to you and say how I'm frightened or worried or have this troublesome feeling because I'm going to make you do the same and that's bad? Well, in some ways and senses it could be used for harm.

But I see the answer to this dilemma in this way. I control your behavior by giving you the acceptance your heart so desires. So I'm controlling my own behavior really, rather than yours. It's like the little rat in the Skinner box who says, "I've got this psychologist under my control. Every time I press the bar, he gives me a food pellet."

This is true. The psychologist had to control his behavior. He had to agree to give the rat a food pellet every time he pressed the bar, before he could control the rat's behavior and keep him pressing the bar.

I ran a class at the University of Minnesota where I was teaching the principles of behavior control. It was an evening class and some of my students were people with no experience in psychology whatsoever. So the first night I explained some of the simple reinforcement systems of controlling behavior. You decide what behavior you want from someone else and then you reinforce that piece of behavior. If there is some piece of behavior you want to get rid of, you just stop reinforcing it and wait for it to go away.

So I told my students to set up an experiment and bring to next week's class a write-up that explained the experiment and their results. And this is one that was read to the class:

The student's mother had not been ironing his shirts and keeping clean clothes in his drawer the way he wanted. So he proceeded in typical fashion (we all love to dish out punishment) to punish his mother for this. "Hey, Ma, get some shirts up here. If you don't take better care of my clothes, I'm going to leave home." Well, I don't know why she didn't say, "Go ahead."

But, nevertheless, that night she ironed a couple of shirts and took them up to his room. And his arms went around her like a blanket, loving her and hugging her and kissing her. And, wow! The clean shirts started moving upstairs.

My son, a sophomore in high school, heard the tale and said, "That boy wasn't really controlling behavior, Dad." I said, "How's that, Jess?" And he said, "Well, the kid had to give up being surly." This seems to me to be a fairly good answer. We must control our behavior first by agreeing to provide whatever reward or reinforcement is needed to change the other person's behavior. When we accept a person as they are this is the one thing they must desire in the whole world, because our complete acceptance frees them so they can change into the kind of person they are capable of becoming. Now that's not too bad a deal for either party, is it?

Reece McGee gave me the analogy of the teeter-totter for this process. If you shift your weight just the least little bit, the other person has to shift his weight, too. Now you say, "I don't have any right to control that other person and the way they respond." And you don't. But you do have a right and a duty to act as you see you must act. And your action will then precipitate change of some kind. And most change of this type tends to be constructive.

When you clean up your side of the relationship by being truly more accepting of the other person their response tends to be a more constructive response. If it isn't, you can't help that. That's not your business. Your business is to make the changes you must make in your life. But you do know that a lot of things will happen because of it.

The idea of controlling behavior really bothers many psychologists—especially those that call themselves humanistic psychologists. I like to think of myself as a humane psychologist, too. But many of my words reflect my interest in learning and experimental psychology. When I use one of those words, a humanistic psychologist is likely to respond quickly and say, "I don't believe in manipulating or controlling people." And this bothered me at first. Then I saw what this humanistic psychologist was doing to me. He was attempting to manipulate and control my behavior by punishing me for using what were, to him, dirty words. The reason I go into such detail on this is that it is crucial that you see that you have *always* been controlling the behavior of the people around you by the way you controlled your own behavior.

A game is just like a tennis match: it takes two to play it. When we walk away from a sick game, we leave our former tennis partner with no one to play with. He has two choices. He can either come play with us on a new, clean basis, or he can get someone else to play the old sick game with him.

Here is where the idea of games is useful. A point Berne makes in *Games People Play* is that we are playing a lot of sick games. None of us are capable of a game-free existence. So the point is, stop playing as many sick games as possible and substitute good games as much as you can.

In my case I substituted the teacher game (which can be a good game) for the advertising-man game (which for me was a sick game because I was unsuited for it). The response I get from students gives me some stroking (in Berne's words) which gives me the strength to help me grow.

This growth can be toward less dependence on games toward a more game-free existence. Which is not me "Author" writing to you "Mass" but Jess talking to you at this minute in time with all that has happened before and what you have done and what I have done completely and honestly available to each of us. That's game-free existence. There's a short section of game-free dialogue near the end of Berne's book.

A crucial idea underlying all of this is that all behavior goes on because it is being rewarded or has been rewarded in the past. Sometimes it is very hard to find what the reward is or was. But it is always there. A young kid may steal cars. Part of his reward may be to look big in the eyes of those who think outwitting the police and car owner is smart. Another part of the reward is excitement.

Okay. Say you're the psychologist. How are you going to get the kid to stop stealing cars? I think you'll have the best luck if your solution has lots of legitimate rewards for the kid that are better than those he's giving up.

Consider this: His father teaches the boy mountain climbing and then the boy takes his buddies out and shows them some hair-raising mountain climbing stunts he can do. The boy gets his parent's attention, he gets excitement and he gets to show off.

I know I'm oversimplifying a difficult problem. But the point is still valid.

There are a lot of people today in our society who are screaming at a lot of other people to change. But what is so ignored is that we won't give up an old way for a new way until we can see that it is more rewarding than the old way.

This is what I am doing with you. It is the same thing I do with my students. I tell them of the tremendous rewards for them when they live this different life. Most already have experienced some of these rewards and want more. Then I tell them how to test out these new ways so they can see the new rewards, and once these are reached, they make a drastically deep impression; it's hard ever to forget.

But my tactic has a limited appeal. It appeals only to those who can admit to themselves that there is a better way of living than the way they are living now. Some people are too locked in to be able to move. And these people may nod agreement and smile at these ideas—but they don't go out and change their lives around.

Near the beginning of one of my classes, a girl raised her hand and said, "Why do you keep telling us we aren't living as well as we can? Why do you keep saying that we are playing some sick games? I'm happy with my life, just the way it is."

At this Tom's hand shot up. He said to her, "If you're so happy with your life, why are you bugging Jess?"

And this I see over and over again. The people who are truly happy with their lives aren't offended or troubled by my floundering attempts to find a better way for myself. They just wish me luck and keep working on their own lives.

So as I say, this whole book is based on two assumptions. One, that you solve all your problems that can be solved by going in search of that unique, magnificent yourself. Two, when you do that you will have the tremendous reward of acceptance of others, which frees them to go in search of themselves, too.

Now this isn't a very perfect or very well-worked out psychology. It won't help you control your behavior or others' behavior very well. But it is the best "psychology" I have been able to find in my forty-five years of searching.

SEVEN

Anyone for Sexuality?

We've got a problem in America. It's a problem, in a sense that all of Western civilization has, but it's worse here.

Put yourself in the place of a college student for a moment. Imagine you are on a college campus and you are walking around on campus and you notice this huge animal. He is ninety feet tall—like an elephant, but ninety feet tall. And he's walking around on campus and he's not very careful where he walks. And occasionally he steps on a whole bunch of people and they are all dead. And you see this going on around you. And you look at your fellow students and they aren't looking at the animal. They are just going about their business.

The animal is just about to put his foot down and they walk right under the foot and get crushed. And nobody says a word about it. Everybody goes on as if nothing was happening. And you see all of it. And you see this animal lie down on a building and he crushes the whole building and gets up. But there is nothing in the newspapers about it. Nobody ever says anything about this animal. Wouldn't you start questioning your sanity?

Well, to my mind, this huge animal represents the spector of sexuality in our society. We are, in my mind, as wrongheaded as I have ever seen any segment of any culture in any society in handling a very basic, overwhelming problem. And particularly this is troublesome for our college-age population who are so terribly caught up in this thing. But it is also very troublesome for everybody in our society.

I speak of this problem in connection with acceptance of yourself and myself because of the terrible obstacles it raises that keeps women from becoming whole, beautiful women and men from becoming whole, beautiful men.

There is an instructive idea in *Zorba the Greek* by Kazantzakis. Zorba was a free-living Greek. And he believed in dancing and having fun together and raising hell. And Zorba had some ideas on sin that, to my mind, the Church could borrow a lesson from—all churches. Because we're Puritans in this country. Even though there are a wide range of religions in this country covering the full spectrum of denominations—most of us are Puritans. We think that because we give so much money to our church we should have some special place in heaven. I don't see anything about that in the Bible. That's a Puritan idea. Another Puritan idea is that if you are very rich and prosperous and very well set up in business or your profession, it is a sign that you've been a very good person. God has smiled on you. I can't find that in the Bible anyplace either. It is a Puritan idea.

But the Puritan idea of sexuality is the one that is raising hell with everybody and has got everybody all screwed up. For this reason:

Zorba the Greek is a man who did immense things for people and he had all these qualities we're talking about. He accepted himself 100 per cent and because of his acceptance of himself he accepted the people around him. He did have a little trouble accepting the dumb college-professor type who was traveling around with him. The professor-type was the kind who every time he had a problem, would go read a book until his problem went away. And he screwed up the lives of all the people around him. He even helped get a woman he loved, in his own peculiar way, killed, because of his stupidity and intellectuality.

But Zorba had one sin he was sorry for. That was the time he was in Alexandria. And the Pasha's wife saw Zorba on the street. Zorba cut quite a figure in his youth and she admired him. So that evening she sent her servant to Zorba's room and said for Zorba to come to her. But Zorba didn't go because he knew what happened to Christians in the Moslem section at night. But he knew she was waiting for him and she needed him and he did not go. And he called that his one sin.

Now when you study the life of Zorba, you see it is filled with all kinds of hell-raising and what we think of as sin. He did all kinds of things that we think would keep him in confession for about a year, but he didn't figure he had but one sin and that was that one.

I was kind of struck by that, but I wouldn't have thought so much of it except that my wife was reading Michener's *The Source* at the same time. I get lots of ideas from Michener. He's not supposed to be a high-class, intellectual-type author, but I get lots of good ideas from his books.

In *The Source,* Michener tells about the time when all the most learned rabbis got together to codify the Talmud—the collection of Jewish law. This was about 1500 years ago. All the most learned rabbis were gathered in one place and spent over one hundred years pulling together Jewish tradition into a single book.

And in the Talmud there is a drastically different view of sexuality than exists in the mainstream of Western civilization. In Talmudic law it specified that a candlemaker shall sleep with his wife at least on Tuesdays and Saturdays. A shepherd shall sleep with his wife on Mondays and Thursdays, a rabbi shall sleep with his wife on Fridays, a sailor shall sleep with his wife at least once every six months. A soldier must return and sleep with his wife at least once a year. And if the husband, under Jewish Talmudic law does not fulfil his sexual responsibilities, his wife immediately goes and lives with his brother. And his brother is then responsible for providing for her keep until the end of her days.

In this crazy, mixed up society of ours, we see sex as the duty of the woman and something for the man to enjoy. Zorba and the Jews saw sex as the thing women needed more than anything else and that it is a man's duty to be there when needed.

As I've told some of my students, it's as if, when a woman gets married she should have a little whistle. And any time she wants to blow the whistle, that's it. Right now. And if she wants to blow the whistle twenty times a day, fine. That whistle has got complete command of her husband's sex life.

One of my young students said it this way: "What you said

about sexuality didn't really hit me until afterwards when I looked at your book and more fully realized what you had said—which was a lot. My husband was in class with me. He's usually away except on weekends.

"I keep wondering if he went out and bought a whistle. I don't know if he'd use it or give it to me. Either way I'm sure it would be blowing all the time. That's okay, though, as I can't think of a more pleasant way to spend a three day weekend—or a lifetime—than showing your husband how very much you love him.

"Love really makes life great—and I am trying to accept myself and others and show my love more although it's really confusing and very difficult."

And this view of sexuality and this acceptance of it is analogous to the situation that creates the specter of the huge animal walking around on campus—and in our society. The sexuality is on campus and in our life, but the whole culture and society and all our rules and regulations and prescriptions are set up to completely deny any existence of it at all. And so the student feels like he is watching the big animal—and no one else will help him or even talk to him about it.

At this point, I have to answer a question I know is in your mind. You're saying, "Jess, you're crazy. I read the newspapers and magazines. I see the hippies. I go to the movies. I know what's going on in this country."

My answer to you has to be, "I'm sorry but I don't think you really do know what's going on in this country."

All the talk of sexual freedom by young and old. All the spouse-swapping swingers. All the movies and magazine articles. All of them are about a small minority who are getting a lot of attention.

I'm willing to grant you that every story is true. But that still doesn't make my argument wrong. Because that talk about sexual freedom you're hearing and reading is very shallow. And it doesn't reflect the bulk of the country.

I know because I've talked to the people who are being written about. One boy had his ski jacket pocket full of rubbers. A girl was such an easy mark that a lot of the guys around her had pushed her in bed. A "hippie" gal was telling me what a great thing sex was (except for an occasional bummer) but her fingernails were all chewed off and there was a sadness on her face like in Death Row at Alcatraz. A couple of women are sleeping with their bosses. A guy is trying to convince his wife by his actions that she would be happier sleeping just with him than all around town (and they are starting to build a marriage).

No. I'm not some old fossil with my head buried in the sand. I know people on both sides of the sexual freedom street. And I believe as strongly as anything I know that much of what is written today about sex is just a pile of half-truths, evasions and rationalizations. It was like the stuff that was written and said about the stock market in the late 1920s. The belief the stock market would always go up and never come down was unreal. It was so unreal that one financier got out of the market because he found the elevator boys seemed to be as knowledgeable as the brokers about stocks. That scared him because it seemed so unreal and he went to his office and sold out his stocks and waited for the fever to subside.

There are laws in human relationships like anything else. Sexual relationships are part of the human relationship, so there are laws working there even though we don't know what they are very well.

A good example is in a story I saw in *Life* about a group marriage in Sweden. Six guys married six gals and slept in a big circle with their heads touching. It was supposed to be complete sexual freedom within the group. But one small sentence in the story struck me. They found that the guys and the gals couldn't switch around freely. A guy had to be with a girl until one or the other broke it off and then it was over. So they found they had to make a commitment to each other. But that's not too surprising because our bodies aren't machines. Our bodies are hooked up to our hearts, and our hearts have feelings.

Many of my students thought they could have intercourse without problems and then found they were wrong.

One girl about twenty said: "I have been blessed (yes, blessed) with some pretty bad experiences this spring which have opened my eyes considerably. I *had* come to believe that any girl could have sex without any hang-ups if she had a good opinion of herself and had decided beforehand that she wouldn't tear herself apart because she had intercourse with a guy she's only been out with once.

"Well, this spring I found out differently. I have learned

that self-respect isn't measured by what bad things I can do and not be torn up about—but how much I can truly love myself and in turn love and understand other people.

"I feel blessed by this experience because I can help other people who have gone through the same thing. There are so many people with a similar problem but are afraid to talk to people about it. Granted, it's a touchy subject. But if these people could realize that there are others in the world who can help and understand them, they could overcome this problem.

"That is precisely what I have come to realize in your class: That other people have a problem and that I'm not alone. There *are* other people who suffer in the same way I have, and it's reassuring to know that."

I have heard so many stories like this from people young and old. I'm convinced that the talk about sex today is very superficial and largely about others. I am convinced that there are an awful lot of sexual problems that are carried inside and have never been aired because there was no one around who could listen with acceptance.

So I don't think there is sexual freedom. I don't think sexual patterns are really changing. And I do think there is still a terrible inability on the part of an awful lot of us—young and old—to accept and voice to someone the burden of sexual guilt we carry so we, too, won't feel so alone. And when we get our sexual feelings out in the open we can better balance all the things in our life, especially our love and our work.

An incident I saw when I was young is a constant reminder to me of how rare it is to find the complete manliness and complete womanliness where sexuality can be handled openly without kinks.

I was sitting in an office in Kansas City one time with a man who was as close to being God-like as I've ever known. If you told me Christ had returned to the world and I had met him in my time, I would say without hesitation that it was this man. He was the kind of person where you were something better and different when you were with him. And I was sitting there talking to him. This was in 1952. At that time I was twenty-five years old.

We had a gal working there who had had polio when she was a girl. She had been told that unless she was physically active she might be handicapped from this. So she started to swim when she was five or six years old and became a tremendous swimmer. She was some kind of high school champion. And along with it, she had a beautifully developed body. Just statuesque. Really stacked, in the vernacular.

And she had about herself a naturalness, an acceptance of her body that you sometimes find in girls. And she came to the door. I was sitting talking and this fellow was across from me. He was a vice-president of this advertising agency and he was about forty, I imagine, at the time. And he looked at Rosie and we were talking to her. Rosie was kind of leaning against the door sill and sticking out all over.

And he said, "Rosie, you've got the nicest pair of boobies I've ever seen." And Rosie said, "Thanks."

Completely open. Not a tone of dirty old man or maliciousness or anything. It was an honest statement of acceptance. That she was a woman and he was a man. And it was an honest acceptance of her womanliness back from the girl.

That man was so gentle that I'm sure that rather than kill flies in his house, he opened the window and let them out. That man would no more look at a girl in the wrong way than fly. I don't think I ever heard him say anything critical of any person in the years I knew him. And yet he was able to recognize that a man is a man and a woman is a woman—openly and honest and straight-forward.

But what is so singular about that incident is that that is the first and last time I have ever seen it happen. And only Zorba, a fictional creation of Kazantzakis, an old Greek on an island, is the only other man like that. Plus the Talmud. And both Zorba and the Talmud are a long ways from our culture, time and era. So only once in my fairly varied and far-ranging life have I seen such an honest recognition and openness and acceptance of a man being a man and a woman being a woman. And that is what I mean by sexuality. Sex is intercourse or masturbation: the physical side.

Now we also have this crazy notion: In the Puritanical life so many of us live, there is only one sin—that's sex. All other sins, like being cruel to each other, oh, they are just little bitty old sins. But that sex, that's that big sin. Well it isn't. Because I don't see sexual sins being associated with very many of the other things that I deplore.

But I see what I think of as the sins of being mean to other people associated with all kinds of other behavior that I don't care to be associated with, thank you.

And oddly enough, I'm not concerned with the sexual values of you young people the way so many are today. We talk about our values and how we need to inculcate these values in kids. We need schools to teach values. The hell we do. We don't need to teach those values. These kids know what those values are in our society. They know them only too clearly. And their problem is not lack of knowledge of the values and not a lack of teaching of the values, but their problem is: "How can I handle those values? How can I begin in any way, shape or form, to live up to those things that I feel society wants me to live up to?"

Some people say, "Well, you're tearing down everything—all of the standards that protect this country." Baloney. I find that these kids are doing a pretty good job at living up to them.

I point out to my students that they are a bunch of liars. They are trying to convince me that there is a sexual revolution on campus. That the girls and boys have completely walked away from the old values and are living together and all this stuff.

I can take the sex surveys and I can take the wildest sex survey I've ever seen. The most extreme. I don't know what it would be, but I'll take any one you can find.

If you want to say that 99 per cent of college kids are having intercourse before marriage, and you want to give me frequencies of intercourse that average twenty, thirty, even a hundred times before marriage, fine. I'll accept any sex survey you want. I haven't seen any that extreme, but I'll take it.

I'll turn it around and I'll use it this way. There is an old proverb that when a couple gets married, everytime they go to bed with each other they put a bean in a bushel basket. And after one year, the bushel basket is full. Then, everytime they go to bed with each other, they take a bean out of the bushel basket. And about twenty or thirty years later, they are still trying to get the beans out of the bushel basket.

Now that's the nature of intercourse. It's like a new toy, and when you're young and your blood is hot, it is a lot different situation than when you're old and your blood is slowed down.

So I tell these kids this story and say, "Okay, you're convincing me that there is a sexual revolution on campus. By that token then, the frequencies in these sex surveys should be not five times or twenty times, because those are the kind of frequencies you would expect from finite human beings."

And so some guy and some gal are going together and they are convinced that they love each other deeply. They get into the situation so common today, with lots of sexual stimulation provided by old people like you and me who are making money at it, or are titillated by it or for all kinds of other reasons (we are the ones who are buying most of these books and movies and producing them). So these two kids are alone in a car and they cross a line that lots of times they would just as soon not. And this happens two or three times and then, lo and behold, the guy or the gal gets sick at themselves and the other person and break up and they don't even get married. Later on one of them goes out with someone else and is really convinced they are going to get married. They walk across the line a few more times and end up married. Hopefully the baby doesn't come until ten or twelve months later—but not always. And so they show up in the sex survey as having had premarital intercourse with two different partners ten or fifteen times.

Well, I don't see that as some drastic new kind of thing. I know of lots of grandparents who wouldn't like to have you check the date of the marriage certificates against the birth date of their oldest child. In the old days, doctors weren't too fussy about when you recorded a birth so we can't find out for sure how bad things were then. But boy have we ever got accurate records today. And we're so good at counting to nine. So I'm not interested in the guy who tells me things have changed so drastically from the way they used to be.

It's like one of my favorite sayings: "I ain't the man I used to be—never was!" And all this baloney about how the world ain't like it used to be when I was young is just that—baloney. In Old Testament times there were all the same kinds of sinning we have today.

I read recently in L. M. Boyd's column that one hundred years ago in Denmark, two out of three brides were expecting on their wedding day. Those were the parents and grandparents of the Danes who immigrated to this country. And I have never noticed that Danes in this country were any freer sexually than anybody else. So I'm not interested in the way things were supposed to have been in some great time that's past.

We are all partly childlike and are frightened by change. But when we are, we risk hurting ourselves and the people around us badly.

I take these sex survey figures and the bean story and say, "Okay, if there is a sexual revolution, I want you to give me the names, not of one or two dollies on campus—because there are always one or two gals who have severe problems— but I want you to name twenty girls who have had intercourse four hundred times or two thousand times." Because they are young and if sex is really like a drink of water like they say it is, then they are going to have frequencies like that. "Why have intercourse just three or four times if you are really liberated? Especially when all of a sudden after the day you get married you have intercourse three or four times a day."

It doesn't make sense. Yet they are trying to say they are liberated. "Man, I'm free." Well, the answer is that these kids, despite their lack of willingness to recognize it, are fairly well dedicated to the principle of chastity and virginity. Now that isn't a very fashionable principle to be for today on a college campus. But I'm a lot more interested in their behavior than their talk.

Kids used to loudly uphold their dedication to chastity and yet have intercourse occasionally before marriage. Now they loudly deny their dedication to chastity and have intercourse only occasionally before marriage. So as near as I can see the so-called sexual revolution on campus is in the way kids talk about sex with very little change in the amount they use sex.

To my mind, a person is dedicated to the principle of virginity and chastity when they take strenuous efforts to preserve their virginity or chastity and when they value it in their prospective marriage partners. To argue otherwise, would be like saying that the nuns who were violated when Berlin was seized by the Russians aren't nuns any more because they gave up their vow of chastity. Well, that's not true. And by the same token, I think that the gal, who under extreme provocation slips a few times, has not strayed that far from the principle of chastity.

Now some argue that one slip and you're a ruined woman, or man. Yet when I look at the lives of people who argue that way, I don't see that the lives they are leading will live up to perfect and rigid obedience to any principle. I know an old man who talks of the noble principles of his day yet embarrasses his listeners with rotten, filthy stories. He waves the flag of patriotism, yet hid out on a ranch to dodge the draft. And all of us adults are constantly breaking speed laws, religious laws, and every other kind of law. We want to be dealt with leniently but we won't extend the leniency to another—particularly to the young. And I think it is because a part of us hates them.

There is another question I would like to put to the person young or old, who wants to talk about all the sex maniacs on campus. How do you explain the girls who are so shy they don't dare walk into the student union alone? Or the girls who are so shy they can't even look people in the eyes? And the guys who go to the dances and stand around afraid to ask girls to dance? Have you ever seen that? I have. Lots of it. Where are you going to put all these students?

You might reply, "Well, you're talking about Minnesota or Montana." No I'm not. You can find the same thing anyplace. But the person who wants to say sex is taking over is looking at some gal in a short skirt shaking her fanny at some guy on a dance floor. And he or she wants me to apply this to everybody. Well, even in the case of the dancers, appearances are deceiving. It may look lewd and lascivious to you but it's just dancing. And the two people involved usually have serious problems telling each other how and what they really feel. I know because I talk to all shapes and sizes and kinds of young people every day. I see exceptional shyness at publicly showing any signs of intimacy. And they are as well aware of the emotional problems of intercourse as anyone else is. The gals are very respectful of who and under what special circumstances they might be willing to give themselves. And they are very anxious and concerned that they maintain society's values and they are trying as hard as they can.

To my mind the interesting thing is that the more open we are to sexuality and its various expressions, the better we can live up to our principles. Again, I see the principle of acceptance operating: The more I can accept myself as I am, the more I can change and live up to the kind of values I see around me and want to live up to. Because these values are in my bones. They weren't taught to me by words from teachers. They were taught me by the lives I saw led by the people who loved me and who I admired. So when I go against those values, I not only go against my society, I go against the memory of my grandfather and my father and my mother and Aura Kingsley and Coach Anderson. I have them in my bones. And anything that I do has got to square with what's in my bones. Sure, I can have all this facile talk in the top of my head about how, "Oh, I can do this and I can do that." But I can't and be comfortable with myself.

It's like one of my students was telling me last quarter. She said, "I found that I could talk myself into having intercourse with the guy I was going with. But later I realized a funny thing. I realized that I was looking at him and thinking that he was going to think differently of me because of my having intercourse with him. And then I realized that because I was thinking that way and expecting him to think differently about me, I was going to be different. And he *would* think differently about me because I was different."

And she said, "I could see all of a sudden as I finally went through that puzzle that, yes, I could talk myself into having intercourse with him. And yes, this was desirable. But I couldn't live with that part of myself deep down in my bones." And while it was hard for her to go with him and not have intercourse, it was not as hard as what intercourse was doing to their relationship.

We need openness to help everyone. Like masturbation. It is a tremendous problem for young people. About 99 per cent of boys masturbate and some high percentage of girls do. And it will carry on sometimes into the first years of their marriages. And it is a terrible problem for kids. Yet who can talk to them about it and tell them clear and clean that all their worries about what they are doing are unfounded? And yet if we could, there would be less masturbation rather than more. How could there be more?

There is a story about the college girl sitting in the front row of psychology class knitting. And the professor is explaining that lots of rhythmic hand activities like knitting are just polite forms of masturbation. And so the girl pipes up with this retort, "When I knit, I knit and when I masturbate, I masturbate." But the tragedy is that of the two thousand college students I've had whose names I know, I can't think of more than five who could handle their feelings about sexuality that openly. One girl, perhaps, could and four or five of the boys might be able to.

Portnoy's Complaint by Philip Roth is the first book I've ever seen that tells of the sexual feelings of a boy and a young man. Everybody says what a wild book. That's not a wild book. That's the way all the boys in Bricelyn, Minnesota, felt as they were growing up. Not a few of them, but all of them. I can say that because the town was only six hundred, and I knew all the kids well enough to know what they were going through. *Portnoy's Complaint* also shows the terrible guilt and suffering that comes from the silence about sex. And it shows how a parent with her or his own sexual problems can add an extra burden to a young person by not handling their own sexual needs directly but letting them out in kinky ways with their children.

I don't know how women feel sexually, so I couldn't say if there is a book that really reflects their feelings truly or not. But the point is the extreme difficulty of breaking down the walls of silence and sexual feelings.

What about some of the movements groups are organizing to prevent sex education? There is going to be a lot of that. Unfortunately. And there is going to be a lot of misguided sex education. But again, this is the kind of chaos that comes with any revolution. It's like the old revolutionist said, "To have an omelet you have to crack eggs, and to have a revolution, you've got to crack heads." And in sex education we're having a revolution. We need one. But there are going to be a lot of wrong things done and a lot of feelings trampled on. The biggest problem will be to find people who can teach the sex education course.

Everybody has some degree of physical or emotional limitations that keep them from handling their sexuality well. If you don't handle sexuality well, it interferes with your ability to accept yourself and the people around you. If you can handle your sexuality well and cleanly it gives an unbelievable extra depth and richness to every human contact you have.

A good illustration is something I experienced while I spent a month in the hospital resting up for heart surgery. During twenty-four hours there were about fifteen nurses coming into our room for one purpose or another. And because of days off and other things I was cared for by about thirty different nurses.

My roommate was a young, good-looking guy so we had lots of cute young student nurses in the room. But wonderful as all those nurses were, there were only two of them that radiated womanliness. One of these was on the night shift.

All I ever saw of her was when she came into my room to wake me up. There was nothing she did or said. She just touched my hand or my shoulder and said, "Good morning, Mr. Lair," in a way that was unbelievable. For those brief moments when she was in my room I felt more at peace and closer to her than I could ever have imagined possible. I think her secret was simple. She was 100 per cent woman and she liked it and it didn't bother her. But because I see this quality so rarely in people around me, I feel we all need to look at this area of our lives particularly closely when accepting ourselves and our feelings.

And when I see the joy and beauty in the people who handle their sexual feelings openly and cleanly, I feel the rewards in change we can make in this area will be especially great.

It is easy for me to tell you to accept sexuality and all the uncomfortable ideas and feelings that go with it. But I'm constantly finding how hard it is. When I first started teaching writing, I was given the idea of having my students write a sentence for each class. I told them to write anything they wanted on a 3 X 5 file card and I would read all their cards out loud at the beginning of class. In giving the direction, I said, "You can say anything you feel." I see now that I was telling them I could accept anything about them.

By the middle of the quarter, Mack, a preacher's son, was starting to feel free enough to be more open. He wanted to say something a little dirty—and a little sexual. So he did and put it on a card. When I came to his card, I couldn't read it and turned it under. So the kid had finally come out with something that needed acceptance so it could go away. And I wasn't able to accept it. I had asked for it—not really meaning to, but nevertheless I had asked for it. And then I wasn't able to accept his particular expression of sexuality when it came. So I fixed him good and put Mack right back where he was. And this was a terrible thing.

Now, I didn't have to read the card. I could have said, "This is a perfectly fine card. It is just my hang-up that I can't read this card." That's a lot different than just turning the card under and giving it the old silent treatment.

How can we teach these things to others? Our wives, children, friends? Only by living example. The better we can work out these problems ourselves, the more the people around us can share in this. Because we teach by example not by edict. We all want to teach by edict. "Do as I say, not as I do."

So, one of the most important parts of the acceptance of ourselves is our acceptance of our sexuality. All of our sexual feelings. Our sexual actions. Look at them as they really are. Handle them. Keep them from being destructive. Handle them so that they are as constructive as possible in our lives. Because much of our very destructive, negative, anti-people behavior comes out of our frustration and denial of our feelings in the matter. I am not saying that they need to be expressed directly, I am just saying that we need to look at ourselves and see that we have them.

The funny thing is that we will be able to handle them better when we are open to them rather than closed to them. And then the other side of that point is that much of the positive wonderful joy that there is in life comes in seeing that you are a man, that you are a woman, and you can see and can have that whole range of feelings and handle them reasonably well.

EIGHT

Letting Go as a Life Goal

You may be making some of the same kind of mistakes in your goals that I made with mine. Now hopefully, it isn't going to take a heart attack and a fifty-fifty chance of living through it at the age of thirty-five to get you back on a decent path. Most of you aren't that stupid. And most of you want something better than what you've heard from me in my story.

Now the problem that I had, and you share the problem, is that I didn't understand that no 19-, 22-, 27-, or 35-year old person could plan out their whole life. That was very low level management that I was giving my life. As I mentioned to you, I was going to be a big advertising agency executive and then own an agency and I was going to make $75,000 a year which at that time was like $200,000 is today. I was really going to do it to people. And I thought this is really me, see.

In my early years I didn't have any idea of what I was going to be. In the family that I grew up in, no one had ever gone through college. I don't think there were more than a handful of college graduates in the whole southern Minnesota town, outside of the school teachers. And who knew the school teachers? I didn't have any idea of what a college was.

So after I got out of the Air Force, I naïvely went to the vocational counselor at the University and said, "Tell me what I should be." He said, "You can be either an advertising man or an engineer, you've got abilities along both lines." And I said, "To hell with the wheels, I'll take the people."

101

And on the basis of that flip remark, I went sailing blindly off into something that scared hell out of me. Because actually I was much more frightened of people then than I am now. I didn't have any notion of what to do, so I went and said okay, I'll be an advertising man. And because some counselor read my profile that way, I threw four years of my college education and many years of my life down a rat hole.

When I was first in the advertising agency business, everybody thought I was going to be an account executive. I looked flashy. I was a fast talker. You know, a natural. Well the only problem was that I was a lousy executive. I had a terrible time and couldn't even make *myself* do the things that I had to do. I would have a list of seven things that I would need to do on a given morning. I would come to work and fight all day long to try and do the first thing on the list. And I couldn't, because I was frightened of it. At the end of the day, when my boss, that sainted man, would say, "Hey, Jess, have you got that done?" I'd lie to him.

After about a year of that and a lot more patience than I deserved, my boss called me in and said, "You know, you just aren't cutting it." And this was no big news to me. "We're probably going to have to fire you." At that time, my wife was in the hospital and had just had a second spinal fusion, and I had about four thousand other problems. You can imagine how that hit me. So he says, "But we'll give you another chance. While you haven't been doing some of these things, you've been showing a little promise as an advertising copywriter, and we'll let you try that."

I tried it and worked hard at it and it was right for me. And within six months or so, I was really starting to produce something because I was a lot better at that than I had been as an account executive. Pretty soon, I was going great guns and I had the help of some fine people who gave me encouragement and support and training. That was what made the outstanding progress possible. But then like an idiot, I said, "Hey, I'm doing great. I'll go someplace else where it's hard, like Chicago, and work for Leo Burnett." And man, it was really hard down there. Lots of those guys carry long sharp knives, and they'll cut you up into little pieces before anybody can find out about it.

I found that while I was a good advertising writer in the somewhat protected and sheltered circumstances of a group of people who loved and cherished me, that ability was not strong enough to stand up under the tremendous pressure of this big competitive agency. I was reduced to almost complete incompetence. All the abilities that I had just evaporated under that kind of pressure. It's like sitting you down at a typewriter and saying, "Type one hundred words a minute. I'm going to stand right here with a gun at your back and don't make any mistakes." Whatever typing skill you had just went right out the window. Well, that's what happened to mine.

I came back to Minneapolis and started my own advertising business and ran it for five years. But I was frightened of it most of the time. I had long periods of depression where for a week I would come down to the office and not be able to do anything.

Okay, now all of this time, I'm not the village idiot. I don't have the lowest I.Q. in the world. I've got some success going for me. But all of this time, I'm a 19-, 20-, 22-, 24-, 26-year-old guy giving direction to my life. Well, looking back as a 45-year-old person having been through all that mess, I can see how dumb it was to try to plan what I should be at 45 and 50 and 75 with the limited experience and abilities I had at those early ages.

The alternative is: *You don't need a plan.* A funny thing has happened. From the minute I looked at my life in that heart attack and said, "From this moment on I'm not going to do anything I don't believe in, I'm not going to do anything I don't really deep down want to do," I've been King Midas. Most everything that I've touched since then has worked great. Sure I've had an occasional failure, I've had an occasional goof. No Norwegian is that protected from error. But my life in those ten years since then, looking at it purely from the standpoint of the successes of the thing I turned my hand to, has been fantastic. And I can do things that I never before conceived I could and would be able to do.

Most important, my whole life has changed. There are all kinds of joy and happiness and wonder in it. I don't care if you want to throw all of those non-material benefits away. I know most of you don't, but I know there are some hard-shelled pragmatists who say, "All that counts is the material benefits in life." I'll take the argument simply on that basis, that you'll go a lot further materially if you will do just those things that you should do and that are right for you rather than all this phony overplanning.

I went into teaching. All I made was just the simple decision that, "Advertising is the wrong business for me. As near as I can see if I were a teacher things would go a little easier for me." I had done some teaching. For a change, I asked some of my friends for their advice. You know, people who really knew me. I said, "Tell me what you think I should do." "You're a teacher," they said. And a couple of people I had worked closely with agreed. In one case a client of mine, a man that I had done advertising for, said, "You should be doing something else, you'd be happier at it."

Just look what happened to me the minute I got into something I believed in. The first year that I was a teacher at the University of Minnesota, I was a half-time instructor, and the next year I was a full-time instructor in charge of a whole writing program. I was assistant professor the next and an associate professor the next with tenure on the University of Minnesota faculty. You can't go any farther than that. But I wasn't trying to. I didn't ask for a single one of those promotions.

My boss just came to me and said, "Jess, next year we're going to give you a new job." And the last couple of jobs that he told me about I said to myself, "Look, you're talking to the wrong guy, I'm not supposed to be able to do those things." And he said, "No, I think you can do it. I think I can get your promotion through and I think you can do the job." He had so much trust and faith in me, it scared me. But, partly, this thing was right for me, and the minute you begin something that is right for you, it goes easy.

Somehow we won't do this for ourselves. We've got such a terrible disrespect for ourselves. We look at ourselves, "I, Jess Lair, am some dumb old object, a calculator or a computer. Let's put it down any place and make it do anything, and if it won't work hard, I'll just kick it a couple of times." That's no respect for ourselves, that's no acceptance.

I talked to you about acceptance and about the difficult thing that acceptance is. The only way it can really be made tangible is through all these other sides of your life. It's got some crucial applications in your work and your goals because if you are trying to be something you shouldn't, you are going to do a lousy job—compared to what you could do. But if your job is the rightest and easiest and best of all things for you, you're going to be good at it.

Again, an example. I am here in the College of Education.

According to my old way of thinking, I would have had my little brown book and I would have had my twenty year plan, see. In three years I would be a lofty department head where all wonderful things happen, where all great things come from. And then five years from now, I'd be a dean in some kind of a setting. And then about ten years more, I'd be a president, maybe, of a smaller college. That's the way you've got to plan this out. You've got to plan ahead.

Well, I've got news for you. I've got no plans. You say, "What are you going to be doing next year, Jess?" I say, "I don't know, I'm going to be doing what I'm doing right now unless something happens to make something different a better thing to do." "Oh, that's terrible," you say. "Yah, that's sure terrible, isn't it!"

Awhile back, I violated my own principle and got worried about money. So I told Dean Ringo, "I want to be a full professor." But Earl says, "You can't do it." "Why not?" "You haven't written anything." "You mean you can't get it with classroom teaching like it should be." "Nope. It's not that simple." "Okay, by golly, I'm a writer, I'll go and write something."

So I went back to my desk and started writing furiously. I've done about twenty research studies, but the minute I find out what the research shows me then I lose interest in it and don't write it up. But I thought I'd write up a couple of dozen of those things and send them into the appropriate places and then I would take that long list down to Earl, and say, "Okay, try to swallow this."

Before I got too far along with that, I went up and talked to some lovely nurses at Big Mountain. And when I got through, the nurses' interest in what I had to offer made me stop and look at this set of ideas. They are ideas that I had been using to try to save my life, to try to get me back into some shape. The nurses were saying that those ideas were a book.

Well, luckily some gal had tape recorded the whole thing, so I put it down and that was the first version of my book. I ended up writing what I really should write, which is something I believe in and something that makes some sense instead of twenty doubtful contributions to the so-called experimental literature, nine out of ten of which aren't worth the paper that they're printed on.

Of course the answer is I also got calmed down again and got some sense. Earl Ringo can make me a professor when he wants to and when he sees a good reason to do so. It just isn't that important to twist your life all upside down just to speed up the process of things.

And I believe and have seen tremendous evidence in my own life of this commonly accepted principle: Out of acceptance for yourself can come the clues that can guide your path for tomorrow, not for twenty years from now, but for tomorrow. The only way you're going to find out what is best for you is really listening to your heart and watching the things that your hand turns to naturally and easily.

Now, there's one big reason why you may not do this. Most people instead take their need for love and run away from it and say I'm going to build this big brick silo. I'm going to have the fanciest brick silo around. I'm going to have a $300,000 a year brick silo with matched white Cadillacs. No one will know that inside here is this impoverished little worm. And the power-mad and glory-mad people that I see are the people whose hearts are aching and dying the most. But the sadness is that the bigger and higher and thicker and fancier you get that silo, the tougher it is to get through. I have seen some of my students (this is almost always students over thirty-five) who are so hard to reach that there isn't a chance, there isn't a prayer. You could no more indulge an honest conversation with them than fly to the moon because their defenses against you are so tough that they just fight you off.

But I can't just tell you, "Hey, there is another way to go," and you'll go. Not a chance. You're not going to go down this path unless you're willing and able to walk away from a lot of foolish dreams. Those dreams are what you are in the process of attempting to substitute for the reality of life—which is the love and affection and the real kinds of human relationships you need so vitally and so desperately.

And once you've done that, once you've said, "Power and glory is fine but it is no way to get the thing that I desperately need," once you have accepted this, then all the rest of it is very easy. And all the times that I am distracted from my own rules, it is that pull toward power and empty goals.

I mentioned to you the time I was reading the *Farm Quarterly,* and reading the stories of very successful and prosperous and outstanding men. I looked at that and thought, "Jess, you should be able to do that. You've got the intelligence, you've got the management skill, you've got certain other attributes. You should be able to do this." Yes, I have some of those attributes, but I don't have all of them. And while I could make myself work along those lines and make some progress, I know I would be miserable and I know I would not be completely successful.

Even though my life today is drastically different and better, I still have to fight my striving for power and glory. I've got something wonderful. If you would have told me twenty years ago that I could have what I have, I would have said, "You're nuts, you're a dreamer. It's impossible for me, Jess Lair." Now, though, there is so much wonder and joy in a typical day. I find that a day has got not just one or two nice surprises, but in the last few years, many days have twenty or thirty wonderful things in them. It often leaves me just blinking my eyes. And I don't mean to put something on. That's just the way it is.

And yet in the face of all that, I can still find myself turning around and saying, "Hey, I want to be a big dealer, I want title, I want money, I want power, I want prestige." Those are the things that are completely irrelevant. The first draft of my book talks about these ideas. And occasionally, I'll find myself distracted even there and say, "Hey, you know, what if my book is a great success?" But that's beside the point. It doesn't make any difference whether it's a complete success or just something that gets published and doesn't make any money. The point that counts is I'm doing what I need to do and love to do and that's all that matters. Sure, there are other things that make nice little distractions, but that's immaterial.

Now, I say we're playing sick games, for power, glory and other kinds of gain to patch up our little egos. It's like Jimi Hendrix said, "We're involved in big ego scenes." We're not going to do anything about our sick goals until we get that need for the big ego scene out of our system. The only way we're going to do that is to go out and get some real honest-to-God love into our lives. The kind I'm talking about is where you can walk up to five people and tell how it is with you in your deepest heart. And two or three of them tell you back. And you get a little fire going in your tummy. And when you see that happen many times, then you are able and willing to walk away from the power and glory.

Now, our Puritan heritage in this country teaches, "Only the good prosper and if you don't prosper it's a sign that you're awfully wicked." So the idea of turning our little leaf loose on the stream of life and letting it float horrifies us. We can't stand it. We want to hook up a little motor to our leaf and buzz around. To heck with the current.

Well, this life is a big and mysterious and infinitely difficult process. And the idea that you or me, in our very finite and limited way, can have any conception of the mystery of the world in our relationship to it in anything past the next five minutes is ridiculous and dumb. We can't. We can't have any conception, really, of where we should be and what we should be doing five years from now. But we have a pretty good means if we live five minutes at a time and follow our nose.

But like I say, there are many of you who are screaming inside, saying, "Don't be an idiot. We can't do that. We've got to control our life. We've got to do something about it." But I don't think so, not in the way that you mean.

Now—some of you will say the other thing. "Oh, that Jess, he's dumb. He's talking about not caring about our life." I'm not talking about not caring. "He's talking about doing nothing." I'm not talking about not doing anything.

One of my graduate students and graduate students are some of the most misguided students in the whole world, heard some of these ideas and thought I was crazy. He wrote, "Hah. You talk about playing all these dumb financial games and other games, but what would happen if all the people who built our financial institutions and who built all the great material benefits of this country, what would happen if they all gave up these games? Wouldn't our chances of living in our own kind of civilization go like it does for the South American people or for the American Indians who just didn't care." He thought he had a criticism of what I was saying.

I said to him, "What have we got that's so great? When an American child is born, he is fifty times more threat to our universe than a child born in India. Now this is the price that we pay for this fantastic material prosperity that we've got. This American child is going to consume fifty times as many of the limited resources of this world. He's going to introduce fifty times as much pollutants and contaminants into the world as the child in India. Okay. We're starting to realize that's a price we don't really want to pay."

Furthermore he criticized the American Indian. The American Indian lived with this land for about 50,000 years. And the land was in as good shape when we took it away from him as it was when he came here 50,000 years before. Now we can't quite make that claim. In a period of about 300 years, we've raised an awful lot of hell with our land, and with our world. The whole globe. We've got all the air and even the oceans as big as they are all screwed up.

Now the person who wants to argue that our material prosperity means anything more than just material prosperity again has got rocks in his head. If you want to look at our country, you can see many serious kinds of problems. I'm not condemning American civilization alone. I'm talking about all the Western culture and the whole world at large.

But we're the only people who have taken this idea of material benefits and ridden it so far and so destructively. There's lots of bad news in our society like our tremendous suicide rate and our tremendous rate of mental hospitalization. We're about the only country in the world that's got lots of psychiatrists and still can't meet the need or the demand. When you see all of these signs, how can you say, "This is a happy country"? It may be a rich country—but not a happy one.

And the happiest people in this country as far as I can see, are the people with less money. What we call the common people. So if we would want to make an argument, I would argue that except for poverty-stricken people, you're happy in an inverse proportion to the amount of money you make. You've got a pretty tough time defending our material success or our material benefits as being necessary or desirable.

I'm uninterested in all that technology. I think that about the happiest I've ever been is when I was on a canoe trip living out of a packsack. When life was stripped right down to things that were simple and basic. And you knew it was all there with you. I could manage this, and I was very happy with it.

We spent time as a family camping on the road for as much as six and eight weeks at a time. Just the family together living under canvas. And the family discord that we had when we were in situations like that was almost completely nil. I don't think we had one fight a week in our family when we were camping. So I'm not concerned about that at all. Sure, I like money as well as the next guy, but I'm usually not willing to beat my life out of shape any more to get it.

Now there's a simple rule to help you do this, I think. You have got an invaluable clue right at your hands and in a way, you despise it. But it's there. And it is this simple rule. A woman asked this question of Proust, the great French poet. She said, "Mr. Proust, is it hard to write poetry?" And he said to her, "Madam, if it isn't easy, it's impossible." If your hand doesn't turn easily and naturally to something, it is impossible for you really.

I grew up with the notion I wanted to do about six thousand things. I wanted to make music on the recorder, and I wanted to do this and do that. I can't tell one musical note from another. There's all kinds of things that I thought I wanted to do in life that my hand doesn't turn to easily.

I wanted to be a football player so bad. I started out for practice when I was in seventh grade in a little school where there were only twenty kids in each class. They hardly had enough guys to have a football team. And I worked and practiced. I was always the last man off the practice field. I did every push-up, I did all the jogging, I did everything. I didn't smoke. I don't think I started smoking until I was nineteen because I didn't want to incapacitate what little physical ability or strength I had. I didn't do anything wrong. If the coach had told me to stand on my head all day long so I'd be better, I would have done it.

Each year, I'd say, "Hey, this guy has graduated and he's not a center any more and this year Jess Lair will start at center." And some kid would come off the farm who had never been out for football before and within two or three weeks, he'd be a better center and he'd beat me out. So I'm second string center again. I finally got a football when I was a junior through the goodness of the coach's heart. He put me in when the game was either so lost or so won that I couldn't do any harm, because I've got four left feet, and I'm always stumbling around. I was even worse in basketball. I was so clumsy, all I would do is foul. Athletics don't come easy to me. They're impossible. I did enjoy the physical conditioning and what have you. I even enjoyed scrimmage, being canned and potted by those bigger guys.

But there are other things that come easy for me—physics and math and algebra. I could just look at most of those problems and see the answers. Those things came easy for me. So what you have to do is follow your nose. And just look around at all those things that your hand turns to naturally.

People say to me, "Hey, Jess, what should I do?" And I say, "Look at your day yesterday. What were the first things you put your hand to? What are the things you like to do the most?" And then typically, they tell me, "Oh, I wouldn't want to do anything like that, you know." They don't realize the tremendous strength and wonder there is in doing something just because you love it, just because you believe in it.

But how many people in any occupation do you see who are there just because they love it? I know an automobile mechanic to whom that is a labor of love and there is nothing more fascinating than the pages of *Popular Mechanics* and that legendary mechanic—Gus. But, you know, very few guys are like that, who really walk in there and do the job. Or nurses. Or teachers . . . each of my students have had roughly fifty to seventy-five teachers. But out of those, only two or three stand out in their minds as really good teachers. So you can see what the odds are on being a real good teacher.

Now somebody says, "You can't run your life without goals, you need goals. You had a goal for a Ph.D., for example, to be a teacher." And the answer is, "Yes, I did." But every goal that I've got now is an extremely tentative one. I would not have gone for that Ph.D. had I found teaching very distasteful to me. But I didn't. I found it a joy. And I found studying to be a joy. I was able to get a Ph.D. in two years while I taught full time and supervised a freshman writing course. I had a family with five kids yet I wrote my Ph.D. thesis and did all kinds of other things, and I never studied past 11:00 o'clock at night and most weekends I didn't have to study.

It wasn't that I was so smart. I loved what I was doing and I did my studying in the daytime, when I was fresh and had the time. So I had all kinds of signs that while I had a goal a couple years ahead of me, it made sense and my hands were turning to it easily and naturally.

Now sure, there were some parts that were hard, like going over in the evening at seven o'clock every night for about two months to write my Ph.D. dissertation. That was hard to do. But I went over and said, "Okay, you've got a job to do. (I set myself a goal of three pages a night.) You've got to write three pages every night." I'd go over and write as fast as I could and come home rather than try to make myself suffer to write three to four hours a night.

A lot of people come back with the idea of challenge. They say, "Jess, you're leaving out challenge completely." Well, Jackie Gleason was being interviewed on the "Mike Douglas Show." Mike was saying to Jackie, "What do you think about challenge, Jackie?" And Jackie Gleason says, "I hate challenge. I don't believe in it." And Mike Douglas says, "Why, you're the guy who has pioneered some great things in comedy like the Honeymooners. What do you mean?" And Jackie says, "Those weren't challenges for me, those were logical next steps in my development."

I would like to see every one of you do something up to and including being the President of the United States, because it was the logical next step in your development rather than this senseless going out and looking for a challenge thing. That's really running away from yourself. And use the simple rule of "if it isn't easy, it's impossible." Or another way of saying it is, "doing what comes naturally." But we so despise ourselves that we have no trust and no faith in what that unique person that is us will love to do and want to do.

In this country, we claim to have some sense of religion, some sense of relationship to a higher power. Each of us are unique and wonderful and beautiful people deep down. Yet we refuse to do those things and to let that uniqueness come out as us. And we refuse to accept it. We are all saying, "I'm bigger and smarter than me and I know what I should be." This shows our contempt for what we are and all the beauty and wonder that is there.

NINE

Trust—the Self-fulfilling Prophecy

When I talk to you about acceptance, a common response is, "Hey, I'm pretty good at accepting the other guy but I can't accept myself very well." Well, the answer is you and I *aren't* pretty good at accepting the other guy. Because if we were, we could change the whole world around us into a different kind of thing. Many of us are very disturbed at the kind of world we occupy. We say, "Hey, man, there's nobody out there to trust me, nobody likes me. And it's a dry dreary place, this world that I'm walking through today."

Well there's one simple answer as to how we can take that world around us and change it. We can't change it by screaming at it and telling it, "World, you're so sick." We need to do something very positive and act on that world and on ourselves, too, in a very positive way. And the best word that I can find for acceptance carried to a real extreme toward others is the word trust. There isn't much of it around. For example, in many final examinations in college, you walk into the classrooms and you sit in alternate seats with your chairs turned around facing backwards. That's beautiful trust.

Many of my students in just a very short period of time are going to be teaching students. They're going to be entrusted with the lives of thirty to fifty people. And yet, people don't trust them very much right now. Well how come, magically at some point, they are all of a sudden going to be worthy of that deep kind of trust?

Trust is so powerful because it is hooked up to the self-ful-filling prophecy, which says that what you expect from the world is about what you get. And when you go out today expecting grief, turmoil, trouble, difficulty, lying, cheating and failing of all kinds, you get just exactly what you expect. When you go out and expect the opposite in terms of trust and when you expect all kinds of good things to happen, oddly enough, those good things are far more inclined to happen.

Now it is not that simple; it demands some change in the people that constitute your world. But if you will change yourself, you will come at people straighter and more hopefully and more expectingly, and you will bring out the best in them. And, if you are willing to give up some of those sick games, you're going to be able to walk away from some of the very destructive people in your life, and stay away from them. This lets you concentrate on those people that are less destructive and more inclined to be a positive force in your life.

I mentioned earlier that people have got two sides to them just like a coin. And when you tell me, "My world is full of tails," I've got to believe you. I've got to say, "I'm sure it is, friend." And you say, "Well, where's this world you're talking about, Jess, where I can change and be different?" And I say, "It's right there. Looking at you. Those coins have got another side to them." And you say, "How come I'm not seeing them?" And the answer I see is very simple.

There's a reciprocal relationship between you and me and other people. And the way we come at them and the way we treat them and the way we handle them determines the side of the coin we see. So we can see heads of coins instead of tails. But the only way we're going to do it is with trust and acceptance, primarily of ourselves and secondly of someone else.

One of my students was telling of her grandfather who trusted her tremendously. She was rather distressed that her grandfather could not trust other people. She could see that his life was very constrained and limited because of his fearfulness and lack of trust. When I mentioned that she was able to trust people because her grandfather had trusted her, it made her very sad to think that no one had trusted her grandfather when he was little and young. Most of the capacity that you and I have right now for trusting was given to us by the people around us.

But we're not completely limited here, either. Like we aren't in love by the amount we got from the people around us, from the adults and our parents. Same with trust. As I was thinking about trust, I realized that trust is really acceptance carried to an extreme. And how are we going to trust other people? Simple. We're going to first learn to trust ourselves, and our trust of ourselves is going to come out of our acceptance of ourselves. When you say, "I just couldn't trust anybody," what you're telling me really is that you're not trusting yourself. Because if you did truly see any good in yourself, you wouldn't have so much difficulty seeing some good in others that you could trust. And if you weren't so terribly uncomfortable with what you see are the negative things in yourself, you wouldn't have so much trouble handling the negative things you see in other people.

A good way to see the importance of trust is to look at our working relationships. It is easy to see how a lack of trust in us can really hurt us. When I was younger and dumber, I used to think that I could work for anybody. And I could work with anybody. But I have found that that is very, very wrong. I can't do that if I want to do a halfway decent job. Because when I'm working for someone, as I have in fairly recent times, who expects the very worst from me, I'm very disturbed at the side of me that he sees. He does see a lot of the very worst in me that he expects. I had the experience of working under two men simultaneously, one who expected the best from me and the other who expected the worst. And I really saw a graphic and drastic example of the fact that we've got two sides to us.

I see now my environment does affect me. But I also see that I affect my environment. We combine the two things and that's how we change the world that we live in. We change some of the people, getting rid of those who will not trust us, those people who expect the very worst from us, and moving toward the people who expect the better from us.

This has some great consequences as to the kind of situations that we spend our lives in. And it says that if we're not comfortable in a situation, if it's not tolerable for us, if it does not bring out the best in us, we should get out of that situation. I don't care what the advantages are for us in terms for our opportunity to distinguish ourselves because we're going to pay an awful price for it.

The minute I tried that new job in Chicago, a lot of the good work that I was doing disappeared. It wasn't built into me strong enough that it could be produced under the worst kind of circumstances. No work ever is. We do have a kind of minimum level that we can operate at even if things are real tough. That minimum level was high enough to hold me my job. But it was not high enough to give me the feeling I was coming anywhere near the kind of potential I saw for myself. So I got out of the situation. Mostly because I wasn't ready for it. And I started my own business which gave me better control of my environment. And going into teaching was another step toward a better environment.

One of the first bosses I had in teaching believed in me so much it was embarrassing. He expected the best from me and that's what he got—the best work I was capable of. And in teaching I have come to see even more how important trust is. Kahlil Gibran in *The Prophet* says of teaching: "The teacher gives not of his wisdom but of his belief and his lovingness." Now how many teachers have you ever had that can live up to that definition of a teacher? Most of them try to give of their wisdom. But so often they don't communicate to you enough belief and lovingness in you to put in a thimble.

I think the same thing is true of our children. We don't raise our children in this omnipotent all-seeing sense that we're inclined to see ourselves—as the father and mother should be. Where are we ever going to get that kind of sense as to what to do in any given situation? The answer is we aren't.

When you become, each of you, parents, you are the same people you were the day before you became parents. And you haven't got any magnificent kind of sense of psychology and fatherhood and all kinds of other things magically bestowed on you. You've got to raise kids with the intelligence and the lack of it that you have right now. So as near as I can see, the only rule that I have been able to find about raising kids is that you try to treat them like people.

You can have your world one of two ways. You can be a part of that warmer, more trusting and happy-with-each-other kind of world as well as recognize that other harsher world is there, but you don't need to deal with it that much of the time. Or you can say, "No, there is no close, warm wonderful world where people can trust each other. No, there isn't any such thing. That Lair is smoking opium again and having another one of his pipe dreams." You can have it either way. But it goes back to the power of that self-fulfilling prophecy.

The only way you're going to see the heads on the coins of the people that you deal with is by expecting to see heads. And staying away from the people who are resolutely determined to show you the tail side of their coin. And you stay away from them, not on the grounds that there's something wrong with them, but because there's probably something wrong with the way that you come at them. Because they're good guys to *somebody*. And the fact that they're not a good guy to me or to you shows me more about me and you than it does about them.

So we control our lives by what we expect of people and the people that we expose ourselves to and choose to be around and choose to live among.

There are some questions you can raise about these ideas. You can say, "Hey, should I always run away from a bad situation?" And I think my answer is almost always, "Yah." If you aren't comfortable with your work, get out. If you aren't comfortable with the neighborhood you're in, get out. If you aren't comfortable in the area in which you're living, the people that you're living with, get out.

Now I grant you that sometimes you would be walking away from situations that you could have cracked if you would have hung in there. But I don't see myself as being that tough. I see this life as a survival operation. This is just like walking a ridge in rock country where the rock is loose. One false step—boom! And you're gone.

It would be very wrong of me to see myself as having fantastic strengths by which I can do all kinds of things that are unpleasant and mean for me. Just because it is good for my character. Or, just because I love to suffer. No thank you. I'm not going to throw away any more days or any more hours of a day than I have to throw away. So, the answer is that if a situation is good for you, you are inclined to feel it right away. If a boss is the kind of person who is really going to be great for you, you're going to feel it right away. Now sure, you've got to make some investment on your part.

Is it always, absolutely the best answer—to run away? No. In some circumstances, you can hang in there, and know that if there are one or two people that are a particular problem to you, they will probably go a lot faster than you will. Because people that are a problem to you and me are usually problems to all kinds of people. They can't stay around very long, usually. Or if they do stay around, there is a way of isolating them and insulating them from people so that they have very little impact on people. So that in some circumstances you can stay.

I know a part of you is inclined to say, "Hey, Jess, what you're talking about, that's so common I know all about that. Oh, I'm so bored with these things you're saying. You're talking this hearts and flowers stuff, and it's so common and it's all over." Well I'll tell you a couple of stories.

If you want to shock some people so much that you will risk killing them, just go out and take these ideas and really practice them. It's like telling people you love them. They'll say, "What's wrong, are you sick? Or, do you need money? Or, what kind of mischief have you been up to now?" Or you try to say the words "I love you" and you choke to death because you can't get them out. Okay. Well this is the same kind of a problem. Now I'll put this another way so you can see this in startling clarity.

A good friend of mine, Willis Vandiver, was supervising elementary teachers down in Colorado. And Willis is the kind of guy who is very thorough about his job. So as a supervisor of elementary teachers, he figures a real good thing to do is to go into elementary classrooms and watch the teachers. You know. He has a real primitive sense of what to do instead of sitting around shuffling papers in his office.

So Willis, with the principal, walked into the first grade teacher's room and watched her teach for an hour or two. At the end of the time, Willis walked up to her, and said, "Madam, I've been in many, many first grade classes, but I've never seen a job of teaching as good as the one you've done." She had taught for about fifteen years. You know what she did? She cried. You know why she cried? "Because," she said, "you are the first professional that has ever walked in here and told me that I've been doing a real good job.

"Now," she said, "all kinds of parents have told me I'm really doing a good job and that they're real happy that their kids have a chance to get in my room." But her fellow professionals hadn't really been that liberal in their praise which came out of trust.

Your experiment for today is to go around looking for the good in situations and really seeing it. I don't care whether it's no deeper than seeing that somebody's got a real pretty yellow sweater on and saying something to them about it. All the way up to seeing somebody doing a real good job of something and saying, "Wow! That's really something."

I was reading a story about Pistol Pete Maravich when he was at L.S.U., and people were always doing the exact opposite to him. Here's a guy that is one of the greatest basketball players that we will ever have in our time. So, you know what they're always doing to him? They're putting him down. "It must be nice for you, playing under your dad." They're implying that he wouldn't be so great without that.

Well if you've ever read the story of Pistol Pete Maravich, that guy has been practicing basketball since he was about four years old. And he spends about four to six hours in a day, year around, shooting and practicing and dribbling. At his age, he has spent more hours on a basketball court, I am sure, than any other man playing basketball. And while all of the good basketball players have practiced a lot, nobody that I've ever read about that is a good basketball player has put in that almost superhuman and fanatic devotion to basketball that he has. And then somebody says, "Oh, it must be nice playing under your dad as coach." Or, "Aren't you lucky?" Or different things that cut him down.

We can't stand to be in the presence of somebody doing good, because it makes us feel horrible, more horrible than we feel right now. So we cut them down—to our size. And we think we are just being realistic about the other person. But we won't be so brutally realistic with ourselves.

You get out there and try some of this and see. And you thought you'd choke on the words, I love you. Wait until you start trying to find something really good about the people around you that you can honestly feel and say. First of all, you're going to have trouble finding it. You're going to say, I'm such a great judge, you know, I really know all things. And what you are, is you are a big criticizer, like me. We know all wrong things that we see about us. But we don't see anything good going on. I wonder how come? You know we're such great judges of this and that, but we don't see any of the good things that go on. And then when you finally see something worth praising, you're going to have trouble saying so. Because you want to think the world has got a taste like lemon to it. And everything in it is that same rotten sour taste.

But you protest, "Oh, I want that world you're talking about, Jess. Man, that sounds great to me." But then you try to do that one little thing that I'm talking to you about and you're going to have trouble, real serious trouble. So you just go around for the day, looking for the good, and saying it and see what kind of success you have.

I think bosses and parents are some of our worst offenders here. The minute most of us get any kind of a leadership role, we immediately figure that our job is to get mean and tough with people, and push them around. It's no wonder, for example, that they still sell whips and canes and rods for use in our classrooms. In fact, in some classrooms, they are very, very common. And punishment persists as a means of handling other people despite the fact that punishment doesn't do a very good job of changing behavior. We've got all kinds of results that shows that.

Some of the interesting studies are the ones that Skinner does. You can put a little rat in a Skinner box and get him pressing the bar so the food comes. After you've got him pressing the bar in a certain way, you can say, "I'm not going to give the rat any more food pellets." So he stops pressing the bar pretty fast. "But," you say, "I'll try a little punishment and see if he will stop pressing the bar even faster." You've decided that pressing the bar is like a kid swearing. You're going to stop it in the kid, see.

So instead of just not rewarding him anymore with food pellets, you're going to punish him. So you put an electric shock on the bar. Now every time that he presses the bar, not only does he not get a food pellet, he gets a jolt. What happens? The answer is he'll press the bar about the same number of times as if you didn't shock him. It's just that it takes longer to get those presses out. He won't go back to the bar as fast, but he'll keep going back, and press it, and boom! he gets this jolt, but it seems like he just needs to press it so many times before he gets rid of the certain piece of behavior that isn't rewarded any more.

The implication is punishment is not a very good way to get rid of the behavior that we don't want. But it persists. We do punish people a great deal. And why does it persist? It persists for the simple reason that punishing is very, very satisfying to us. The person who's doing the punishing enjoys it.

As a parent, as a teacher, as a boss, you and I just love to pound on people and punish them. But you're doing this, not because it works so well, but because you love it so. And because I love it so. There are times when my kids are noisy and cantankerous and it makes me feel good to beat on them a little. But it doesn't help them very much in terms of them changing around to being different.

So that's the opposite end of the world from the end of the world that we're talking about. But it's more typical of the kind of life that we're living today. We're living among people where we are punishing each other. And we're living in a life where we are punishing life and pounding on it, and saying, "Life, you sour lemon." And then we expect good, wonderful things to come back to us, like banana splits.

Well, it doesn't work that way. The self-fulfilling prophecy is what works. And this is why this set of ideas is not a bunch of idealistic nonsense. It is not a delusion.

You ask, "Well, how can you expect me, Jess, to take these ideas out in that hard cruel world and keep them going out there where everybody's trying to put out my little flame?" Well, the answer is very simple. You just go out there and look at yourself and expect the best out of yourself. To do that you've got to accept yourself as halfway decent. And then you can expect the best from other people. All of a sudden you're going to find that's a different world out there than it was yesterday. And you're going to be welcomed with open arms, if you can look for the good and see it and say it.

Now this is simple. It isn't easy to do but it is simple. It works. If you don't believe me, go out there and try it for yourself. You're going to see how hard it is for you to look for the good. But if you think what I'm talking about is common then ask yourself again, how long has it been since somebody has seen some real good in you? Compared to how long it's been since somebody has seen trouble in you and problems.

Another way we can look at this problem is: Imagine you are going to work under me and I say to you, "You are no good. I won't trust you any further than I can throw you. I'm going to give you a job, then I'm going to watch you like a hawk every minute of the time."

I guarantee I can make you look real bad. On the other hand, I can come up and say to you, "You are probably God's greatest gift to your line of work, and I am the happiest person in the world because you are working with us and I'm convinced you can set right many of the problems we haven't yet been able to solve."

Do you see what a difference this could make in your life or the life of the people around us?

So here is a magic weapon that each of us have in working with every person that we are working with or along side of. We don't have to be supervising someone to believe in them but particularly it is crucial to those people over whom we have some responsibility. There's no one I can think of who doesn't have some responsibility for at least a part of some other person's activities either at home, on the job or in some kind of social or service activity. In fact, I think you'd be surprised how much responsibility you have for others once you sat down and thought about it.

I've got a responsibility to my family. I've got a responsibility to my students. I've got a responsibility to my fellow professors. And oddly enough your and my responsibility isn't just limited to the people directly around us or under us. In a sense, I've got a responsibility to believe in and accept all the students and all the professors at our university—not just the ones around me.

The more you trust your associates, the more you believe in them, the better they are. The less you believe in them, the worse they are. And yet they are the same people, it's just a difference in what you expect of them. And this is a very powerful tool.

In the self-fulfilling prophecy, I see a fantastic power to change the things that go on around us. We aren't powerless. Granted we don't have the power to move the whole world but who says we should have that much power. That's grandiosity.

But we have an amazing power over all the people around us for good. And oddly enough, the way we do it is just by believing in them. Not by messing around with their lives. Not by putting my grubby little finger in your life.

I'm just saying "Whoopee! We've got a good group. And we can do a lot of things." And everybody calms down and gets to work and gets their full weight against the wheel in their own way.

So that's the point of the self-fulfilling prophecy. When you believe in people, accept them as they are, then they can change—and grow. When you accept people, you expect the best—and you get all they've got to give. But expect the worst —and you'll get much less than their best.

That's why it's such a fantastic tool. When I believe in my students, trust them, expect the best from them, they are surprised. Why? Because they claim it doesn't happen to them often.

TEN

Accepting Grief and Death

Another trouble that you and I have is our lack of acceptance of grief and sorrow and death and suffering. We find it very, very difficult to understand how sorrow plays a part in the world, and we use it as a way of running away from ourselves and from the world.

A guy came in my office the other day, a student who has been a good friend of mine for a number of years. He said, "Jess, I've got a twenty-one-year-old cousin who is dying of leukemia. What kind of rotten world is it that this kind of thing would happen?" This is a tremendously egocentric view of the world when we see ourselves as the center of the world, and that all things that happen are aimed at and are vicious attacks on us personally.

We can't understand why death will come at any particular time. The only thing we know is that it's going to come to all of us. Someone we love is going to be dead before the year is over. And there really doesn't seem to be any reason why it should happen.

But again there isn't much sense as to why it shouldn't. We've each got to die and get out of the way of the people who are coming along behind us. It would be a pretty crowded world if we let people die when they wanted to die. Because all the people who had ever lived would be running around the earth right now. Because nobody that I've ever seen has ever been in a big hurry to die.

So this is something that we've got to do. The answer as to when it happens seems to me to be pretty meaningless. With a family I know, I've recently gone through the death of a young man. And they've asked these questions of themselves a lot. The crucial question is: What is life? And the thing that I see about life is it isn't some specified length of time. Life isn't living to the average sixty-eight years. To me life is a process, and this is where the five-minutes-at-a-time idea comes in. Life is a process where we either live five minutes at a time or we don't. And how long it is, it seems to me, is pointless. It is a process in which we are either engaged to the best of our ability or we ain't.

This was the sadness that I felt when I had my heart attack at thirty-five. If you would have asked me, "Jess, were you engaged in this to the best of your ability?" I would have had to say, "In a way, yes, but in another way, no." And if something happened to me today, and you said, "Jess, are you engaged in this process to the best of your ability?" I would have to say, "Yes, as much as I humanly can, I am." And a lot of you have been struck by the fact that you, too, after you work on these things would find that you could answer that question the same way. You don't need to get hit with a heart attack to do some things differently in your life. And this, as I see, is the process of life.

Now the grief that we get and the suffering and sorrow, I don't see as particularly related to anything. We're suffering partly under the notion that sorrow and trouble and misery and misfortune and financial woes are all signs that we're some big fat sinners. Well I've seen an awful lot of sinners who didn't get much trouble. And I've seen some people, who it seemed to me didn't do much sinning at all, who just got a ton of trouble. And again I don't see the nature of the particular troubles that we come across in life as being particularly meaningful in and of themselves.

There's a family just outside of town where there were eight children. They've already lost four of their eight children in accidents, war, things like that. Why should that be visited on them? Well, there perhaps is some mysterious plan to this that I will never see. And I'm sure that's the case. I'm a very finite person, and this is an infinitely complex world.

But the thing that I see about the sorrows and sufferings in my own life is that what has counted isn't so much the particular nature of those sufferings or sorrows, but what has counted is what I do with those. And I see that under the burden of each of the various sorrows of life, we either grow or we die. We take that sorrow and suffering, pick it up and use it as a means to a richer and better life for ourselves. Or it just kills us. No I don't mean to suggest that these sorrows are for that purpose. I would never argue that someone's death is for the purpose of making those who are left behind lead a richer life. I wouldn't argue that at all. I would just simply say that that is one of the things that can happen because of it.

I saw in the cerebral palsy organization that my wife and I belonged to that an awful lot of the fathers in those families had run away from home. The mother was raising the handicapped child by herself because the father was not able to stand the terrible sorrow and suffering that was there. And rather than grow from it, he chose to run away from it and in a sense die from it.

And I've seen people who were very burdened with sorrows, in a sense, almost die from their sorrows. But I've also seen people who haven't had any sorrows at all die from the lack of them. I think it takes sorrow to open us to life.

We are very hesitant and very frightened to accept the certainty and the knowledge of our death. Before I had my heart surgery about five years ago, I went to my best friend in Minnesota. I was looking for sympathy. "Boy, old Bitz, I'm going into surgery and it's going to be dangerous and they're going to cut great big holes in my chest and take my heart out and play games with it." And I was expecting old Bitz to say, "Oh, Jess, that's so sad."

Bitz was working alongside the barn. He looked up at me and said, "Jess, you know there ain't a one of us going to get out of this thing alive." I was just about crushed. I could have hit him. But it is very true. There ain't a one of us going to get out of this thing alive. So we better get on with living. Bitz had this tremendous acceptance of death and his life showed it. He's one of the happiest, easiest-going guys you've ever seen. He's not about to twist his life out of shape for an extra nickel. And this seems to me to be the lesson.

But this is why death and sorrow in others is so terribly hard. We see it as a personal affront to ourselves. And we see it as a very personal and deep reminder of our own death. That's why we have a terrible problem handling the grief of others. The typical response that we make is to deny their grief. A child dies and we go to the parents and say, "Aren't you lucky, you've got four living yet?" Well, you're not lucky because you've got four living, you are terribly sad because four of eight are dead and that is not only false comfort, it is the rottenest kind of thing to say to people who are sad and sick.

We owe it to the people who are grieving, who are sad, to let them grieve, to accept their grief, to accept their sorrow. But we won't and can't do it.

Grief suffered by the people around us is particularly troublesome for us. They need us more than ever. Yet their loss of a loved one or their suffering frightens us because we can see ourself losing the same thing. And their strong need for us bothers us too. So it is very hard for us to really accept another person's grief.

Grief isn't just when people die. Grief is in all kinds of things. Like I grieve at leaving Minnesota. It has a horrible climate—it's colder than the North Pole in the winter and hotter than the tropics in the summertime. But it's got a pretty spring and fall. So I grieve at leaving a country and friends I won't see much anymore.

People grieve at many of the difficult spots in their life—not just death. And in a way death is an easier kind of grief to handle because it is clean and definite. The worst grief of all is suffered by the people who must bear a lifetime of sorrow. Someone who has to commit a wife or child to an institution. Or a parent whose son is imprisoned for murder. That is a terrible kind of grief that just won't end because you are continually thinking about what might have been and what will be. It's like being impaled on the point of a pin and being held up so you can flop around and try to get off.

I accidentally drove through the grounds of Warm Springs Mental Hospital recently. We were going to stop at the town of Warm Springs for a cup of coffee but found there was no town there—just the mental hospital. I was sick at the sorrow and suffering and anguish I felt as I watched husbands or wives walking with their mentally ill spouses. At one place on the grounds I saw what looked like a severely retarded young man kissing a retarded young woman. It was a poignant, sorrowful scene.

But the big thing about grief is just to see it as a factor in your way of life. Accept it. Understand it is there. It is a problem. You have to handle it.

I see this in all the feelings and difficulties we have. Rather than use the word acceptance, you can just use the word, openness. Once you are open to what's going on inside you, once you open the door to your mind, your feelings, your heart, you can look inside. Once you've got a window, you can look in and see what's going on in there. It's some kind of honesty about yourself.

What about the special sadness of watching a young person die? Can a young child be ready to die? I don't know. I have only seen one young person die of cancer. He was a lot calmer about it than all of us around him were. I just don't know. There is a saying in large families that each child brings his own loaf of bread. And I've seen some truth in that. And there is another saying: "When you get married, God guarantees you enough help to get you through the problems of marriage if you will ask for it." I think that might apply to any death—old or young.

The people I've seen die have all died well—with dignity. Sometimes there is pitiableness to dying. My grandfather was just pleading to die. He was a very sad, depressed man after my grandmother died.

When I was very near death during my heart attack, I was struck by the tremendous calm I felt. I even said to my wife when she got to the hospital, "You know I could die, don't you?" and she did. I don't know why you get through something like that in that way but you seem to.

The big principle I see here is this: When my oldest daughter was born handicapped, people would say, "Aren't you lucky she isn't worse." Don't do that to me.

Now we do this partly as a well-intentioned effort to help the other person. We are not helping the other person. We are refusing to accept them. And we're saying don't bother me.

Now the extreme of denying and failing to accept feelings is to try to hide death from a dying person. Maybe the wife doesn't want to tell the husband he is dying. Sometimes this can work it out. The wife has the solace of thinking she's fooling the husband and doesn't have to talk to him about his feelings, but he knows he's dying. We always know.

But don't give me this baloney about, "Look on the bright side." Damn it, look on the bad side! Double it up. My wife is always doing that. It works great. She always says right out the worst it could possibly be. She comes bombing into a situation and says, "Hey, are you worried about dying?" And you say, "No, I'm not worried about dying but I am worried about being incapacitated for a long time." Which is not as bad.

That's the way to do it. And that's the way to open people up, too. Say the worst, the most horrible thing. Get the feelings out in the open. Your next door neighbor comes over and says, "Gee, I've got an awful problem." So you say, "Did your husband run away with another woman?" And she says, "Oh, it's not that. My kid got a B in school."

I was so struck by an incident. One of my students wrote me from Nebraska. Her next door neighbor's husband was a traveling salesman and died. She said, "I baked some pies and while they were baking, I got your book out and read the chapter on grief where you said just this. So I went over to her with my pies and said, 'I'm sorry.' And the woman cried and I was sad with her and let her be sad. But I noticed running through my mind were all these thoughts like 'Weren't you lucky that he died at home instead of out on the road someplace and all these other things you warned me against saying.' But she said, 'Luckily I didn't say them.' But what she was so struck by is that they were there."

Now sorrow has its uses and purposes. It won't make me feel worse when you respect my sorrow and accept my sorrow and my grief. I need my sorrow, and there's nothing wrong with it. Acceptance makes anybody I've ever seen feel better. And also it's pretty rare and I need your acceptance pretty bad.

Now as I see it, one of the things about sorrow that is not a mystery to me is its value to us. Gibran says it beautifully when he says, "It is by the depth of our sorrows that we know our joys."

And this is the thing that I've seen about sorrow. You can liken sorrow to the winters. You can take a little seed and it lies in the ground for twenty years. But each of those twenty years, there's a frost and it makes a little dent in that seed. In the twentieth year, there's a frost and the little crack is finally widened open to the point where it is broken enough for the seed to come out. And the seed says, "Boy, that twentieth winter, that was an awfully big, bad winter." And the answer is, no, it wasn't. It wasn't just the twentieth winter. It was all those nineteen that went before it. So I've seen that our sorrows can open us to the world and can open us to ourselves if we will not run away from them.

A student asked this: "Could you accept the idea that our lives should be lived as preparing for the day we die? I read an article by a person who knew she was dying of cancer. She spent her last year doing good things for others and things that she had always wished to do someday. She made the statement that she would rather live forty-two full, rich years than twice that long in dull tempo. Is this essentially what you are trying to tell us in a way? Should we live each day as if it were the last? How many of us really do?"

We should live each day as if it were the last, but at the same time we should live each day as if we were going to live a thousand years. This keeps that kind of franticness out and makes us go on. We need the balance between the two attitudes.

What I've been saying is this. The funny thing is when grief or death confronts us, we are touched deeply. A good way to understand this is to use an analogy. Put just one drop of red food coloring in a glass of clear water and the whole glass of water turns red. You can add twenty more drops of food coloring and the water only gets a little redder. Grief's like that.

When you meet grief and death, accept it. Don't give false comfort by saying to someone, "Buck up, it could be worse." Their whole life has changed. Someone else's problem means nothing to them.

It's not a blessing the baby dies. It was their baby—deformed or not.

It is not a blessing her husband is no longer suffering. He was her whole life—and he is gone.

Why can't we just say—I'm sorry. And let our friends weep if they need to.

ELEVEN

If There's a Problem Here—
I Caused It

I talk to you just about hard things in this book because they're the only problems I'm interested in—the hard ones. One basic idea is: *If there is a problem here, I caused it*. This runs exactly contrary to what you want to believe. I've got news for you. It runs exactly contrary to what I want to believe, too. But I don't really have that much choice.

My experience, my own story, has led me to believe that if there is a problem here, I caused it. Now that's very sad, but in another way, it's very happy. Because it says, that if there's a problem here, I had an awfully big hand, if not an exclusive hand, in causing it. So I can get to work on it.

It says that one of the most crucial things we need to do in our five minutes at a time today is to look for problems that we are a part of. Look for arguments. Look for troubles that we have. Like something we should have done but didn't. And because we didn't do it, we'll have a problem tomorrow. Okay, how did I cause it? Well, I start looking at it. For day after day, I put the job away and don't do it. Then I'm violating one of the central principles of life and I know it. So all of a sudden I come up to the deadline and the job isn't done. So if there's a problem here, I caused it. And there are just tons of those during the day.

This has even greater implication in the people-problems in

our life. My first law of the classroom or any other human relationship is: Bug and thou shalt be bugged in return. A number of my students have taken that and put it on a little card and set in on their desk in front of them. Bug and thou shalt be bugged in return. It applies to all of life. I found out about this because when students would bug me in class, all I would need to do is look back five minutes, ten minutes, an hour, a day, and I would see the thing that I had done to them.

Now this isn't very surprising because as a scientist of behavior, I see great evidences of the lawfulness of behavior. In fact, the only way there can be a science of anything, of chemistry or behavior or anything else is that behavior does follow basic rules and basic principles. Now this does not mean that we aren't free. It's an altogether different thing than that. It does mean though that each of our behaviors has certain, immediate and inflexible consequences. The problem in behavior is that the consequences aren't near as immediate as they are in terms of physical law.

What happens if you walk to the top of a building and step off? Boom! Broken leg. Right now. What happens if I bug somebody in my class? Do I get it right back? Probably not. Most likely, you see, I won't get it back for five minutes, ten minutes or a week—or even two weeks. So this is hard to learn.

They find, for example in learning, that when you put a rat in a Skinner box and have him press a little bar, you must give him a food pellet the instant his paw presses that bar so he learns very fast. But when he presses the bar and you don't give him a food pellet until maybe a couple of seconds later, he learns very slow. And if you get that food pellet to that rat five minutes after he presses that bar, it's going to take him a long, long time, if ever, to learn that pressing the bar has got something to do with those food pellets.

And here's what you might find the rat doing if you give him a food pellet five minutes after he presses the bar: He will press the bar and then he'll go over and sit in the corner and then he'll walk to the center of the cage and be kind of sniffing around in the air and the food pellet will come. So he will make a funny kind of connection. He will think that what he was doing just before the food pellet came is what got the food pellet. So it encourages patterns of behavior where many of the behaviors in the pattern aren't important. The rat's got the notion that when he circles around in the cage, that's when the food pellet comes. So he maybe circles around some and goes and sits in the corner and goes over and presses the bar and goes back and circles around some more and boom, there's a food pellet there. And it increases the rate of accidental behavior unrelated to what he really did to bring the food pellet.

This is very analogous to what we do in life. Not only do we not see the true consequences of our behavior, but we are inclined to feel that some other aspect of our behavior was rewarded when it really wasn't and it wasn't really consequential. So what we are in search of, is that ultimate reality in life, that ultimate lawfulness that lies there beneath the surface. And it is there.

In a classroom as in other groups, I find that most of the troubles that I have seen are problems that have been created by teachers or other kinds of leaders. Now it seems to me that it makes a lot more sense for us to avoid creating those problems for ourselves than it does talking about how to handle problems after we've created them.

For example, a number of fine teachers don't think there is such a thing as a discipline problem. You say, "You're crazy." And the answer is, "No, I'm not crazy. I haven't done that much teaching in all kinds of grades, but the teaching I have done at different grades, I didn't ever have any discipline problems." And there's a very simple reason I didn't have any discipline problems. That is, when I talk straight turkey right into the eyeballs of my students, they will listen to what I'm saying. When I use some kind of imagination to see how the world is for them and with them, they feel it and respond.

When you talk to people like that, which is one of the few times someone has talked to them like that, are they going to goof off and run and throw their chairs around? No. They're going to sit and listen, that's what they are going to do.

So the discipline problems come, when you walk into a group and start talking about something people are completely uninterested in, in ways that people are completely uninterested in. You say, "Well, that's the nature of school. It's just got to be dull like that." Well that isn't the nature of school, that's the nature of the way school has been handled for so many people. But there isn't anything that uninteresting. There isn't anything that can't be invested with relevance to you.

In some cases, it might be quite a ways from what you think of as being a hot burning issue. In some cases, I might find myself on some certain subjects or some aspect of the subject, saying to the student, "Hey, Sam, I know you just haven't got a prayer of getting interested in this thing. You and it have just never agreed." It's just like me trying to make a meal out of rutabagas which I hate.

But you can say, like I said to myself, "Okay, Jess, my own grandmother made those rutabagas and I'm not going to break her heart by not eating them. So I'll eat them because, while they taste bad, it would hurt a lot worse to leave them on my plate."

Well, the same way in some aspects of school. While you can't see any sense to it, just do it and get through it because it's one of those hard spots, it's one of the lumps in the oatmeal. And you'll at least get the satisfaction out of it that you did it. If you can't, okay. You can forget it. And of course, you can't ask that of students very often. You can't have very much of their studies of that nature. Most of it has to be things they can see and understand and believe. Same with work and family life.

Cheating and stealing works much the same way. The cheating that you find in a classroom will be directly related to the amount of trust that the teacher has in the students and that is communicated to them. You aren't going to be able to communicate any trust in them that you don't have. So the cheating or stealing will be directly related to the amount of trust you have in your people and that goes back to the amount of trust you have in yourselves. Do you see how these things fit in? And to all the other groups in life?

Like the question of motivation. In learning, I find that when I can make something crucial to my students' interest, they will work quite hard. I don't need to stand over them with some kind of new stick or whip and beat them with it. I don't need to use the fear of tests and all kinds of other things to make them learn. I've found amazing amounts of learning in a completely open setting where there are no tests, and they grade themselves. In the tight setting where I do all the grading and we've got two or three tests, I see less learning and more fear. Motivation is a door you open from the inside.

Now there's little chance that I could convince most people in educational circles of that because they're so wedded to the idea that you have got to have a lot of proper tests for there to be any real learning. Those are advocates of fear as a force in education. And I don't think fear is a real force in education.

Freud said: "There are two things in this world a grown-up person should be able to do. To love and to work." And really the work needs to be work done out of love so there really is just one thing in this world which is to love and to love your work. And I think that there is only one reason to do something. That's because you love to do it. It fits in with you. It's got some relationship to something you value and feel is precious.

I think fear gets in the way of learning. I think fear makes you submissive. I think fear destroys your independence.

Now, this is no fun. The biggest reason this is no fun is because we are face to face with ourselves and reality which is ourselves. When we take responsibility for our actions, we can't blame them on someone else or the world. If there's a problem here, I caused it. That's our bitter medicine to take. It is no fun. And you and I will run from that thing every chance we get. So while I recognize that taking responsibility is a crucial thing in my life, it is still hard to do.

This is one of the reasons why I need this five-minutes-at-a-time idea. So often we are in a problem and don't even realize it. And when we're doing five minutes at a time, it's much easier to realize. Something's wrong. Something's going on that isn't right.

Now you can say, "Your idea that if there's a problem here, I caused it, is dumb. What about the other guy? What about the other lunkheads and knotheads and narrow-minded, closed people in this world?" Fine. Sure. But the funny thing is that I've seen that when I do my part of the job right, very seldom is the other person a problem to me.

I'll give you an example. I taught freshman writing every quarter for three or four years. They would throw me fifty students drawn at random. They weren't there because they knew me or because they wanted to be or anything else. I got fifty scared freshmen in the worst subject in the world which is freshman writing. The flunker course in college.

The thing that I found at first was that sometimes I would have better luck than I would have other times. When I would give an assignment one way, everybody would do real well. But when I would give an assignment poorly because I was in a hurry or something, everybody would do badly. So I saw that if I wanted to make my students look bad, all I needed to do was give the assignment poorly.

But if I wanted to make them look very, very good, all I needed to do was find a good assignment for them. One they could really get interested in, then give it to them, very, very clearly. They would all do amazingly well.

What I found in teaching those classes was: When I got so I could really overcome most of my problems, most of my students' problems disappeared. I love teaching writing. I've been a writer. At the start I was a terrible writer, and I had gotten to the point where I wasn't so terrible anymore. It's a little like Benchley said about his writing. "By the time I realized that I was a bad writer, I was making so much money at it that I couldn't afford to quit." No paper that any student ever wrote was so bad that I'd look at it and throw up my hands and say, "This guy is a low-type scholar and will never make it. He should be flunked out of the company of distinguished men." I would always see some problem that I had solved for myself and be able to help him solve it.

So I got to the point where I could take fifty kids in a freshman writing class and get all of them to turn all of their papers in on time. None of them would get sick on me. None of them would drop out of school that quarter. And all fifty of them would end the quarter with at least C grades or better.

Now, what was the difference in this miracle of selection of students that all of a sudden I got this better quality of student? That was no miracle. The point is, that good work was in them and finally I was not bugging them. I was coming at them calm enough and easy enough and straight enough and hopeful enough and encouraging enough that I was getting the good work out of them that was there. And freshman writing is a very hard course for people.

If you get a mean, tough freshman writing instructor your first quarter in college, he can knock you right out of college to say nothing of flunking you in that course. So I saw a crucial demonstration, that if there's a problem here, I caused it. And I've seen that happen over and over again in all the other areas of my life.

Now, you say, "Yah, Jess, but a lot of times I'm in arguments where the other guy is 100 per cent wrong and I'm 100 per cent right." Well, that's beautiful, that's just beautiful. I'd like to meet you, God. You know, I've always been kind of looking around for you. You just don't find that. I know we want to look at things that way a lot of times and we'll do everything to clear ourselves of any responsibilities.

We'll say, "Yah, look how wrong that guy is, he has been wrong all day long. So it's no surprise that he's wrong here. A hundred per cent wrong." Well, he isn't. So what I'm saying is all we need to do is to shoulder that responsibility in the situation that is ours. And usually it is very sizable. When we do, we do drastic things for the problem.

One of the ways we do this is first of all to really try to see the other guy's side of the problem like the old Indian adage of walking in the other guy's moccasins. So we must take a look at that guy's position and see if we really can find some things in it that we can respect.

And the best way to do that is start off by respecting the other guy's position, and say to him, "Hey, Sam, what do you feel about this situation that we're in? Tell me." And then do a very hard and surprising thing to him. Listen to what he's telling you and respect what he's telling you. That's a fellow human being who's saying that and he's got some reasons for doing what he's doing.

Okay. Respect his position. Then, too, once you understand something about his position, then you can take another step which is share with him your position. And you can say it like this. "Hey, look. You know, you and I seem to be at odds in this thing. But that's not very surprising to me. I'm at odds with most everybody else in the world most all the time anyway. So it isn't very strange that you and I should be having difficulties."

You say, "Oh, that's not true!" The heck it isn't. You just follow me around during the day and you will see how cantankerous I am. Now you say, "I'm not mean like you, Jess, I'm kind of a sweet person." And if you want to say that to me, I might ask to follow you around for the day and maybe might be able to find just one or two single acts of cantankerousness showing up that you hadn't even noticed.

Now I wouldn't want to be so spiteful to predict that this would automatically happen, but there is a small chance. Okay? So, you share your position with the other guy. You say, "Now look. I'm as wrong-headed, probably, as a person can be. But this is what I'm thinking in this situation. This is why I want to do this and why I want to do that. You feel this way in this and I feel this way." You tell him how it really is with you.

Now this should have a familiar ring to you. When you're respecting his position, you're suggesting there's a real him and it's something pretty good. And when you're telling your position, you're trying to tell how it is with you, baby, really. And it's in this connection that one of my students contributed something to me that I have never really seen before.

"I was happy to hear that when you don't get a response that you want from another person, it's because you weren't being real enough with that person. It's encouraging to know that when a person doesn't respond to you in a real way, it is because you weren't real enough to him. It isn't because of what you are, but it's because of what you did. So there is nothing wrong with the real me. It's just the way I came at the person."

And this is something that I had never seen before. We've said that when you are real and someone isn't real back, it's a sign that you weren't being real enough. But, you see, we aren't saying that's a sign that you *can't* be real.

And this is something I see very strongly lying right at the center of all these things we are talking about. When my students are willing to tell it like it is with them from their hearts really down deep, there has never been a situation when that didn't just wipe out the whole class. And it created instant openness toward that person on the part of everybody else who was around him at that time. So that I've never seen a real you that was repugnant or a problem to anyone. The difficulties that I'm in typically come out of dealing at too much of a surface level. Mostly out of the anger that's in me. And as near as I can see, an awful lot of anger comes out of fear anyway. And neither of them are the real person, the real me, in the deeper sense. And this is the answer to this business of why I think it works better to talk about being real than being congruent or being honest.

Like many of you say, "Hey, I've got to be honest." But the minute you tell me that, "I got to be honest, or I got to be congruent, or I got to tell it like it really is with me," what you really mean is telling your anger and being your anger. You know, I've never lied to you but I've always wanted to tell you that and now my psychologist says I should be honest, and boy, I'm going to take advantage of this and really tell you off. You know, you really need correction badly.

But that's not really us. And this is where I think the idea of being real is so much more helpful than the idea of being honest or being congruent or telling it like it is. What I'm talking about is telling someone how it is with you in your deepest heart. You know what that means. There isn't any anger or fear there. Some apprehension perhaps, and it is hard, but, nevertheless, it's a feeling that is very deep and very true.

Now you understand that. And an awful lot of you are able to do it. So to the person who says, "I've got to get rid of my anger. I can't repress it, I can't bottle it up," I say, "That may be true. But I don't see how that has ever been really constructive." If somebody says, "Well, you've got to let it all out, all of the feelings and truly express your anger and say a lot of it's my fault and I'm sorry but it really bugs me so that you cut in front of me in this line but it really does."

I have never seen any good ways of doing that. Now I grant you that I'm terribly prejudiced because I'm as frightened of anger as anybody can possibly be. I'll run away from anger and yelling as fast as I can. So I grant my prejudice in the matter. But, nevertheless, I have found that not only for me but for an awful lot of other people, working at the real them underneath and getting a real relationship going helps get rid of that fear. The fear goes away and when the fear goes away, a lot of anger goes away, too.

So we started out with a simple little thing like: If there is a problem here, I caused it. This says that each day that we look around us and if there is a problem in our lives, we recognize our responsibility in the matter. And here we end up again right back with ourselves, in the deepest part of ourselves. And that's very simple. There is only one truth. And that is the reality of us and our relationship with the world. There is a lawfulness and a beauty in our relationships. But we are inclined to run away from them every chance we get. We will escape and there are a million ways to escape. But there is only one way to face ourselves. There is only one way by facing ourselves then, to face life.

Here is an important quotation. Anais Nin tells what fiction really is, but I think she also tells what reality really is. She says Jung, the great Swiss psychiatrist, defines the self as a virtual point between conscious and unconscious which gives equal recognition to both. And this is the thing that I think gives so many of us so much trouble. The fools are those of us who use intellectualization to run away from themselves.

In each of our small communities there are what can be described as common people. Some of these common people often have a great deal of very uncommon and very fine wisdom and they are quite happy doing what they are doing. So they don't take the trouble to come away to college and separate themselves from the people they love and value for four years. And we look down on these common people but some of them are very much in harmony with themselves and with everyone around them. In any small community that I have ever been in, there are a few common people who are very, very uncommon.

But we're so often running away from that half of ourself that lies below our consciousness. We're dealing with the conscious part of ourselves exclusively. Life is a slide rule. Life is wholly rational. If I just work a little longer, I'll get it all figured out. And we're in flight from the lower unconscious half of ourselves. That wild frightening reckless part that has feelings and that wants to do things. But we can't live separated like that. We've got to put ourselves back together again. And ourself has to be enriched not just by our mind, but by our feelings. And what the self means, as Jung says, is mind and feelings working openly and freely in some kind of harmony in each other.

So the reality of ourselves is something pretty tremendous. And when we can bring that to bear on the world, we don't have any problems. And when we have a problem, it is a sign that the real us isn't working, that the real Jess isn't at work. That Jess is in the process of bugging out and he's escaping from something. And half of his mind is working and ain't doing very good and that's why he is having problems. And we take that medicine all day long, every day. And we find that if we do so, there will be fewer problems that we have created. Then we won't have to say so often, if there is a problem here, I caused it. Then we can be a part of a lot of happy things, a lot of happy solutions, and happy answers and not near so many problems.

TWELVE

When We Go in Search
of Ourselves

"How am I going to avoid money nerves?" Money nerves are just a symptom of a broader system of nerves. It's got to do with, I think, a fundamental mistake that we're all inclined to make. And that is that we are too tied up in the things that we can see, feel and smell. We don't have enough sense of the things that lie beyond.

Basically the thing that I see is a funny thing. When you and I stop our mad, frantic dashing around the world and our mad frantic running away from ourselves, and when you and I finally go in search of ourselves, it seems to me that we almost always find not one thing, but two: I find that most everyone finds himself or herself, but they also find something else outside themselves. And this is the thing that to me is a very striking characteristic of someone who has made progress toward being that better person that they want to be.

In the program that I've mentioned to you so often, the program of Alcoholics Anonymous and Emotions Anonymous, they talk about a higher power. Or God as each one understands Him. The funny thing that happens in that program is that when people first come into it, they usually can't talk about anything beyond themselves. As they become freed from their alcoholism, or as they become freed from their neuroticisms, they are far more able and willing to talk about something beyond themselves. And they can talk of God and spiritual things easily.

So I've seen that this ability to see something outside of ourselves goes along almost exactly hand in hand with the kind of progress in terms of changing our lives around that we see here. Now—one of the things that's involved here, as I see, is the expression I use of being your own boy. If you're going to go your own way, then you've got to free yourself from my control. Now you're not going to free yourself from my control as long as I've got things that you need and want. As long as I can buy you with money. As long as I can buy you with cars. As long as I can buy you with jobs or anything else, you haven't got a prayer of being free.

And this is where money nerves come in. The guy who has a lot of money nerves is not a free person. He hasn't got a chance of being free. The person who was like I was, continually seeking a bigger and fancier job and bigger and fancier income, has no freedom. He's for sale to the highest bidder. And his behavior is under control of the guy who's controlling the money, or the people he thinks might control the money. So he's got his whole life turned inside out, trying to please a bunch of people that might pay him something.

There are more kinds of payment than just money. There's the social prestige and recognition that comes out of income. If you're going to belong to the polo-playing set in Connecticut, your final rewards aren't financial, but the reward that it takes to be a part of that set has got to be pretty heavy financial and pretty heavily material.

Now we have often talked about what I say is the thing that every one of you need and want more than anything else in the world. And with it I can control all of your behaviors in the ideal sense of the word. The problem really is all of you want this thing to some extent, but not all of you want it to as great an extent as you say you do—or as you believe you do.

That thing that you all want is acceptance. You want me to accept you just exactly as you are right now. Not if, but just exactly as you are right now. Out of that acceptance, you will be free to do and become those things you're ideally capable of becoming.

Well, you see, there's nothing material in that. That's a purely non-material and, in a sense, a spiritual kind of reinforcement. And yet I'm saying, and I have a great deal of evidence in my own life to justify this, this is the most powerful thing that someone can do for us.

Some people feel I make too big a point of this, but I think our whole school system is intensely focused on, "if you do this, you will get this." And someone else is deciding for us the things we should do before we will get rewarded. And there is very little in our school system of accepting us just exactly as we are. There is a great acceptance of those things that agree with some particular teacher's idea of what we should be in a given moment. And if we are in a science class, and we're under one particular kind of teacher, there can be a fantastic stress on certain aspects of that science and not on others. But there are all kinds of research to show that a lot of people don't look at the world the way their particular science teacher does, and very often that is a clue to the person's greatness. It even goes down into fourth and fifth grade kids. Some place, I read of a study where an awful lot of guys with great accomplishments (like Churchill) were a real problem to their teachers in fourth and fifth grade. And of course, their individuality, and their strength of character and all kinds of other things made them very much their own boy even at this very early age. That's a kind of a tough kid to have in a fourth grade class.

I had a nightmare just the other night about being in a fourth grade class. The teacher was saying, "We're going to have a spelling test." And I had said to myself, "Well, gee, I can spell halfway decent. I've been a writer most of my life and here I am in the fourth grade class. So I don't need to worry too much about that."

Then it turns out that the spelling test consisted of having memorized ahead of time the words in the order and giving myself in a sense my own spelling test. Well I didn't know what words to write down. So obviously I didn't know how to spell them. When it came time to correct my paper, it was chaos, of course, and here I was with this blank paper. And I quickly, in my great Norwegian intelligence, saw now how things had to be done so I said, "Oh, oh. I see. Next time I'm going to have to really pay attention here and just really get this just right."

I had a very sick feeling in my stomach at some of the implications of this. So many of us have not found much acceptance by the people around us throughout our life. This was why it was so striking for me to have walked into some groups and been accepted just exactly as I was. No ifs, ands or buts. And once you feel the warmth and power of that kind of acceptance, it is something that transcends reading about acceptance in books and makes it meaningful.

I imagine each of us in psychology have read about acceptance perhaps a thousand times. But it doesn't mean anything. It's like you can walk into your garage a thousand times, too, and never come out an automobile. You can read about acceptance a thousand times and nothing ever happens 'til somebody makes it go and applies it to you and makes it work. And that's what acceptance is about really.

We are outside the material world now; we're talking about the highest kind of living being conducted without any concerns about money. You let the money take care of itself, and you get along on whatever money you've got. And this is the thing that is a puzzle to people.

There is another side of it too. The more we are locked up in our egotism and egocentrism, the more we're locked up in our various inferiorities: "I am an awful person. I am a terrible person." This keeps us from not just ourselves, but from all of the things and all of the people around us. And the minute we stop and look at ourselves and say, "I ain't much, baby —but I'm all I got," then all of a sudden that grandiosity that is in an inferiority complex disappears.

A lot of you have asked the question, well, what about this inferiority complex? Where does that come from? Strangely enough, from the very idea that you or I should do some grandiose thing. In alcoholics, you see this particularly strongly. Even though they may be on skid row, they have this grandiosity in them. They will never admit it, but you can see it in their conversation. They have the feeling that if the world would only recognize their fantastic genius, they could pull the whole world out of its mess.

If the President would only call them up each morning and confer with them as to just what he should do that day, they could really tell him. They conceive of themselves as being godlike in their ability to see all things and know all things. In that kind of conception of themselves in relation to the world, they cannot help but feel inferior.

There is an interesting experiment that gives us a better understanding of how grandiosity and inferiority fit together. McClelland and Atkinson have worked with achievement motivation. In one of their experiments, they give a five-year-old some ring quoits and tell him to throw them on the peg. But they don't tell the kid how far away to stand. They find the kids who are failure-oriented stand either very close to the peg or very far away. Only those who can take success, stand at a reasonable distance.

I think this is what the grandiosity of the alcoholic does for him. He has such big dreams for himself (like standing too far from the peg) so who can fault him when he fails all the time. So his goals are self-defeating, but he likes that. To accept himself just as he is would mean he had no excuse for what he did. He would have to take responsibility for his own actions.

So we are able to continue a sense of inferiority only by having some very exalted sense of what we should be and what we should do. And that inferiority represents a tremendous alienation from ourselves and from the people around us. The minute we turn and say, "Hey, Jess, I ain't much, but I'm all I got," that calms us down. We're in *search* of ourselves. And it's the first step in *finding* ourselves, and that's crucial.

But what is also crucial to me are some of the side benefits that we get from that search. We find for example, that there are lots of inconsistencies. Like a lot of people just scream at me, "Jess, what you say here doesn't agree with what you say there." Well, the answer is of course it doesn't. We can't see all things and know all things and have this fine certainty. Granted, uncertainty and inconsistency is a very frightening thing.

It's as if you started on a trip to New York and somebody gave you six maps and all six of them showed different paths. While they agreed that New York was somewhat to the east, some of them had it a lot further south than others. That would make it very hard for you to go on that kind of voyage, wouldn't it?

Such is the voyage of life. We don't have very good maps, and they're inconsistent. But the funny thing is that as I see mental health, you could almost characterize it by the ability to tolerate inconsistency. The more able you are to handle confusion and inconsistency, and make just the best choice you can make at any given moment, and then live with it as well as you possibly can, that's an awfully good measurement of how healthy you are.

Yet there is the person who needs this rigid certainty, he

must know all things. The extreme example of this is when I'm in an algebra class. I love that. Because when I'm within the walls of that class during that time, I know everything will work out absolute certain. All I need to do is to just study hard enough and I will get 100 on all of my tests, and there will be no questions ever of any kind that I don't know the answer to. Well, that's a nice little artificial, closed, mechanical system, but that is not the world.

The best description that I've ever seen of this is by Sir Jeans Eddington, the great British astronomer. He said, "Imagine that you were asked to describe marine life and you were given a net with two-inch mesh. You would cast it into the ocean, and pull it out. Then with the specimens you had, you would describe marine life." Well, immediately you see the problem. You lose all marine life smaller than two inches. So you can't describe it. It's obvious to you. You say, "I can't do it that way." But the point is, you see, no matter how fine a mesh we use in our net, we're still missing some things that we can't see, that we can't know about.

When they first discovered the microscope, they started making cell drawings, and the first men who started to do cell drawings left out the chromosomes. And one day someone was looking through a microscope and saw that blob—the chromosome—and drew it in. After that all the people drew in the chromosomes because they knew they were there. Well, before, they were there, but they hadn't expected them to be there, hadn't looked for them or hadn't seen them.

This is the nature of life. And the funny thing is whether you choose to see this thing that's bigger than yourself and myself and just how you see it, that's a matter of your own individual deciding. But, nevertheless, it seems to me it's there.

I was particularly struck by this because after that heart attack of mine, I went in search of myself. And I had available to me at the time a religious system. In some ways, it did guide me. But I wasn't particularly looking in that area. And the thing that I've been surprised at, is the further I've gone along the lines that I've been working on here in this book, the more people of religion have come to me and said, "Jess, come and talk to our church." I feel like I have my own private ecumenical movement. I've been to all these different denominations, but nobody has asked me what faith I am, if any.

And, a drastic example of this was about a month ago. One

of my philosopher friends down the hall from me came running in and he said, "Hey, Jess, I'm really glad you wrote that book. I've just read it and I think it is just tremendous." And I said, "Why?" And he said, "It's really got a lot of Zen Buddhism put forth in a practical way." Well, up to that time I hadn't read more than two or three paragraphs of Zen Buddhism in my life, so I was kind of struck by this.

About a week later, one of the other people in the philosophy department came in and said, "Jess, this book's given me the theme for a new approach to the letters of the apostle Paul." So I thought well, I don't know anything much about Paul either. I said, "Well, that's fine, I'm glad you get that out of it."

I was telling one of the ministers downtown about these two startingly different views of my book. He said, "Jess, just tell them, thank God, it's all the same God." And this was a minister's response to this matter which again isn't the traditional response but nevertheless, one that was very interesting to me.

You young people are screaming against this materialistic age and the materialistic adults and the things that you have. But I think that, in a way, you're in danger of fooling yourself pretty bad because it's an area where talk doesn't mean very much. It's awful cheap. And in some of these student parking lots I see a lot of pretty gaudy automobiles for a bunch of people who are purely spiritually motivated, and who want to be non-materialistic. It's pretty easy to talk about these things, but it's awfully hard to do them. Joe Lewis said, "It isn't that I like money so much, but it sure calms my nerves." And I think we're all inclined to feel this way. But the thing that I'm struck by is how little money does to calm the nerves of myself and my friends.

When we go in search of ourselves, we see really that the world is lawful. It's like being real: When you get out and be real, it works. And when it doesn't work, you can say, "Hey, I wasn't really very real." But it wasn't that there was something wrong with you. So when you start out in that process, you see that there is a tremendous amount of lawfulness and order in the world and that each of us are only able to see a very small fragment or small fragments of that.

And it is as if the world were some gigantic jigsaw puzzle and we've only got six or seven pieces put together here. Then over there, we've got ten pieces put together, and further over there we've got twenty. And we can start to see the glimmerings of some kind of an outline as to what this picture is going to be about, but only very dimly and vaguely. And we can see, too, that we're never going to get very many of the pieces put together.

So we see this beauty and order that there is the minute we start coming to grips with the world as it really is rather than in this kind of grandiose and wild and very egocentric sense that we are so used to. This is surprising to me. We do what seems selfish, which is to be concerned about ourselves, but we are really in pursuit of something that ends up being much less selfish than that, a relationship to something bigger than yourselves. And many of you are resentful of any discussion of religion and God and things like that. I can't say that I really blame you. There have been a lot of things done in the name of religion that are pretty bad.

I think that Dante in his Inferno has a nice low spot in hell for the people who did horrible things under the guise of religion and helping other people.

It's like a story that came out in a Minneapolis courtroom. A woman brought a Thanksgiving basket to a poor Negro family down in St. Louis. The son remembered the woman saying, "It's my Christian duty to bring this to you, but I want you to know that I despise the way you live. And I despise you for living this way."

Well, some of you have had that kind of charity visited on you. And while it is no deep reflection on religion, you've been inclined to see it that way and it's not really strange that you should. It may seem kind of strange to you to be looking at some of these things and be talking about them. But they're very much involved with this process of changing our lives around. We can't be the better people that each of us would like to be, or get to that deeper self that we see lying within us, without looking at lots of different aspects of ourselves. All of the research that we have on occupations indicates that while you need to know a lot, the best predictions we can make on our success will have to do with your basic attitudes toward people and things and the world around you.

So when we go in search of ourselves, we find ourselves. And we find, too, some sense of a power higher than ourselves with whatever name you personally want to put on it. But this search takes a long time. Cliff in A.A. says we won't stop working on this problem until two days after we're dead.

THIRTEEN

Touching People

I had never realized how big a part touching other people plays in our lives until recently when I read of a striking piece of research on touching in Sense Relaxation by Gunther. He said Sidney Jourard observed in a European city that when friends were talking to each other, they touched the other person a hundred times per hour. In the Midwest friends in conversation only touched each other three times per hour.

I had always been fairly expressive and touched people a lot but hadn't realized how few people did. So I talked to my students about this and they found it was a revelation to them. Many were surprised to find they couldn't make themselves touch people at first. When they were able to, things went better. I think touch is an important part of really communicating with others and is very expressive. When we don't realize this we can more easily kid ourselves about the level and depth of our communication. But then when we find we can't touch that person or be touched by them we are forced to really look at the quality of our communication.

Now I'm not saying touching is completely essential to communication. But it is a bigger part than we usually think. And the touching I'm talking about is only gentle touching, not poking in the ribs, slapping on the back or leaning on someone. Those are appropriate in fun but not as habits.

The biggest value of touching was for those people who had

touched a little but could do a lot more. One nurse reported back to me later. She said, "I started touching all my patients constantly. I held their hands, patted their shoulders, hugged them, even kissed a few. Right away there was a change on my floor. My patients were less confused and they needed less medication."

I think part of this is that when we go to the hospital we become like little children, so far more touch and more personal touching is appropriate in the hospital for those nurses who can do it. But all my nurses agree that as far as the patients are concerned, they all love it.

One of my students was a minister. He started touching people more and he said he could see a big difference. He could talk so much more personally and directly when he was touching people. He found this especially true on his sick calls. He had one old patient who was alone and dying. After he started touching her, she clung to him like he was life itself.

A woman told me of seeing a friend of hers very upset during a nervous breakdown. She wanted to reach out and hold her friend and finally was able to. She said, "I will never forget the magnificent, sensual and almost supernatural feeling of holding her. I feel I benefited from it more than my friend."

But a story like this frightens us. We are so afraid of our sexual feelings that any touch is suspect. School officials tell their teachers on hall duty not to let boys and girls walk holding hands because it shows a lack of respect for the girls. Some principals are offended by young girls dancing with each other. What a bunch of dirty minds. And what it tells me, not about their students, but about their own problems accepting and handling cleanly their own sexual feelings.

We have taken our Puritanism and used it to build a rigid taboo against touching. The taboo is so extreme that it hurts our ability to convey to each other our love for them.

One of my students told of an example. A friend of his had seen me walking down the hall of our office building with my arm around the shoulder of one of my old beat-up fellow professors. He asked my student if I was a homosexual. My student said he didn't know. But my student added, "A few days later you told us about touching and I felt like a big turd. Here I had just blindly accepted my friend's condemnation of you based on our stereotyped morality."

Something like this is frightening. But the alternative is to

walk away from the idea of touching people, and the consequences of that are even more frightening to me.

Listen to another one of my students. She was a widow
who lost five loved ones in separate accidents in one year. She
had tried to build a wall around herself and live without feeling but then she started to come back to life.

She said, "My first encounter with how desperately people
need telling and touching love was with my young daughter.
She has always kissed me hello, good-by, good night. My reaction to this had been to turn my head (ever so slightly). A
couple of weeks ago I didn't wait for her to kiss me good
night. I kissed her and told her I loved her. The beautiful
smile, look and extra kiss were all I needed to tell me that
this is what she wanted all along. But I thought this worked
with her because she is the type of person she is.

"I was sure it would never work with my youngest son.
(His outward appearance reminds me too much of someone
else who was in the family.) I started telling him exactly what
I thought instead of assuming he knew how much I appreci-
ated him doing the dishes for me without asking. I even got
the courage to say, 'Hey, knucklehead, you know I love you!'
That was the first time I had ever seen tears in his eyes since
his father died.

"It's amazing how fast young people learn. A couple of
days later (before he left for his summer job) he hugged me,
kissed me and told me he loved me. He hadn't done that in a
long, long time.

"All of this love I have had for my children is spontaneous.
I've just been afraid to show it."

This kind of touching is much, much easier to pick up and
handle than touching that gets close to or right at those
deep, hard-to-change sexual problems we have.

A woman in my class had been, as she put it, "walking
backwards into the past as my way of living." She started
looking at areas of her life so she could start living.

"I have been very reserved almost to the point of not even
being aware of my feelings. I can't put into words the power
of the feeling when I've been 'touched.' My husband and I are
beginning to use this idea and talk to each other about these
inner feelings. Before we talked at each other never giving
considerations to emotions. The real turn from walking backward into facing the world straight on was on Saturday.

"I never wore a two-piece swimming suit because I hadn't accepted my physical part. This morning I made one and wore it to the garden. I was unaware John was coming to the garden. He slowly came up behind me.

"John put his hand on my back and said, 'You have a beautiful body.'

"And I said, 'Thank you, so do you.'

"His eyes, his touch and his feeling communicated through me. For the first time I heard what he said and I believed him. It was a precious moment when we both realized how wonderful our inner feelings were."

Most of the students on our campus claim they are big lovers and they may be in a parked car. But it is fairly rare to see couples holding hands on campus and it is seldom that I've seen couples walking with their arms around each other. So this next student is an exception.

She said, "I have been touching people all my life, but didn't realize I was doing it and how it really attracted people. Nor did I know how lucky I was, because it was habit and a common occurrence to give love socks in the belly and arms and to hug the people around me at any time just because I wanted to.

"My parents still, after twenty-six years of marriage, mash every chance they get, and if they don't get a chance, they take it. I saw and felt so much love, that I accepted the role of spreading it very easily. Like every time I saw my guy, I thought nothing of squeezing him around the stomach at first sight, and interlocking our arms to go where we are going to go because holding hands wasn't close enough. Or wrestling with my brothers or kissing my mom and dad each morning. I took all this for granted until you said most people just don't do this. And then I saw it was true and how lucky I was."

Why is a story like hers so unusual? I think the Zulu story helps us see the answer. The Zulu babies are touched and held for two years solid and lots after that. They get enough touching so they aren't desperate for more. I think most of us got way less touching than we needed as babies and kids. It wasn't our parents' fault. They just carried on a trend from their parents and that's in our society.

I think that's part of the reason our young people have so much trouble with petting or making out or whatever you call it. Both the boys and the girls need touching and holding so badly and are so starved for it that they have trouble controlling themselves. We see some evidence of this in that our most promiscuous girls are those who were most rejected and got the least love in their homes.

I think adults have the same problem. I think we are afraid of touch partly because of our deep need for it because our taboos and customs on touch restrict it so greatly. But there is only one way out of such a dilemma. Societies change their ways when those ways become obviously harmful or not useful. So you and I can change society by touching people when it is the appropriate thing to do.

Students find that they have enough sensitivity right now so that almost all the time they touch people it will be in the right way and it will be the right people. We all know who are the touch-me-nots. And we all know when people are in the touch-me-not moods to the point where we'll damned seldom ever go wrong by just taking the lid off and doing what comes naturally.

Now, you might feel, "You're opening the door to fantastic sexuality and everybody sleeping with everybody else, doing what comes naturally." It has been my experience that the women who are most sexual are the women who are truest to their husbands. I'm not saying that this woman who is very sexual can't, on some occasion, slip. She can and possibly will if the conditions are difficult enough for her, but it has been my experience that she handles it a hell of a lot better. Her sex just bubbles out of her. And because she is free and open to her feelings, she is not so damned busy fighting it that it comes out kinky. And because it is bubbling out all over the place, she has no trouble drawing a line around a certain area of her sexual relationships and saying that these are for me and my husband alone. But she doesn't automatically then turn all of the other dials every other time and every other occasion so everything else is turned off.

Touch is used a lot in encounter and sensitivity work, and I understand the results are good. But, while I want to stress the importance of touch, I don't want to overstress it either. Touch is a crucial part of our communication, but it is still just a part. And all we can communicate is what we are at the moment. Usually when there is a deficiency in communication, I feel it comes from not *being* deeply enough rather than from not *communicating* what we are.

While I believe in the deep potentialities that lie in all of us, it is very hard to develop those potentialities. It is a long, hard struggle and we never reach our goal. We just move toward it. I don't understand the person who says, "If I could just release everything in me, I'd be great today." I don't think it's that easy. I don't think living is a natural, easy thing with us that we had as children but that was beaten out of us by our society. Our particular environment may have hindered or aided our development. But what I'm talking about is a lifelong process of struggle to find what's easy and right and natural for us. I know it's a contradiction to talk about the struggle to find what's easy and natural, but it's the only way I can find out to say how I feel and think.

In everything, I see the people I respect moving slowly and patiently. So with touch.

Touch is an essential part of communication, and it is something where each of us should be free to find our own style. At the beginning and end of the hour in all my classes, I have students hold hands around the circle. A few people look at me and wonder what is wrong with me, am I nuts? No. The answer is that there is a minimum level of touch there and the point is for each of us to look at this idea and find our own style of touching. Whether it's one time a year or a thousand times an hour. We should be free to find that level of touching that is our own. So find out what part touching people can play in your life by more clearly and eloquently conveying your feelings.

FOURTEEN

Youth—and the Generation Gap

Some of us are going to be teachers, some of us are going to be nurses, some of us are going to be parents, some of us are going to be friends to other people. And there's a crucial thing that stands in the way of our being the best we can. One way of talking about it is in its most visible representation—what's called the generation gap.

I know there isn't any such thing as a generation gap. I've seen a lot bigger generation gaps between some of my students in their discussion sections than I have seen between any eighteen- and eighty-year-old person I've ever known. My students sit there and many of them are inclined to say, "Hey, Jess, those are awful modern ideas for an old man." Well I've got sad news for them.

I was down talking to fifty or sixty St. Joseph nuns recently at Lewiston, Idaho. A couple of them were so old they were practically carried in in a basket. I was warned ahead of time by the young swingers who had brought me down, "Now don't you worry when Sister Mary Michael starts going to sleep. And then when Sister Ethel gets up and walks out, that's just her. She can't stay very long in these things."

Well, a funny thing happened. I started to talk. My wife was watching Sister Mary Michael particularly. About the time I would get halfway through a sentence, Sister Mary Michael would start smiling because she knew what I was going to say. My wife saw that Sister Mary Michael could finish most of my sentences for me. She's only eighty-five years old. And she was laughing in all of the right places. And she was doing a better job of listening and understanding these things than some of the young swinging nuns that invited me down.

The point is—these ideas are pretty universal and they reach across the age groups. But the problem, as I see it, is when you are young, you underestimate how terribly difficult it is to accept other people and life just as it is. My students all sit there, and when I ask them, "Do you guys understand these things?" they all figure they do understand. But then when I point down the road and say, "Look at those forty-year-olders who are giving you so much grief. There aren't very many of them that can accept you and listen to you are there?" And they say, "Oh no." But they aren't impressed by the odds of what this suggests for them. They don't see that twenty years from now they will very likely have the same trouble listening to people that their parents have. Some of them begin to see that they can't listen very well either.

Well, I'm impressed by the odds. It scares me to death, not just for them, but for me, too. Accepting life as it is, is hard. It's the hardest thing I've ever tried to do. This is why I stress that every moment needs to be treated almost as an emergency, like your life boat's going down. It's hard.

Now in a way, it's easy. Just like when Sam Snead hits that golf ball, it looks easy and it is easy in the sense that it goes a long way and he doesn't have a lot of waste of motion in there, but in another sense, it's very hard to learn to do it that easy way. This is one of those many contradictions in life. I got a letter from a graduate student at Missoula the other day. He had bought my book up there. He said, "Those of us who like these ideas feel so lonely and ashamed of them, that it's good to see somebody put them down in black and white." Well, again, this is simply the sadness of the thing. My students find the same thing in their discussion sections. The minute they let their hair down and start talking, they find they are not alone. Nearly everybody believes the same way they do. But the sadness and tragedy is that they didn't know it. And unless you can get honest with yourself about what you really are and open up with others about what your feelings are, you aren't going to know it either.

We had a student who was really working hard in his discussion section last year. I ran into Phil in the middle of the next quarter and asked, "How goes it?" And he said, "Awful. I kicked the dog, and yelled at my wife and just raised general hell around the house this morning on the way out. My wife told me, 'I sure wish you were back in Jess's class again this quarter.' " As he told this kind of funny story on himself, it illustrated how hard it is to use these ideas once we get away from the support of a group of people who are as open to us as these discussion groups are. There doesn't seem to be that much going on in them—everybody kind of sits around and looks at each other a lot—but occasionally somebody will say something about himself. And then they are struck by the feeling this graduate student had when he read my book.

But here's a guy sitting up there in Missoula, and he thinks he's all alone. He thinks he and I are the only two nuts in the world. All this illustrates the tremendous gap between us. No, the generation gap isn't a gap between old people and young people. Those of my students who are most prepared to discuss this set of ideas could have been sitting in a chair down there in that Mother House of the St. Joseph nuns. And they could have been talking, and Sister Mary Michael at eighty-five could have been nodding her head and smiling at what they were saying. But they don't know that. And you don't know that.

This is the sadness. We are so busy, not just building walls but being the big judge, that we don't have time to find, "Hey, there are a lot of other people just like me out there."

A story I tell about my dad fits in this connection. I went to a little Baptist church in southern Minnesota. There were all those pious down-in-the-front-row sitters in this church. Oh boy! When it came time to hang their checks and money on the clothesline to raise money for this little bitty church, oh, they were quick to go up and pin their check or their money to the clothesline. And they were very well known in the church for their deep and prominent giving.

Well, this was back there in the depression times. And the minister's suit got pretty frayed around the edges. None of those pious front-row sitters noticed that this man of God was not dressed properly or that his feelings were certainly damaged each Sunday as he stood up in the pulpit to talk about God and the crucial important things of life. My dad, who went to church only on the high holidays, noticed that. And so among his cronies down at the tavern, where he spent most of his Sunday mornings, he took up a collection to buy a thirty-five-buck suit. I can still in my mind as a little boy see that list. All of the sinners in town were on that list; they each gave a buck for the minister's new suit.

You know how we all are when we walk into a clothing store. Our eye inevitably picks out the highest priced suit on the rack. It turned out the minister bought a forty-five-dollar suit instead of a thirty-five-dollar suit. So my old man had to go out and hustle ten more bucks. But the minister had a new suit. And it wasn't the front-row sitters that got it for him. And my old man was the guy that all the people in church were sitting around praying for. Because they were the big judges.

Now as far as conventional sinning goes, my old man did as well as the rest of us. But some of those sins that Dante in his *Inferno* rates so low—like being mean to a little kid—he didn't do that kind of sinning. Not at all.

Things really aren't as they seem. Yet we've got this fantastic tendency to judge others. I think that all this judging is our anger coming out. Where does our anger come from? I think it comes from fear. Where does fear come from? I think it comes from the thing that graduate student wrote me about. "Jess, I'm so lonely and ashamed of these ideas. They're mine, they're the ones I want to live by, but I'm afraid to say anything about them to anybody else."

It is so fashionable to either sneer at the world or to say that the world is going straight to hell in a hand basket. And on college campuses, the primary posture is sneering at the world. "Oh, this world, we've got to whoop it up right now, and man, we've got to go for trips. And we've got to do this and we've got to do that." And then all the old people are sitting around having a beautiful time talking about how all the young people on campus are going straight to hell.

Well, let's take a look at that. We've got some drugs on campus, for example. But I don't see very many students walking around with glazed eyeballs. We've got some drugs in the bars downtown, and on any Saturday night you can find a lot of people walking around downtown with alcohol-glazed eyeballs. And a lot of them get into cars or trucks in that condition and try to drive home, but kill or get killed on the way.

Now, I'd like to talk to you about drug addiction because I'm an addict, myself. I was on the worst kind of drug you can possibly be on. When I was a young person, I'd get into a jam. I found that the adrenaline that would be produced by my fear of that emergency would energize me and get me out of it. As I became a businessman, I found more and more that by putting myself into jams, I would get the burst of energy that would get me out. What happened is I became addicted to my own adrenaline.

So I was one of the worst kind of drug addicts. Instead of buying it for five to twenty-five dollars, I produced it, by getting my whole body out of balance. Now that happens to be a kind of addiction which will kill about 500,000 people this year. It's very fashionable. In fact when you die of a heart attack, everybody is a bit sorry. But they think, "Man, he must have been a real worker. He must have been a real goer."

Yes he was a real worker and a real goer to the point of almost insanity. And he, like me, was an adrenaline addict. And he, like me, had his whole body physiology beat out of shape. There are an awful lot of us cats. Coronaries are the number-one killer in the United States. Dying at that rate means that there's about ten million of my kind of adrenaline addicts running around in our society. And most of them are pretty busy sneering at some young guy who's smoking a marijuana cigarette.

That doesn't make much sense to me. Particularly when in the same house with that old, bald-headed drug addict, there's another drug addict. She takes benzedrine every morning, or "bennies" as the boys call them. Then she takes sleeping pills at night, and she's in a constant buzz. Typically she's got her connections, which are two, three, four to six doctors, all of whom think she's their patient exclusively. But those are her connections. And they are very precious to her and she won't move away from her connections. Because she needs that many connections to get as much drugs as she wants and I know lots of these women. This is a very, very common problem.

So, here we've got the spectacle of all these millions of households of drug addicts, sitting around reading about the awful drug problem. And they're saying, "Isn't that an awful drug problem out there in California, or up at Missoula? Oh, that's really ferocious, isn't it?" Yah, it sure is.

We take a problem which is very near at hand and close to home, inside us, and we take and stick it out on somebody else, stick it on you. Well, I don't think that's very smart.

Now a lot of people hear me talk and they say what I am talking about is permissiveness. Well, I'm not. There are two kinds of things that people mean when they talk about permissiveness. There's the kind of permissiveness that says I don't care about you nor anybody else in the whole wide world. You can just go and do anything you want, and I don't care.

There's a different kind of permissiveness that permits the Missouri River and the Mississippi River to keep flowing to the Gulf of Mexico. Yes, I permit them to flow. And I permit my students and you to find the best paths for your lives and to find them in your own way and in your own pace. And to say that I permit the world to go on around me as it chooses, really isn't saying very much. But it does not say, I do not care.

Now there are people who like things around them very orderly. They don't really care too much about what's inside them, but they like the things around them to be very orderly. And these people's view of society is a simple one. All we would do is arm most everybody in society with a high-powered electric cattle prod. And every time every one of us saw a no-no, we would give the other person a jab with the cattle prod. Pow! And pretty soon, those of us with cattle prods wouldn't see very many no-no's. Because anybody doing a no-no, would see the guy with the cattle prod and he would say, "I'll just go around the corner, man."

So we could convince ourselves very quickly, "Oh, the world is a beautiful place because we don't see any no-no's anymore. And with our little electric cattle prods, we done stamped out all the no-no's." But sooner or later, we're going to have to see some of the consequences and effects of the delayed reaction. The things going on behind the corners are going to start leaking out. And then we're going to have to wear dark glasses to avoid seeing the effects of a world where we use that kind of punishment that much.

When you talk about permissiveness in the sense of I permit you to make your own mistakes, and you talk about that as being bad and as if there were an alternative, I'm very curious about what the alternative is.

Well, often, they say, "No, no I don't want to punish people like that. I want to tell them about the good. We'll put out *Reader's Digest* every day instead of every month and it will be filled with testimonial stories of how I follow the straight and narrow path. And everybody will be forced to read

Reader's Digest every day—the whole issue. And they'll spend two or three hours in meditating on these good examples."

Well, there are two problems here. We will be continually distressed, I'm sure, to find that some of these good examples have got feet of clay. But there's another problem here. How many of us ever learned anything, really, by reading about somebody else's struggles with it. Very few people that I've ever seen. Most of the people that I've ever seen, have learned by doing the best they could, and learning from that. And that's the way, it seems to me, it's always been.

Now we can benefit from other people's experiences, but to a quite limited extent. It's like this book. I'm telling you about a certain set of experiences. I'm hoping you can benefit from some of those. But I'm trying to emphasize as much as possible the need for you to go out and try these things out. See how they work for you, rather than just borrow from my experiences. Because if you copy me, it will be with great disrespect for the uniqueness that is within you. You can't know what's right for you until you try it, until you take yourself the way you are.

Now other people say, "Hey, Jess, you're doing away with all standards. No standards in your system at all are there?" And I think the answer to that is a troubling one for this reason. I grew up in a little town that my grandparents helped start. So my parents and relatives knew everything about everybody in that town. When I was a kid, I thought all the things that went on in that town were just normal. I see now how screwy some of them were. In the thirties, there were rumors of some wife-swapping. Every once in a while a husband would hang himself. A minister took in a girl from a poor family but she didn't like living with him because he was always pinching her. There were all kinds of petty wars and major wars going on between people.

You say, "But there were a lot of good people in town." Yes, there were some but they're harder to find than we're inclined to think. So when we're talking about standards, usually we're talking about a set of standards that somebody else is going to have, but not us. We're Mister and Miss Purity and we don't have any need for standards. Those standards are for somebody else and we sure wish they would obey them. We sure wish they'd be halfway decent like we are. We're awful blind to what we are.

Now one advantage of a small town is that you can track

down these interrelationships. And you start to see what the situation really is. You know what the trouble with you and me is? We preach one thing and do another. And then we wonder, "How come the kids think we're hypocrites?" How come, would you imagine? We've got such high standards. How can they possibly think we're hypocrites? Well, we've got such low conduct. You say, "Well, that's not me, friend. I do a lot of nice things and I don't do any of that dirty sinning."

There are a lot of people who have talked to us about sinning and they say that there's a special place in hell, not for the drunkards of this world, not for the adulterers of the world, not for any of those messy kinds of sinning—but there's a special place in hell for the person who could have said a kind word to someone and didn't. That's a grievous sin. Those other things aren't so grievous. You say, "Well, that's not my idea of sin." Well fine, but that's an awful lot of people's idea of sin, especially the young.

This is something that a lot of us have trouble with. I'm still trying to figure out the answer to the riddle of acceptance. When I say acceptance, the thing I'm really saying is that we accept our feelings, we accept our needs, but we don't accept all of our behavior. We're trying to change our behavior. But that really isn't so much change in us. It's more in the way we look at ourselves. So we can accept ourselves but today we can be determined to handle some specific thing better than we did yesterday. But at the same time, we must be accepting of our feelings, our needs, accepting of the way we look at the world, that's us.

I think this is possibly a distinction that you and I need in this idea of acceptance. Acceptance does not mean approval.

So the whole point of what we're talking about here is to get our eyes off our neighbor's fault or young people's faults or old people's faults and get our eyes onto our problems. They are the only ones we can do anything about. But that's so hard for you and me to do for the simple reason that when we are thinking about our neighbor's problem, we don't need to do anything but just kind of wring our hands and indulge in some wonderful self-congratulation. "Oh, boy, I'm not like those people out in California who think they're witches. They're having these satanic rites and stuff."

Well, to me, that's like looking at somebody in a hospital who's lost both arms, both legs and his eyesight, and saying, "Oh, boy. I'm sure glad to be alive today, because I'm not in his boat." You're congratulating yourself because you're able to walk around. Well, that to me is kind of a sick way to get any satisfaction out of life. It seems to me far more instructive if we would look at ourselves, and say, "Hey, Jess, how are you going in this five minutes compared to the Jess that you could be?" And to heck with what somebody else is doing.

In this furor about what's going on in southern California, there's another sadness. And that is there are some very peculiar chambers of horrors in every town and village and even homes in the whole United States. Some aren't quite as weird and erotic as others.

But someplace in Bozeman, as in every other town, there is probably a little kid who is tied to his bed all of the time so that he doesn't run around and bother his mother too much. In Bozeman, there are a certain number of husbands and wives who got tired of each other's company, so they're switching around to get a little excitement into their lives. And while that's not that bizarre, nevertheless some of the specific things that are happening in the privacy of those bedrooms, I imagine, would start to be pretty bizarre. But nobody's reporting on these events. And it's almost as if, by tacit agreement, we all agree to talk about the extremes, about way-out drug addicts and what they're doing. The guys who have really freaked out.

When I talk to my young students, they say, "I wish the old people would feel this way." When I talk to my old students, you know what they say? They say, "I wish the young people would feel this way." But the saddest part of all is that none of you know what the other person really feels and thinks. That's what is so terribly and overwhelming sad.

And this goes right back into teaching and nursing, and parents, and brothers and sisters being all of these things. How in the world are you going to teach some kid, big or little, if you don't understand that their concerns and yours run right along the same path?

How are you going to be teachers when you aren't able to even talk with your other teachers and realize that the things that you want to do in your class, which you see as so far out, are the same things all of the other teachers want to do in their classes? You say, "But they aren't doing it." You know why? They aren't doing it partly because of their fear and terror of what *you* will think. And here you're in favor of what they would do, but yet they think the opposite because of our tremendous inability to walk up to another person and tell him how it is with us in our deepest heart. This is the thing that we just cannot bring ourselves to do. We will practically choke before we will do that.

A lot of you think, "Hey, I'm really tough and I'm really smart and I'm really strong. Man, I really see these things." Okay, if you do, then go out and open that door for somebody. Because each of you in your lives are going to touch thousands of people or even tens of thousands of people. In some cases, some of your lives will touch hundreds of thousands of people. And if you want to do something drastic and something gigantic and something big and stupendous for the world around you, all you need to do is find some way of living your life so that to those thousands of people whom you will contact you will convey this feeling of "Hey, you're not alone."

My wife was over at my little boy's school to see a teacher. As she was standing outside a room she heard a teacher talking about the moon. One of the little kids in the back row said, "Hey, wouldn't it be nice to go to the moon and see the men on the moon?" And the teacher turned on the kid and said, "Really, men on the moon, how silly. What do you mean, men on the moon?"

Isn't that something? Isn't that bravery? That teacher, that big teacher was willing to speak right up to that little kid. And intimidate him and tell him how stupid he was. Isn't that a wonderful way of handling people? But no, that's not a sin. Not when compared to a man who's been without a wife for two or three years for reasons beyond his own control, and some gal, after too many beers, looks pretty good to him some night. So they slip across a line. I can excuse that and understand that a lot easier than I can what this teacher did to that little kid.

Now that's why I feel a lot of these standards and things we've got are just so much baloney because we're thinking about them as a set of rules and we want everyone else to follow them but not us. Not Mr. and Mrs. Purity. And because each of us has enough trouble on his own hands we shouldn't be distracting ourselves from our own problems by yelling at other people. If we did a good job of working on our own problems and staying close to life, we wouldn't be out of touch and there would be no generation gap—just hearts talking to hearts.

One of my older friends raised the question of short skirts. My reaction was, "I'm not kicking about short skirts. I'm not bothered a bit by them." I don't know if that is completely true about myself, but it makes a point that I think is fundamental. We need to get over blaming others for our problems. When some others have any real control over us in a destructive sense, then we're not really free but are puppets. But usually we blame others for problems that aren't their fault. If everytime I see a girl in a short skirt I have long sexual fantasies, then it is because I enjoy having long sexual fantasies. Blaming them on the girl's short skirt avoids the problem so I can keep on with some behavior that I don't believe is really me. If I can see this and get at the problems in my life that are making me respond this way, then I can get some control over my life. Hopefully, I can get to the point where a girl can wear the shortest skirt possible, or none at all, and I would still be in reasonable control of myself. In fact, I've heard that this was a mark of a great rabbi long ago—that he could keep his mind on his theology even if a nude girl were to walk by.

Not only is this important for me, it is also important for the other person. When young people know that wearing short skirts (or long hair on boys) is a good way to bug older people, then part of their decision is influenced by the reaction they will get from us. When we stop reacting to them, then they are forced to decide just how short their skirts should be to please themselves and their own ideas of what they want to be.

At the University of Minnesota, students wanted to form a DuBois Club. Some people advised the then president, O. Meredith Wilson not to give them the right to start the group, arguing it was a Communist front organization. But Wilson said, "No, I won't refuse them. I won't give them that wall to bounce their ball off of." So the group started up, had difficulty getting enough members to stay alive and finally died. Had he refused to allow them to organize, they could have had a hundred pickets outside his door by the next day.

I think this is what we do when we react against other's actions. We give them "a wall to bounce the ball off of." And to the extent that we do, we lock them in and keep them from finding the thing they really want to do because it is right for them rather than something that will get a rise out of someone else.

What about discipline? The only meaningful kind of discipline there is in the world is the discipline we freely and willingly impose on ourselves. I've seen people try the idea of will power as a way to solve problems. I've tried it myself with a notable lack of success. But what I'm struck by is how hard someone will work for something they believe in—and how hard I will work at something I believe in.

The bad side of discipline is shown by the kid who is sent to school and told to get good grades so he can be something in the world—preferably something to please his parents. So he learns to work at any job people give him to do. And if that family is lucky enough they will produce a person who never asks, "Is this job right for me?" but simply does it. We saw the logical conclusion of that kind of acting without thinking in the men around Hitler who just followed orders.

True discipline, to my mind is imposed out of a real love for the work and not blindly. One of the best advisers of graduate students I ever met was Dr. Cyril Hoyt. One night he told me, "Jess, I've found that I don't want any more graduate students with straight A's in their undergraduate records. They make lousy graduate students. I want graduate students who had A's in the areas they liked and then B's and C's in other areas. I've come to see that as a mark of a student with the independence needed for successful graduate work."

I think the best advice I've seen on raising kids was in a study which suggested that kids could adapt to a wide range of discipline styles as long as there was mutual trust and consistency. The home could be quite strict and authoritarian but if there was mutual trust and consistency it was okay. But it was on the two extremes without mutual trust and consistency that the trouble came. Extremely harsh discipline without consistency produced adults who were violently aggressive and frequently committed crimes against other people. The homes with the complete lack of concern for their children produced adults with self-destructive tendencies.

When I became a parent, I didn't get any divine writ from on high telling me just how to raise kids. While I felt a special responsibility to them, all I could do was the best I knew how. And the best I knew how was to treat my kids as much like people as possible—and as little like slaves or robots. But that's hard to do.

I wasn't a psychologist until after I had my kids fairly well raised. They were from thirteen down to three when I started my Ph.D. I don't see that I'm doing things much different because of the studies I took. I'm trying to apply all these ideas to my relationships with my kids, but most of these ideas came from life and reading—not my studies. My studies just underline and support these ideas. And I'm horrified every day at how poor a job I do applying these ideas to my family. I'm not the big expert—and I never will be. I know what I am trying to do. But I know how far I fall short of what I want to do.

I think the way to solve the generation gap is to ask a person what he thinks about something and then listen to what he says. And then don't argue but accept what is said. And then don't start setting him right and telling him the error of his ways. "But," you say, "if you don't do that, how are people going to change?" When they want to. Are they going to change because you tell them to do that different? Hell no. What are they going to do when you tell them to do something different? They're going to say, "There's such a generation gap here, isn't there?"

Now the point of all of this is that you and I love to be the judge, the judge—here comes the judge. But there's only one person whose story we can know anything about. This is all I know, what's inside this skin. And I can't know what's inside you, I can't know what's right for you, I can't do anything else. But the funny thing that I have seen about life is this, the more I concentrate on doing what I should do and being where I should be, that has more influence and more effect on helping the people around me do and be the things they should be than any other single thing. That sure beats that cattle prod. And it's sure the answer to make certain that you and I stay in touch with the people around us.

FIFTEEN

Love—Come Fill Your Cup

I think there is a great misunderstanding about love. Many people argue that love is natural with us and that it is easy to love if we can just get over our hang-ups and inhibitions. But I think we can better look at love in another way.

I see love as something we are starved for. We crave it. We scream for it. We will go to any lengths to get it. We will play sick games just to get a sick love because it is better than no love at all. I don't think we can give away what we don't have. I don't think we can give real love until we find a way of getting some real love.

I think it is like Mother Hubbard trying to make supper out of a bare cupboard. You can't do it. So this is what I mean when I say, "You've got to get something going for you." I mean you've got to find some ways of being real with other people so they will be real with you. I think that's love. Your feeling this closeness, this realness, this love, will give you something you need.

By getting love, you will be able to be more real, more of the time and this will be you giving love. And your realness will generate more realness in the people around you and you'll get a bigger and bigger love return on your love.

One of the most vivid illustrations I have ever heard for the loving process is from the psychologist Maslow's levels of needs. He saw our needs as a series of cups that are interconnected. The cups started with our immediate physical needs, warmth and safety. And then when that cup gets filled up we go on to the next one, which is kind of the need for developing ourselves as some separate entity—and so on up to the highest levels.

My wife and I, as we were bringing up our kids, were constantly aware of these cups, the basic cups that needed filling. And, however much aware of things you are, it doesn't help that much because they are so hard to do. I think the saddest thing of all is that you and I and everybody else in this world are terribly misled by the ease with which we can talk about love and loving. But I hope you are starting to see more clearly (I know I sure am) how terribly hard it is to love.

A student asked, "You mentioned once that people often or never have their cups filled with love. Could it be possible too, that someone might have gotten a hole in the bottom of their cup at some time so from then on they feel unworthy no matter how much praise they get for what they accomplished that is worthwhile?" Right. This is the feeling that because you aren't loved you are not worthy of love. And this makes it seem like you have a hole in the bottom of your cup. Because it seems like nothing that you get can be enough. Nothing that I get can get me over this feeling that I am unworthy. We have also taken not just individuals in our society but broad segments of people in our society and made them feel unworthy. But it just seems that there is a hole in our cup. It ain't really there. The answer, in my experience, is that it is just a very deep cup.

A student gave me a poster that said, "Because you are afraid to love, I am alone." So now it hangs in my office. But it now says, "Because I am afraid to love, you are alone."

If we were to take the good lovers in this world out of it, the population wouldn't be decreased much. Because the good lovers that I have met in my life are just awfully rare. Very, very hard to find. And when you do find one, you are struck and overwhelmed.

I think, not only is love a terribly hard thing to get to, it's a terribly hard thing to handle, it's a terribly hard thing to understand. It's something that people are really going at in an awful lot of wrong ways.

One of the biggest bars to our loving is our anger. The minute I talk about "tell it like it is, baby," what all of you and I are inclined to think I'm talking about is to go and speak of your anger. And the minute I talk about being real to people, so many questions are so constantly centered on, "How do I handle those angry feelings? I've got all those people around me and I really want to tell them off. I am going to really tell them what I've always thought about them, or I'm really going to tell them how these things bother me. How do I do it?" Well, that's not very loving.

Each of us had loving experiences. We have had periods of our life, where we have for brief moments been great lovers. And those moments are laughed at and ridiculed pretty much because usually they occur when we were quite young, fifteen, sixteen, seventeen, maybe eighteen, maybe sometimes nineteen. But by then we are trying to get so sophisticated that we aren't capable of that whole-hearted, all-out kind of love that is more common earlier.

When we are younger we can look at someone and for some reason, they are transformed magically into a white knight or a fairy princess. And we just love them 100 per cent and we are completely blind, fortunately, to all of the faults that they have. For some brief time, while this spell lasts, there is nothing wrong. Then society gets a hold of us and wakes us up and says, back to hate. This person has buck teeth and poor hair and poor complexion and poor figure and poor this and poor that and they've got sloppy habits.

Now, the kind of loving that you do when you are older, when you're old enough to understand that no one is perfect is mostly feeling, but is partly an act of the will. You say, okay, here is a person who may have some difficulties, may have some problems, may have some things about them that I don't find particularly attractive, but so what. Don't we all. And you choose to ignore those aspects of the person. So that what we're talking about here is something that you do knowing that the person has some problems. When we say, I like you because, I love you although—we know about the although and we don't let it bother us. So that this is the thing, one of the many things, that is involved in this process. It's an all out kind of feeling.

In a previous chapter I mentioned talking to a group of nuns, forty or fifty of them from four or five states. And because of the kind of things that you and your fellow students before you have shown me, because of the kind of things I've seen in Alcoholics Anonymous and Emotions Anonymous groups, I was in a position of telling them to love, and telling them how to love. And they were in the unfortunate and contradictory position of arguing back frequently to suggest that you can't love that way and that much. And I was saying, the heck you can't. I've seen dummies, eighteen-year-old dummies and forty-three-year-old dummies doing it. I've seen rummies, old beat-up stinking alcoholics and neurotics doing it in the way a group of nuns were saying, "No you can't."

For example, I was saying that the most loving thing we can do is tell it like it is with us in our deepest hearts. And they said, "Oh, you can't do that. If you tell it like it is in your deepest heart, people will immediately run and blab to somebody else." I said, "No they won't. When they run and blab to somebody else, that's just a good sign that you haven't really gone very deep into your deepest heart.

"You have partly faked it and the person listening to you, hears that fake and feels that fake. And they say, hey, this person is not really telling it like it is. And you don't feel any necessity to respect their confidence."

But I've seen that the minute somebody opens up and tells it right out of their deepest heart, we feel the honesty of their story. And this doesn't need to be any fantastic, hard feeling, it can be nothing deeper than, "Hey, you know, it bothers me that my grandfather can't trust people."

I heard an old alcoholic say this very effectively one time. He said, "You know, I see these people come into meetings. They tell about how they did all their drinking at fancy bars, drinking high-priced whiskey. I know that man ain't telling it all. Cause he's an alcoholic and that isn't the way it is. But after awhile he really gets down to business, and decides he wants to live instead of die. He starts telling about how he took a copy of the Denver *Post* and laid it out underneath the box car so he could drink his wine out of the rain. And then I say. 'Yah, he's telling it like it is.' "

He said, "Because I can feel those real stories. It's just like I wrote every one of them myself." See?

Now it isn't that any man has had every experience, but in a sense, we have everybody within us. So the minute we feel somebody telling it like it is, the little switch goes on inside us. And we say, "That's real, man. That's the way it really is." And the minute that happens, we know that we are part of something very precious. And we know that someone is trusting us more deeply than probably we've ever been trusted before. And this is the self-fulfilling prophecy, that when you or I are trusted that deeply, we could no more violate that trust than go to the moon.

So here I was telling these nuns that no one that I had ever heard tell their story from their deepest heart had ever had that trust violated. And they were saying, "No, no, no! It can't work, it can't work!" And I was telling them, "Hey, shut up you guys. I know. You're telling me the world is flat. Well you and a lot of my students from other classes and other people I know and respect have been around the world. We started out east and ended up west. And when you've done that, it's hard to have somebody tell you. 'No, it can't be done.' "

Why would they say this? Here are a whole group of women who have supposedly dedicated their lives to loving. And it's very simple. The answer is that it is so very hard to do. It is very, very important to us but it is very, very hard to do even though we can recognize the almost life-and-death urgency of something like this.

I can tell you that if you don't love, you are going to wither up and die as a woman. You may live on the outside. You will have to turn to using blackmail, coercion, whining and crabbiness to get your way as you get older and older. And if you're a guy, and don't learn how to solve this problem, you're most likely to die of ulcers, heart atttack or various other internal ailments as you turn your fear and anger and stuff it back inside you. You let that fear and anger lie within you without doing anything about it.

The opposite is doing something about it which is getting some love into your life. That's what makes the fear and hate go away. Or you may live on to be a crabby old man who again uses blackmailing and complaining and other means to get what he wants out of life instead of people doing for him what he needs because they want to do it.

Now, the basic principle that I see here is—see, ...mendous their separateness from people, young and old, it is their aloneness, knowledge that we are not alone. And for you and me the edge that can be brought to any of us is the most crucial knowl- process of talking about what's in our deepest heart as so im- portant. We see that we are not alone. We see that there can be some kind of bridge between the thing that is inside my skin and the thing that is in your skin. This is crucial and necessary to us. And the best name I can think of for this transaction is love.

The word love scares a lot of people. And like all words, the word love is tricky and slippery and subject to misunderstanding. And love is something that is subject to a great deal of misunderstanding, but it is the best word I can think of for what we're talking about here.

Originally, when I started talking about all these ideas, a lot of people got nervous about talking about loving each other. Because the minute you say love, you are talking about intercourse. You are talking about escalating right into sex. And there is a very simple explanation for that because for most of us, these feelings are so very rare, that when they occur, escalation to intercourse is very frequent and very common in their presence. And this has misled us to feeling that this is necessary.

Well, it isn't. Because guys can love other guys. Girls can love other girls. Guys can love their wives with whom they're the only person in the world where any range of physical intimacy is available to them. But guys can love other women, and women can love other guys when they understand exactly what's involved and they understand that this is something that is fairly common. The minute that you see and understand that is and can be pretty common, then it's pretty obvious that intercourse isn't going to be the result. Whereas someone who has experienced love only once or a few times in their lives at most have it closely tied to physical intimacy. A lot of marriages are entered into, really, with very little experience with previous loving. It's like coming out of the Sahara Desert after two weeks without water. You see a water cooler and run up to it and try to drink it dry. And you hug it so no one can steal it. And you have ~~never~~ ~~~~ away at ~~any~~one who tries to ~~get~~ you w~~~~ would just f~~ine~~ who tries to ~~get~~ you ~~~~ hundreds of water c~~~~es a little you.

If you would do that, then y~~~~d see the value of going from water cooler to water cooler, ~~~~sting the water from each. Then, when you came to the water cooler you wanted to spend your life with, you would have made your choice freely. Not out of desperation and fear, but as a free, loving individual.

But the sadness is that when I use this analogy, I find it necessary to say that I'm not talking about physical loving but I'm talking about mental loving where the emphasis is on two people's minds and hearts being open to each other instead of just their bodies being open to each other.

Some of the problems we have in talking about love were well put by a student of mine once. She found a quotation some place that said: "There are many literary efforts turning on the Rip Van Winkle theme, a man from the past awakes in our alien country and cries at the sight of automobiles and electricity, etc. What the devil are these? We expect him to have a terrible time understanding, of course. But he doesn't really. Someone would explain that is an automobile. Its power is covered up. It is powered by a fuel which by little explosions run it. And these wires are carriers of harnessed electrical power which is really like lightning. And those little machines that cut and sew and mix are all powered by that electricity. After a short lecture of how things were powered, I'll bet our friend from the past would say, 'I see.' For there isn't a man or woman who doesn't understand power, it's love they don't understand." And that is very, very true.

I know I'm not explaining this very well because I don't understand love either. But I think I understand it well enough to see it as necessary to keep me alive. And I'm amazed how many of my students young and old want more love in their life.

Now. Love can take many, many forms. It can take as many forms, in fact, as there are people. And one thread that I see in most forms of love is emotional honesty. In a way you don't really need to call it love, but in a way again, there is no reason why you shouldn't. One of the nuns that my wife and I met had a special way about her. Her name was Sister Elaine, and she was working in the pediatric ward. One sad day every kid in the place was crying. Well, you can imagine what that was like.

Instead of saying, "Oh, gee, somebody better go out there and quiet those kids down while I go down for my coffee break," she said, "If these kids don't stop crying, I'm going to jump out the window." And she let out a yell.

You may say that's not good nursing procedure. Well, that's what she did. That's what she felt. That's what she said.

Well, what does this do for the three to four other nurses around her? It does a very great wonderful thing. It says,

"Hey, I'm not alone in the fact that I'd like to get out of here, too. If this noise is driving the boss crazy, no wonder it's driving me crazy."

When Sister Elaine did this, she calmed everybody down around her. She didn't pick a fight with somebody else just to kind of increase the uproar. She was honest about herself. She didn't scream her anger at the kids for yelling. She talked about her own feelings about kids yelling. She didn't let fear, the fear that they were yelling just to spite her, control her. They were yelling because they were sick or uncomfortable. And they missed their mothers.

So, Sister Elaine said to the nurses, "Hey, each of us will go and take the noisiest one and hold him and rock him until we get him to shut up. And then we'll take the next one and we'll see if we can't get some quiet in this place—or a little bit more quiet." So they all went and did that, but they knew that each of them were doing it out of their own sense of desperation rather than any great fantastic love of God and love of fellow man.

In handling this situation this way, Elaine did a powerful, valuable and exceptionally rare thing: She expressed rigorous self-honesty about her emotions. This wasn't honesty aimed at the other person.

Some people just want to see honesty as something to be applied to someone else, not themselves. I don't think that's honesty. I think it's anger. I don't know how to handle anger like that. I don't know that there is any good way of handling anger. And if somebody ever discovers one that I can see works for all of us, I'll let you know the minute I see it. So far the only way I've found of handling anger is by handling our feeling of separateness from other people which makes us frightened.

So I see that as we do the kind of things that Sister Elaine did in that situation, our anger tends to fall away. It is a side effect. And I don't think anger needs to be handled directly. I don't think, in a sense, it deserves to be handled directly. People say, "Yah, but if I take all this anger and stuff it back in me, it's going to kill me. True, if that were the way it is. But we're not taking our anger and stuffing it back in us, we are just seeing our anger and letting it lay there and walking off in another direction and occupying ourself with other problems.

But the funny thing is, as I see it, that we occupy ourselves with these problems, our anger does drop away.

It might be that love is just rigorous self-honesty about our feelings. But see how much difference there is between knowing and saying how you feel and the opposite? One of the most painful things in my life is dealing with people who are blind to their feelings or who aren't blind to them but refuse to admit them. We are each one of God's creatures yet look what we are doing to each other. We are saying I don't dare to tell you the truth about myself. Or you don't deserve the truth. Or I want to keep on lying to myself about myself despite your obvious need to know I'm human, too.

Here is a woman who is a nun. She could have easily pulled the nun fake. "I am a happy nun going about God's work and I will smile and I want everybody around here to start smiling." You just kill people with that kind of thing. And you can't live up to this fake picture. So your response is, "I'm a happy nun and all you nurses should be happy nurses, so as a happy nun in charge of this place, I'm going down for a cup of coffee and I want all you guys to be happy while I'm gone." Or "Sister needs me down the hall for some important administrative task, I just remembered just this instant." She uses that as her excuse to run away from the problem.

So that as I see love, it is the process that ranges anywhere from a rigorous self-honesty about our action and feelings up to telling it like it is in our very deepest heart where we dig down and take that thing out that we have been hiding from everyone and tell it to someone. And I see that whole range of things as love.

Love doesn't mean sex, but when a man and a woman are involved in a situation like this where there is some kind of gentleness or kindness or openness, the other person out of their need and out of their hunger is inclined to respond to that and kind of keep on responding past the point where it is appropriate for the two of them to respond. I find it helps my students to know what to expect. Then, when they run into a problem like this, they are prepared for it and can handle it better for what is in their bones. And in real loving relationships, I have seen that there is a great deal of "taking care for what is in the other's bones." It isn't easy, but it can be done.

There is an awful lot of cheap talk and loose talk about,

"Oh sex, that's easy for everybody to handle. We handle it as easy as drinking water." Well if that's true, try to make up some dirty jokes about drinking water. You can't, because everybody handles it well. It's only about things that you don't handle well that can be a basis for this kind of sad humor.

For most of us, it is deep in our bones that physical intimacies are to be reserved exclusively for husbands and wives after marriage. Any violations of this are likely to be severe problems for us and very hard to handle. It is for this reason that we need to see loving for just what it is and for no more than it is. Just what it is is the most precious thing that someone can do for someone else short of marriage which is to show them they are not alone. But what love isn't is going anywhere past the personal encounter. The physical side of loving is reserved exclusively for married couples. Period. It is as simple as that.

I find that some of my students have misinterpreted and misunderstood a lot of things that I've said when I say accept your sexuality, when I say accept your sexual feelings, when I say accept the problems and difficulties that you have handling your sex and your sexuality. Some have twisted that to say, "Hey, Jess says that anything goes." I don't say anything goes. I'm saying the exact opposite in that very little goes. I'm saying that there is only one place for physical intimacy and that's in marriage, after marriage.

And I'm saying that while I know and understand this 100 per cent, I know that there are occasions when despite your own views on this matter, you will have some difficulties and problems, and I'm saying, Okay, let's accept this. This is the way the world is. But I don't say that this is the way it should be, but the way it is occasionally.

We need to accept that so that we can keep those experiences from distracting us from the fact that we've got a new day and a new leaf today. A new thing to work with rather than stewing about any of the mistakes that we have made yesterday. That way we can concentrate 100 per cent on today—free and clear, on the next five minutes.

Because of its dangers for the people involved and the difficulties, there isn't much mental loving by married people of the opposite sex. Most of the "loving relationships" that we read about in Dear Abby are just the opposite. They are two people *using* each other for their own sick enjoyment. That's not a loving relationship because it is not love increasing in both their lives. It doesn't make them better at loving their wives and their husbands.

The real loving relationships don't make Dear Abby because there's little hurt in them and lots of good. An example of this is a friend of mine of about 50 who lost his wife. They had a very close relationship and when she died he was just devastated.

He came to see me in the hospital and told me about his problem and asked me what he should do. I asked him if there was anyone with whom he could talk about this problem and the rest of his feelings from his deepest heart.

He said, "Yes. Now that you put it that way, there is a woman across the street who just lost her mother to cancer. I can go over and talk to her and she really understands.

"But I think her husband thinks we're both crazy because we sit in the kitchen talking to each other and crying like babies."

I told him I felt that was just what he needed. All he had to do was be aware of how close physical intimacy was to mental intimacy. So he could protect what was in his bones as well as what was in the woman's bones by just seeing her when the husband was home and not going there at any other time.

The weaknesses and inadequacies in our loving relationships show up most when we're in a time of sorrow or trouble. I told this same man that I felt part of his problem came from a lack of loving relationships formed through the years.

He and I had been friends for a long time. We had been in a group that met once a week for five years. We liked each other. But neither one of us had gone below the surface of our feelings in all that time.

I asked him who were the men he loved—men he could tell how it was with him in his deepest heart. He named a mutual friend, Paul. I told him I didn't think that counted in a way because Paul has deep relationships with lots of people, so it wasn't much credit to him that he was open with Paul. He saw my point and realized he was paying the price for years of neglect. During that time he had really been able to love only two people, his wife and Paul. So when he lost his wife, he had almost nothing left.

I saw this happen to my grandfather. He seemed to be the patriarch who ruled the roost. He even bought Grandma's pots and pans and dishes. She was just a little bird who was glad to see everybody, full of hugs and nice words. They were extra special to me because they raised me for a couple of years when I was little. But when Grandma died, Grandpa crumbled and wanted to die, too. He didn't die physically until some years later, but he was never the same man again. He was so sad.

Because my Grandpa was a deacon in the church most everyone thought he was the holy one. An aunt and my grandfather were saying to each other that they were sure Grandma was going to Heaven. This was more than my dad could stand. He said, "Hell, if Grandma doesn't go to Heaven, there ain't one."

I was sad about my grandfather again recently. I ran into a man who was eighty-one and looked a lot like my grandpa when he was happy. This man looked fifty or sixty but not eighty-one. His eyes danced with humor and laughter. He looked at you and really saw you instead of ghosts out of the past. His wife had died twenty years earlier, but while I'm certain he loved her deeply, he could still go on—alive and loving. In fact, one of my students wrote a card that said just about exactly that—living is loving and loving is living.

So this is why I feel one of the crucial tests of a loving relationship is in the rest of our lives. If a relationship is truly loving, it is love increasing rather than love destroying. I'm not saying there is no hurt and trouble in loving. There is plenty of it. Gibran in *The Prophet* speaks of the hurt and pain in loving. But it isn't a hurt and pain that destroys. It is a hurt and pain that signifies that you are open to life and like the winter frost breaks open the shell of the seed so does the hurt and pain open you even more to life—and loving.

When you look at life this way, it is easier to see that we build loving relationships like we build a house, a brick at a time. All our life we can be laying bricks. If we don't, we pay the price in broken relationships and diseases of the body that started in our head, heart, stomach or guts.

Young husbands and wives keep coming to me saying their marriages are no good after the sex has worn off. When I ask them if they are laying any bricks and speak to them of how I'm trying to make my own marriage a better one, they see what I mean. They thought a marriage happened on the altar. It didn't. That was just an opportunity to work the rest of their lives building a marriage.

So these are some of the problems of loving other people. I saw this in a good friend, old Quentin Brewer in Kansas City. He loved guys and gals almost indiscriminately. Everybody that ever met that guy felt that he was their very, very special friend. And most people could handle this and took it in the sense in which it was meant. But some people could not. They gave it a twist; they felt that because when they were with Q, there was something magical going on between them, they felt that that was because of them. They felt they and Q had some peculiar magical thing that had not ever happened to anyone before. You see, this is this starved for loving thing.

The real significance of Quentin's lovingness was that you carried that around inside you. And the point wasn't being continuously and incessantly with Q. The point was that you took his love for you and created new love between you and other people. And in that sense you would make the love that he felt for you meaningful and alive and really mean something. Instead of taking it in this narrow, destructive and exclusive sense.

You see it in high school kids who are in love with each other. They are just locked in 100 per cent in each other's company and if the guy or gal so much as looks out of the corner of his eye at anybody else, the other one is hurt and offended and angry. You see? This terrible narrow and exclusive and jealous view of love is as if there are only three and one half pounds of it in the world. And I got all three and one half pounds here and I don't dare give up a bit of it. Well real love is the exact opposite of that. It's the funny thing about it.

The more you hold your hand open, the more mercury you can hold in your hand. And the tighter you squeeze it, the less room for the mercury there is. Well it's the same with this business of loving. And it's an even funnier thing in the sense that the more you give it away, the more you have to give away. Because the faster that you give it away, the faster it comes back tenfold. So the point of Q. Brewer loving somebody is that when you are together, that's great. But when you aren't together, that's great, too.

He died about fifteen years ago, but there's a part of him still inside of me. I can do certain things today because of him. You see? The point of all this is for us not to see love in a narrow, tight exclusive sense.

Now I respect the fact that everyone has feelings of this kind for other people that they don't want to label with the word love. I respect those feelings. I admit that I feel a little creepy about even saying that I love some other woman or women or people than my wife. But it helps me to see love this way and I can accept it fairly well. And I think the more clearly I recognize and accept my feelings about other women than my wife, the more it helps me preserve and live up to my need to be true to the ideal of marriage I got from the grandfather who is in my bones.

There is another problem for me when I say I can love other men. I don't know that I would ever be able to say this to some other man. But I was very struck by something I read when I was writing the first draft of this book. I was reading a Sherlock Holmes anthology to calm down at the end of the evening.

I was startled to find that when Sherlock needed Watson's co-operation yet couldn't explain his reasons he yelled at Watson, "Watson, if you love me, do it now!" If an old dried up Englishman like Holmes can tell Watson that he loves him even indirectly, then why is it so impossible for all of us?

Love is the thing that everybody—especially on campuses —is talking about. "Oh, man, we love 'em. Love. Love. That's just all over the place." I've got news for you. Love is an awful lot easier word to spell on a poster than it is to do. Yet with all these people talking about love, it seems to me that too often they're shouting it at me. And too seldom are they coming up to me easy and soft and saying, "Hey, stranger, I hope you and I don't stay strangers long." And saying that in a loving kind of way.

To me it would be far more fitting. Because I think it is cheap hypocrisy to just talk about something and have your talk drastically unrelated to your actions. It bothers me to see people talking about love and then not showing much of that love that they are talking about. And I think that there's nothing we could do for a protestor that would be more appropriate who's carrying his love sign, than go up and give him a big hug. Now, I don't know how well he or she could handle this. You know, here they are carrying this big love sign and you're loving them and they're wanting to get out of there. But it kind of makes the point.

And then, too, we talk about love as if we've got a ton of it. I don't see that we do. I mentioned to you before the little analogy of the farmer having five grains of wheat that's going to have to feed his whole family. Well, it's that kind of a problem with love. We've got five grains of wheat and we plant them in separate spots and water them and eventually we've got a big crop. And then we've got enough wheat so that we can eat some and still have plenty for seed.

But most of the people I know are still starved for love. We had better start giving it away so we get a lot back. If we don't, we'll be in real trouble. You see this so often in young married couples who have their first child. You see this young couple just beating the dickens out of the little baby of theirs. They're just disciplining the heck out of him, but what it is, is here are people like you and me who feel, "Hey, I haven't got half the love in my life that I wish I had or that I needed and all of a sudden I'm in a position of having to give it out. And I don't have any to give." And that makes you mad.

This idea that everybody can automatically love little kids is again just baloney. And if you see some of the beat up little kids that come into the hospital, you would understand that even clearer. We don't have that ton of love and it's misleading to think we do.

A lot of times as parents you're going to be sitting down to make a meal of love for your children and you're going to be making it for them out of an empty cupboard. You're going to be giving them love that you didn't get from anybody or anyplace, you're just going to take it out of heaven knows where.

But the answer is when you're digging it out of those kind of resources, you aren't getting very much of it out. Granted there is a lot of love passed on to children that was never given to the parents, but that isn't the best way to do it because it isn't going to just flow out like a gusher, like water out of an artesian well.

This is the kind of love that I can understand or that makes sense to me, and it comes only when you get to work on your loving and work on it hard. And the more love there is, the more that comes out, the more you get back so the more there is. And in that kind of situation, there is plenty for everybody.

I'm firmly convinced that it isn't easy to love and be loved at first but it gets easier. And I'm convinced that the wide ranging loving that I'm talking about does not create problems but solves problems instead. As far as the best way for you to express your love, that's a matter of your personal style at the moment and whatever change occurs in your style as you become more loving. But consider again my little experiment of telling five people you love them and see what happens—and see what you learn. And then tell five people how you feel in your deepest heart. You'll find that's lots harder.

SIXTEEN

Higher Power and Spirituality

A student of mine turned in a card one day for class that said:

> God is love
> All people want love
> Therefore all people want God.

I think that card expresses the matter well. But from my experiences working with people, I find that the most troubled people have the most difficulty even admitting the existence of any higher power. They have trouble believing in anything more specific than a belief in an order in the universe, or a belief in the group as their higher power.

As that alcoholic or neurotic recovers, he typically becomes more and more spiritual. And formal religion becomes easier for him.

If all of us were living in a fairly close harmony with the laws of life, we wouldn't have many problems. But there are many of us who have lived for a long time, a long way from any laws of life and our thinking and behaving is pretty badly bent out of shape.

My wife says, "Religion is for well people." And I believe she is right. This book reflects my personal program for getting rid of more sick games and getting more well games in my life.

So as near as I can see this is my program. It has steps in it just like Alcoholics Anonymous and Emotions Anonymous programs.

1. I saw I was on the wrong path for the inner person I felt myself to be.
2. I decided to do only those things that inner person believed in.
3. I went in search for myself to find more cleatrly who and what I wasn't.
4. I found the warmth of acceptance for me as I was.
5. That helped me see that I was afraid of what I really was.
6. I saw my need for other people and the love they could give me.
7. I found the way to get the people I needed was by telling them my story and by letting them be free to need me back or not.
8. The deeper I went into myself the more love I got back from people.
9. This helped me see deeper into myself and value myself more.
10. The more I was able to value myself and yet see and accept my limits, the more I was able to see a higher power.
11. I realized that the only way to run my life was to give up fighting for complete control and accept God as I understand Him so I could let my life run itself—five minutes at a time.
12. My relations with others would take care of themselves the more clearly I was able to see my need for them and for deep, warm relationships—rather than looking at other people as needing me.

Where is God in this program? God as I understand Him made me the way I am for some reason. The more I, like a tree, a mountain or a frog, start being me, the more I am in harmony with God.

This is where I am today. Where I will be tomorrow, next week or next year, God only knows.

I feel deeply about the place of a Higher Power in my life. I try constantly to ask: "Hey, God, what should I do in this next five minutes." But deeply as I feel about this, I am still troubled by my memories of Grandpa's God. Not my specific grandfather's God but that frightening God of my childhood. There's no human for me to blame that fear on because our ministers were kind men, but I still have that childish feeling to fight.

It is very hard for me to speak honestly about religion, higher power and spirituality. So I'm going to try again just to tell my own story as much as I can. I don't know what goes on in anybody else's body. I barely know what goes on inside my own skin.

Before I try to say more about my feelings about religion, I'd like you to remember that I'm trying to speak about the unspeakable. And consequently everything I say to you is wrong. And for God's sake, don't listen to my words, but try to, like you read a love letter, read between the lines. Because it's in between the lines that there is any meaning but nothing in my words.

Also, most of my words won't agree with the other things that I say. They are either contradictory or wrong. So don't listen to the words. Listen between the lines like you do a love letter. All that is there is in between the lines.

For me religion is not piety. The word scares me and bothers me. An example is in a survey a psychologist took among religious people. He did this survey among the most pious people. Those with the most pious attitudes and statements about their faith and church attendance and all of these things.

The thing that he found was that the pious church goer had some extremely negative attitudes toward Jews and blacks and poor people. And he found it was very difficult to reconcile their pious statements with the kind of behavior that you would expect to go along with piety.

Now these people trouble me very, very deeply. They shouldn't. I should be a big enough person not to be bothered by them. But I know I am. And a lot of other people have told me they felt the same way I do about walking into church and feeling the hostility and anger and fear that is there and feeling it so strongly that it makes religious services very, very difficult.

I just read recently that a boy was going to be an Eagle Scout. Then, all of a sudden, they found he didn't believe in God. His father was an atheist so they said, "Well, you can't be an Eagle Scout."

I can't understand that. I know it says in the Scout oath that you believe in God and your country and things like that. But I also am acquainted with Alcoholics Anonymous and Emotions Anonymous. And there, what they do is talk about a belief in a higher power—God as each person understands Him. And most atheists that I have ever seen have a lot more God in them than they will ever care to admit to. But God as we understand Him, gets away from that dilemma of a word that is a problem to some people.

So I don't like piety. I had an experience which to me is the height of piety. And it shows why piety can be such a terrible problem. Because always we have to walk out of church or whatever other setting we talk to our higher power in. We have to walk outside and deal with people as they are. Not as some little hearts and flowers concoction which we have in our minds. Because they ain't that way. And you and I ain't that way either. And piety gets between me and people. It gets between me and seeing the people. So that the kind of piety that I have had experiences with is a very harmful thing to me in dealing with the world.

When I was twelve years old, I was baptized in the Baptist church. My grandpa was a deacon in the church. I had been a regular attender at Sunday school. My mother was very close to the affairs of the church. And I really liked going to Sunday school. It wasn't anything my mother had to force me to do. In the Baptist church at that time you were baptized by immersion. Up on the altar they had this cover that you take off. Under it was a tank with steps. You went down the steps to the deep part of the tank. The minister would stand in water up to his chest. You'd walk down there and he would say, "I baptize you in the name of the Father and of the Son and of the Holy Ghost."

He would dip you backwards and your head would go under water for an instant and come back up.

We wore washable clothes that looked nice because you wouldn't wear a suit in that situation.

There were three of us boys who had known each other from the time we were little kids and three girls in this Baptist Sunday school who were going to be baptized. And I felt very pious, very holy. This was an important occasion.

The three of us boys went down and I was the last of the three boys up. And then one of the girls was baptized. She came up out of this tank up the steps. She was really stacked.

And it was so obvious in these wet clothes that really clung to her. And I noticed this instantly in all its startling detail. But then I was just terribly shocked and horrified at this. In fact, I was so shocked at it that it wasn't until just recently that I was able to tell somebody else how I felt. You know, it was just one of these things that you carry around with you and are horrified at for so long.

A good friend of mine has a ready answer for the questions: "Who am I? What am I?" She says, "You're a child of God and an inheritor of the Kingdom of Heaven." This is her way of saying this. And what she is saying was an admonition to me, you see, at twelve for coming out of there, seeing what I saw and having the thoughts that I had that I was immediately horrified and repelled by.

"Oh God, that's not me," you know. "That's sin and that's awful and that's ugly." But that is me.

The problem I see for me in piety is this. You can buy a road map of the state of Montana. It will show where most all the highways and most all the towns in Montana are. The state of Montana is a finite state with finite roads. There is either a road at a given spot or there ain't. And there is either a town in a given spot or there ain't. And there are some finite number of miles between towns.

But when we're talking about a higher power, we're talking about road maps of something that's infinite. So there ain't very good road maps of the area we're talking about. And the pious person so often is one who has finite road maps of an infinite world. And for the kind of world we're talking about, there isn't a single path to our destruction, there's a bunch of paths, and all we know is our destination is someplace east. And it's about so many miles. But we don't know, we don't ever know how far it is there. And we've just got to head out in that general direction. It's like using the North Star to get out of the woods at night. You ain't ever going to get to the North Star, but you are going to get out of the woods.

So piety is having finite road maps of an infinite world. And that's a lousy kind of road map to have.

The pious person is going straight to heaven because he never jumped in bed with his neighbor's wife. Well, that ain't the point. No place in the Bible does it say that. It is suggested in the Bible as a guide line that we stay away from our neighbor's wives as much as possible.

So that's why I'm agin' piety, as I understand it.

What am I for?

What is religion to me?

To me, religion is epitomized by a statement which I think was made by Tillich, the Protestant theologian. In any situation, the moral response is that response which is most loving in that situation. Tillich is talking about response because he doesn't care about thinking, he's only concerned about your doing. What your hand turns to.

In World War II the Germans captured a bunch of Russian pilots and used them in some very terrible experiments. They also had at that time in the concentration camps a bunch of Jewish women. One of the experiments is mentioned in Shirer's *Rise and Fall of the Third Reich* which is a terrible book to read because it takes you ten to fifteen years to get the memories of what you've read out of your mind because it's that horrible.

One of the experiments they did was they put these Russian fliers in ice water. And they took their body temperatures down as low as they would go and still have them alive. And then they would put one with a Jewish woman. And see if this woman could save his life. So here was this woman and this Russian flyer. Probably both were married. And the woman would hold this flyer and caress him and even have intercourse with him as a means of trying to get him warm and save his life.

Okay. Was God outraged at that? Not the God I understand wasn't. Now that violates the commandment. They're both going straight to hell. No, it does not violate the commandment. It seems to me it is an example of what Tillich says.

One way to read Christianity is as a protest against legalism and against a foolish belief in laws alone. Even the Commandments aren't paramount. When asked which Commandment was greatest, Christ said none of them but to love thy neighbor as thyself. So the only law is the law of love. And how are we to know how to love our neighbor? Simple. We look at him as he is at the moment and do for him what he needs rather than doing what we want to do or ignoring him.

I was talking to Karl Menninger about this recently when he visited our campus. He was afraid it would lead to us doing what was most expedient, what was easiest for us. But I have seen many people avoid the expedient thing and do the hard thing using the law of love. And I have faith that even when we want to justify an action, it isn't that easy. Also, we are unlikely to be able to continue to justify it for long. Because when we constantly ask, "Hey God, what should I do now?" we aren't likely to be misled very often, very seriously, or for very long. I know there are problems, but I would rather bet my life on "what is most loving?" than the negative "am I breaking any of the million possible laws?"

This doesn't say we don't need laws, rules and forms. We do need them, badly. But we can't follow them blindly and routinely. We must use them as guides to help us find the best answer we can for each situation we face.

Now does this say, "Hey, if I'm going to give up my finite road maps, then life, each day, is going to present some real tough dilemmas?" And the answer is yes, it sure does. Because I'm going to be dealing with people. I'm going to be dealing with humanity. But that's kind of neat, because I ain't God. And I can't ever be.

So it's like Vance, an old A. A. member told me: "If we're going to live the abundant life, we've got to stop fighting for complete control. If you want to live abundantly, you must surrender. It ain't easy but it can be done. There ain't no money nor job in the world that can help us get rid of grief. We've got to either accept God—or be God."

If we decide we're going to be our own higher power, then we've got to worry about everything that goes on all around us. So we're controlling everything. We're just like a puppeteer and we're jerking everybody's strings.

But if we're going to accept God—instead of trying to be God, then all we've got to do is worry about our own little puppet and where it's going to go. And what it puts its hand to. And that means that what you do is your decision. And it's under the control of some higher power not mine. And you are free then to go, each of you, and do what you choose.

So that this is the thing that I see. Most of our trouble comes from the fact that we don't want to accept God. But we want to be God, because we are so terribly frightened of all the things we see in ourselves. And the things we see around us. And we don't like all these shades of gray that we've constantly got to choose between.

But that's life. That is our finite condition. We are limited people. I'm a dumb Norwegian and there's very little I understand about anything. And my job is simply to do the best I can, always.

Now there's another terrible thing about Tillich's idea of doing the loving thing. We talk about love so easy as if we've got a ton of it. But I haven't met that person yet.

Very, very few people that I meet, perhaps only a few out of a hundred, are very loving people. The kind of people that you can feel their love in them. Because when you walk in the room, they look up from what they're doing and they look at you, and they really see you.

And they say, "Can I get you a cup of coffee?" Because they're looking at you and they've got their eye off their own damned navel. And consequently they can see you. And this conveys a fantastic message. But those people are like one in a hundred.

As for the rest of us, in my experience, and Jess Lair I know for sure, there isn't much love in him. I mentioned the story about the farmer with five grains of wheat who has to feed his family. He plants them carefully and waters them carefully. His situation is dangerous.

In my experience this is the way love goes and I start with about five grains if I'm lucky. So I'd better love the easy ones. And I'd better plant my wheat where it will be returned to me.

But my students say, "Oh, Jess, you should love the hard one." I can't. To me life is a survival situation. To me, today is a life-or-death matter. Because I look at yesterday and what it was. And some of the grief I was confronted with. And some of the gut wrenching dilemmas that I was confronted with trying to live up to that very simple statement of Tillich's. And having the agony of not having a good finite, definite guide. "Yes, Jess, this is right. The next is wrong. This is right. This is wrong." I can't have that kind of a guide. And it made yesterday terrible, terrible hard.

So that today I need all of you. But the ones who are looking at me the most and seeing me are the ones I'm going to concentrate on the most. Because I know that's a sign that they're inclined to need me back. And I haven't got so much love that I can go out and just sow it to the winds. Because I have very little of it. So I'm inclined to put it where it is most likely to come back to me.

One reason I don't think we have a lot of love to give away

is I don't think a lot of it has been given to us. Very few of us were loved well.

A lot of people say, "Oh, Jess. No. I was really loved. Man, my parents just loved me to death. Oh, they were just so great." But they are saying that, and they ain't even seeing me. And in my experience, a person who was well loved, loves a lot of people. Not necessarily me but the people around them. And they're very easy on the people around them. And they're not hard on the people around them.

But the people who are so frantically asserting to me, "Jess, I was loved so deeply and so well," those people are hurting a lot of people around them that I see. And this is a sign to me that they weren't loved very well. But it is so hard for them to admit. And I understand that.

One of my students who felt this way for a while, later said this:

"You have taught me to slow down and breath the beauty of life—to inhale the warmth of man. But the hardest part is yet ahead of me. I know what it is but can I do it? Can I find it?

"Oh, God, I'm trying. I'm trying to accept me—as I am and as I was born to be on this earth. I'm trying to accept my faults and my virtues. I'm trying to learn how to forgive myself. And how to pat me on the back. It's the hardest thing I've ever done. I don't know if I can ever do it. But at least I'm trying. Thank you, Jess."

One of my students said on a card, "As Christians, we are constantly being admonished to 'love thy neighbor as thyself.' Maybe we do and that is the problem."

I've seen that I'm like a little car. And I need gas stations. I need people. And that if I'm going to make any kind of voyage in this life, I need people who love me.

How am I going to get people who love me? The answer is simple. I know what love is. Well, not really, but I know what love is well enough that it works for me and a lot of other people. And love is when you tell someone how it is with you in your deepest heart about yourself. Not about your anger but about yourself—your imperfections.

When I share the imperfections in me with my fellow imperfect being—that's love. Because I let them know that they are not alone in their imperfections. There is somebody else who's just as damn weird as they are.

So each of us needs people. And the way to get them is to

tell them how it is with us in our deepest heart. And tell them that way. We don't need to say, "I need you." When we tell how it is with us in our deepest heart, our need stands out there and is obvious. It's screaming. And then some of them will choose to need us back. Those who can. Those who happen to resonate on our particular wave length will.

I'm not everybody's cup of tea. Not everybody can stand me. But some people can, fortunately. And that's great.

And what does that love do as it comes back to you from another person when they tell you how it is with them in their deepest heart? That love coming back to you calms you down. It calms me down. It helps me see deeper into my heart. So that there is something more the next time I go to somebody to tell him how it is with me. So I am calmer. And I am a different person than I was before I was loved.

When you tell people how it is with you, it's a way of building some gas stations for yourself so your automobile has some places to stop.

If you don't do that, if you put up the shell, then you're going to get the shell so high and so hard you ain't ever going to get out. It's like being shot in a rocket to the moon and you're going to be doomed to circle the moon forever.

I've never seen anybody who was able to defy the idea they need people.

Now this is my idea of what I think religion is. I don't have any difficulty squaring this with any kind of theology I've ever seen. It squares with Tillich. It squares with the way I read the Bible, which is the friendly Bible. The part of the Bible that says: "As ye shall do to the least of me, so shall you do unto me."

There is another part of the Bible that says, "An eye for an eye, and a tooth for a tooth." I'm going to throw that part of the Bible away because it scares me to death. I can't handle it. I don't want that part of the Bible. I don't need it.

I'm interested only in the friendly Bible. And I think that in the days of Rome in the early days of Christianity, I think why so many people came rushing to Christianity was because of the things that are in the friendly Bible. "If you will love one another, you will live forever." That must have been a pretty interesting idea to people in Roman days who were superstitious and afraid of all the gods and their terrible wrath and were trying to appease the gods in any way they knew. And they didn't know how to go about it.

And then some people came along and said, "If you'll just love each other, you will have everlasting life."

All of this crust that we've added through the years has been the human fallibility showing itself.

A minister tells a good story about this. A group went to the ocean and formed a life-saving club right on the shores of the ocean because a lot of people will drown in the ocean in rip tides and accidents.

The life-saving club was pulling people out of the ocean and saving their lives. But then things got kind of encrusted. And the club turned into a country club. They moved it away from the ocean because they forgot why the club was ever set up in the first place. Pretty soon a bunch of other country clubs were formed along the same lines and they didn't save anybody's lives anymore.

I don't mean to suggest the church is exactly that way. It isn't. But there's an awful lot of things in a church and in a religion so a person has to be careful. It's like what's been said about philosophy: "Too much of it rots in your mind." Or, "You can sicken and die of too much philosophy."

All you need is enough philosophy like a little flashlight to guide you in your path through the woods in the night.

Someplace I was reading about a man who said it wasn't important to know a lot about religion. He said, "I don't want to know a lot about religion because we're trying to know about the unknowable." He said, "It's enough to say 'I believe.' I'm not interested in knowing any more than that."

So I'm interested then, in taking that belief and seeing how I can translate it into action in the next five minutes of my life. The next five minutes.

I'm not interested in living a day at a time. I'm not interested in smiling. I'm not interested in loving people in the sense of, "Oh I love everybody." I'm interested in the next five minutes which is all I can handle and stand and understand. And I'm interested in telling how it is with me in my deepest heart because I know when I do that people come back at me straight and good and true.

This is what I understand—my need for you. And if I don't get some of you, I will die, and if I do get some of you, my life, the rest of today, will be something far better than it was yesterday. And the day before that. And the year before that.

I've seen many drastic consequences of this in my life. And some of the consequences I've seen in my life are exceptional-

ly hard to handle. But when I understand that there are no finite road maps in this infinite world, it is easier to understand
my mistakes.

The Jesuits make a big point about something I used to
think strange. They say religion isn't an emotional thing. Religion is one of the most cold-blooded processes in the world.
And they are terribly distrustful of the emotion in religion.
And I know why. Again this goes back to, we want this little
sugar-coated world. We want this pious, beautiful, all is love,
sunshine and little birds singing and flitting around the little
ivy-covered college.

Hell, that ain't the way life is. And that ain't the way love is.
And that ain't the way the church is. This is a world of very
finite, limited people. And when you paint religion in this
glorified manner, you cannot but be defeated. Because nobody
can measure up to that. And it's a way of intimidating yourself and a way of running away from the world. Just as much
as hiding in an alcohol bottle is, or running away into any
other kind of thing. It's just a hideout.

But it is very simple. Each of us are exceptionally limited.
Each of us exceptionally finite. And each of us can do only a
certain, few limited things. But we should be thankful for
that.

The day I can say, "I ain't much, but I'm all I got," is the
day I start. "I ain't much, but I'm what God made me." You
see. And if I scorn that, I am putting myself above God.

If I say, "Well, when God made me, he sure must have
made a mistake," I put myself above God.

When I say, "Well, when God made me have some of those
feelings I have, he sure didn't know what he was doing," I put
myself above God.

As Vance said, "I've got to accept God—or be God." And
when you put it that way it simplifies the matter. There ain't
no choice between the two when you bring it out in the open
like that. But there's an awful lot of people in the world who
think they're God. And they've got an idea how people should
be. And it's a hell of a lot different than they are or I am.

I'm a mess—a basket case. And I know it. But God must
have had something in mind when he made me like this. So
my job is to do with it what I can.

SEVENTEEN

How to Die—
at a Very Early Age

I've always felt that it was love that kept people alive. We have a number of recent experiments on monkeys that give some scientific backing to this point.

You can take a pair of monkeys at birth and have them raised by two different kinds of mothers. One is the regular loving monkey kind. The other mother is bare chicken wire with an artificial nipple. The monkey raised on the bare chicken wire gets no attention at all. And he turns out to be very queer. He exhibits a great deal of behavior that we humans would call neurotic or psychotic.

But an even more striking thing happens if you raise a boy and a girl monkey on bare chicken wire mothers and then pair off these two mixed up monkeys. Their children, when raised artificially are even worse and seem to have no sense of their sex or anything else.

Now these are sad experiments because you hate to see something like this happen to animals. But we even have some human evidence along this line. In the old days, there wasn't a big demand for illegitimate babies for adoption so they went into orphanages. Some of those orphanages were horrible places and way understaffed. Some of these little babies were only handled to feed them or change their diapers occasionally and there were some drastic consequences in their physical and emotional health. So we see many signs that physical love like touching, holding and handling is vitally necessary. And if we don't get enough of it when we are little, we will have a deeper than average craving for it all our life.

When we get bigger much of the love we get can come from words and actions of others but unless we get love of one kind or another, I think we may decide inside to die. So that's why I feel that love keeps us alive. And unless I can find a way of running my life that brings me a minimum of love, I'm in danger of dying.

I've always figured that when people who weren't loved enough wanted to die, they just grabbed the nearest available disease and died from it. I've seen too many people die where there was no very good reason for their dying. And I've seen too many people live when it didn't make any sense that they should live. They were shot to pieces. And they were supposed to die. But they refused to believe it and they were damned if they were going to die, thank you. They were not ready to die yet. So they are living and walking around today.

Any time I see someone who doesn't want to live very bad get in an automobile or get near any kind of germ or anything else, I worry about his life. Because to my mind, we die when we don't want to live any more. A lot of times many of us don't want to live any more at an awfully young age.

I think a lot of our automobile accidents hinge on what we do in a fleeting instant when we either choose death and let the car go—or choose life and try to save ourselves. The accident may have even been caused by something completely beyond our control like a faulty steering mechanism. But when that car starts to go off the road, there are a lot of things you can do in that instant. But some of the things you can do in that instant are just give up.

If I'm in any kind of dangerous situation, I don't want anybody around me who doesn't want to live real bad because it is so easy to die.

It may seem dumb to you for me to put so much emphasis on loving. But Reverend Ellertson said the Zulus had little or none of the diseases that are such big killers in our society like heart attacks and ulcers. But he also said they didn't have much cancer.

I thought that a little strange but I sure didn't want to argue with that man. Recently, though, I saw some new research that suggested a basic cancer causing agent was produced in the stomach. And we know what worry does to upset and change the chemistry of the stomach.

When I see how my stomach feels when I am in a desperate emotional situation, I'm not surprised when you tell me the byproducts of my stomach can be harmful. And I'm used to seeing young girls, nineteen to twenty-one, walk in my office with one or two bad ulcers. And they don't need to tell me their story. I know ahead of time what it was. I say, "You didn't come out of a Zulu home did you?" They all say, "No way. Our home looked fine to outsiders. But there was no real warmth or loving there. I think my folks are seeing the problem clearer now because now my younger sister has ulcers, too."

Does love solve everything? Almost everything, I think. And the problems it won't solve are made bearable because of it.

A woman came to see me who had heard me speak. She was widowed with three children. She said, "They tell me I don't know them. They tell me 'We are different when we are away from you.'"

I told her, "If they say that, it is probably true." I asked her if she thought she could get out of her silo before they all left her. She said, "I don't know."

I told her that if she didn't it would be like sealing herself into a moon rocket that loses control and is doomed to circle in outer space forever. And when that happens, you either die or kill yourself.

At this she nodded and said, "Yes, I know about that. My husband committed suicide."

So there are many ways to die—but only one way to live.

I have had a little experience with would-be suicides, who tell me to tell them why they should live. They already know they should live or they wouldn't take the trouble to call me. Someone who really wants to kill themselves just does it quickly. And they leave very short notes.

So I don't try to tell them they should live. I just try to tell them from my deepest heart of both my fears and hopes for my life.

The most poignant suicide I've heard of was by an American Indian college student in Billings. He was married and a potential basketball star, but he evidently couldn't stand the world and killed himself. His name was Star Not Afraid.

May there be enough love in your life that you choose to live.

EIGHTEEN

Teaching These Ideas—
I Am an Expert
Only in my Own Story

As my students get hold of these ideas and see them working well in their lives, they want to teach them to other people. This is a very good thing. But I find we have some tendencies when it comes to teaching that can be very destructive.

The only way I have seen these ideas transmitted from one person to another is by example and by being an expert only in our own story. As a teacher of these ideas, by far the most frequent problem I have is to avoid yelling and preaching at people and instead concentrate on telling my own story. The world is full of people who are telling us to do one thing and they are doing another.

There is a lot of talk today about the dangers of smoking. But how much of this talk comes from smokers. A recent study showed the biggest factor in whether a kid smoked or not was the example he saw. If his family and friends smoked, he smoked. The fewer smokers there were around him, the better the chances the young person wouldn't smoke.

The power of example is even more crucial in this set of ideas. They strike right to the heart of a person's being. If you attack him, he closes up to protect himself. If you work on your problems out loud and concentrate on being an expert in your own story, the other person is not frightened. He is calmed down and is free to move toward these ideas if he wants to.

I see this working most strikingly in my big classes. I just finished three classes with a total of two hundred students. I spent 60 to 70 per cent of the time talking about how I used these ideas in my own life—being an expert in my own story. While we all would have liked a little more discussion opportunity than we had, most all of the students were calm, felt free to speak on anything in class and got the support they needed to go out and apply these ideas to their lives. I mention this not because it is the most desirable situation but because it shows how crucial it is for the teacher to concentrate on his own story.

So the only way I have found that works in teaching these ideas is for me to use them as continuously as I can and then try to be as real as possible with my students as I tell my own story. Now that sounds simple and fairly logical, but I find my students and I have lots of trouble doing it.

I think our biggest problem is that it is much easier and nicer to see these problems as being in other people than in ourselves. Much of our seeming desire to teach these ideas is really a distraction that we use to run away from ourselves. So the first caution I make to myself is to be sure I'm working as hard as I can on these ideas before I start using time and energy to talk to others.

I think our next biggest problem is that as learners we need to be free. The only kind of learning that I see around me as significant is that which people pick up and learn freely. When I try to teach you by shouting at you and preaching at you, I take away your freedom and independence. If you do something because of what I yell at you, it is really me that is making you. And you see your dependence on me. If I tell you my story, and because of it you decide to try certain things, you do so freely and independently.

It is for this reason that I place such a high value on personal freedom in my classes. I try hard to avoid asking a student to do or say anything until he is ready to. But oddly enough, I see evidence that he will be ready faster if he isn't pushed.

So while we might like to go and pound these ideas into someone else—there's just no way we can do it. One of my students said that when my first book was ready, she was going to tear out a page at a time and give it to her husband. I told her that a better way to give my book to her husband was through her life—five minutes at a time. This same student told me previously, "If you didn't practice and work at all these ideas yourself, they wouldn't have meant a hill of beans to me or anyone else. Every person in that class felt your acceptance of yourself and of us. That's why we could open up a lot of our feelings to you and to each other the way we did." She saw that example is the only teacher, and I was just turning around and applying the same thing to her.

When we see someone near to us who is in trouble and who we would like to help, we can go to them. But all we can do is be as real about ourselves as we can and tell our own story. I have found that can help a lot. But it isn't perfect. And the person we are talking to is free to take these ideas or not. If we really let him be free, one choice he has is to not do anything. If that is his choice we must respect that and not try to force change on him.

When someone hears these ideas and starts working on them, so often he looks around him and sees all of the other people who need these ideas so terribly desperately. "Wow! Jess, does my roommate ever need these ideas." Then you start going to work on him. That's the handiest way of running away from these ideas: to see how somebody else needs them.

But there comes a second stage when you honestly feel, "Hey, you know, I've worked three months, or six months, or nine months, or a year or two years on this set of ideas and I feel that I'm making some progress. And I see somebody in deep trouble and I'd like to help them." And you say, "Jess, how can I help them. My neighbor's about to have a divorce or there is a terrible problem with the way they're treating one of their children." The list of problems of people that come to me with them go on and on.

When they say, "Jess, how can I solve this problem?", there's an insistent quality as if they say to me, "Jess, you tell me how to solve this problem or I'm going to beat your head against that wall." But always I have just one answer for them, and it never seems to be good enough. And yet, it's the only answer I find I can use in all my teaching.

I have to say, "Well, maybe it isn't good enough for you, sunshine, but it's good enough for me and it's the only one I can find." And that is: *the only way of teaching these ideas* and in the broader context, the only way of teaching any idea to anybody else, *is through your story, through your example, through your life.*

If your neighbor's marriage is breaking up and you honestly want to do something about it, I'll tell you something to do and most of you haven't got the guts. And that's to walk up to them and tell them the story of all the difficulties and all of the problems that are in your marriage. Tell them your own story, that's the only thing you're an expert in.

Maybe in their case, divorce is the only answer, maybe it's the best answer. But it is so typical of us that we presume to be able to judge the other person and know what's best for them when so often we've got very little idea of what's best for us. But, oh, our vision on the other guy's situation is always 20-20. So the answer in teaching these ideas to others is to *tell your own story.*

It's the basic principle that comes out of Alcoholics Anonymous and Emotions Anonymous. They use it constantly and it's coupled with another caution. The only negative thing that you are ever allowed to say in their program is: "Please don't criticize anybody else. In your last comment, I felt you were criticizing and it would be best, I think, if you would stick to telling your own story." That's the only place where criticism is allowed which is to say: "Please, we're not to criticize each other."

This just underscores this point that we make here, and that is, to tell your own story. You see this is so terribly hard for us. By now, as you near the end of the book, you have probably seen how difficult it is for us to face into ourselves and to face into the way things are for us. And when you're faced with telling your own story in all of its grim detail to someone else, you are really brought up face to face with yourself. I know you honestly believe as people continually say to me they do, "This other person, Jess, has a problem and I really want to help him." But if you do honestly believe that, that's all the encouragement it should take to reach down inside yourself and to tell your story.

Oddly enough, the best time to tell these stories is before there is trouble. My neighbor and I have conversations with each other that seem to be somewhat on the light and seemingly facetious level. We seem to be joking and kidding with each other a lot. But there's an awful lot of telling our own story going on between Dave and I. I'm telling in a somewhat humorous and whimsical fashion some of the problems of living with five kids and living with a wife and living with an employer—and most of all, living with myself. And he's doing the same back to me. And this is the best way, of course.

When the couple is ready to get the divorce, that is not the best time to go running over to them and tell them all the troubles your marriage has had. Ideally, you see, we should be doing some of this all along the way. And this again is something I am struck by when someone comes running up to me and says, "Jess, my friend is in this terrible trouble." And I say, "Well, tell them your story." And they say, "Well, I couldn't. I can't." And I say, "Well, maybe there is nothing you can do." And they say, "Well, this is my best friend. I've got to be able to help this person. It bothers me so to see this person in agony."

Well, all we need to do is look back two months, three months, six months. How come this "best friend" of theirs hasn't deserved any part of them before now? And how come there needs to be this emergency action of rushing to them and unloading their story all of a sudden? And, how come, if, this person is their best friend, they haven't had part of their story continuously? How come they haven't been real with them before? And regularly? And a piece at a time?

Again that's another important lesson about learning. We can swallow learning in small hunks a lot better than in large. I'm continually confronted by this problem and I'm doing lots and lots of one, two and three hour talks on this set of ideas that we spend a whole book on here. But it is really amazing to me how little happens in those brief talks because of the fact real learning and real change happens a piece at a time. It takes time for it to sink in and time for reflection. So again, in teaching these ideas to others, you need to think about that aspect too, which ties right back in with being real.

If you with your best friend had been blazingly real, they would have been blazingly real back to you and you would have known about their difficulties a long time ago, and you would, furthermore, have discussed them in great detail, many, many times because this is the most pressing problem for them. But so often, the mark of our friendship is that only at the eleventh hour do we find out. "Gee, our friend has got a problem." Yah, what kind of friend are we that we've never created any better opening than that for our friend to tell us of his problem and dilemma.

So, while essentially, I see our concern and preoccupation with teaching these ideas to others as pretty much a distraction, there are legitimate places for them. And I would give you then just these two simple rules in teaching these ideas to others. One, is tell your story, and then secondly, after you've told your story, you can make whatever point it illustrates. You can tell your story about trying to accept yourself and some of the difficulties you've had and some of the horrible things that have happened to you as you've tried to accept yourself. And then at the end, you can make your point. This is just an illustration from me that in my life, acceptance is something that's crucial and something that's hard.

Now most of us want to preach at others. In fact, I think by and large, all of us would a lot rather preach at other people and tell them how wrong they are rather than we would yell at ourselves. This is something that is a real concern and a real threat, it seems to me, to learning and change. There is nothing sadder than somebody saying one thing to us and doing another. It's when someone says I love you, and they're kicking us in the shins. We say, "Hey, hey, wait a minute here. There's a contradiction between what you're saying and what you're doing." And while we have a certain ability to handle these contradictions in life because we see them so much and we get lots of chance to practice them, the less we treat other people to these terrible contradictions the better.

It seems to me that almost without exception, that in practicing these ideas, I have to concentrate 90 per cent of the time on doing it myself. I'm talking about my own applications. And it seems to me that the times that I get into trouble, are the times when I turn from myself and start yelling at my students and start pushing them. Ideally, you are completely free to move toward those things you want to move toward and only when you want to move. And that freedom it seems to me is very precious.

But we don't like freedom. It frightens us. We want it for ourselves perhaps, but we sure don't want it for other people. It is right here that the restrictions come in, because we see how little willingness there is in us to give freedom to the people around us. But I've seen that the only kind of learning that really counts is the kind of learning that occurs in a situation where we are free to make up our own minds. To do the things we want to do and to do them at the time we want to do them. Now this frightens a lot of people because as teachers, as parents, as members of society, they see their roles as imposing some kind of a rule on other people. They see their role as parents in taking and making the world go some certain way. But there is no way. You can get all the appearances of order. But don't be fooled by appearances.

I thought one of the best examples I've seen of this is the story I read in the papers recently. This gent blew into town from the East. He had a criminal record as long as your arm, but he started baking fancy goods for the ladies' bake sale and all of a sudden they thought he was some kind of a knight in shining armor. Later there was some talk that he insured his building and then burned it down for the insurance, and then gave the land under it as a kind of a park. So again he endeared himself to the ruling members of the community and to those who ask only that your outward appearance should be very proper. And he looked like some kind of a white knight while at the same time he was carrying a gun, using a little strong arm tactics and running a prostitution ring on the side.

So the world, it seems, is very happy if all of our outward appearances will give the kind of comfort and assurance to them we want. And then inside, we can do whatever kind of thing we care about. Oddly enough, that doesn't work very well. It seems to me that a far better rule is just the reverse of that. If we get the mess inside straightened out, then the public and the society has got this responsibility to accept whatever outside variations in behavior they see as long as they are somewhere within the normal realm.

Another question that comes up when we talk about letting the people around us be free to learn when they want and what they want is the issue of motivation. Everybody wants to talk about motivation. I talked to a bunch of businessmen and I talked to them for four hours. And one of them at the end said, "Hey, Jess," he said, "you've never talked about motivation in all of these four hours. Why is that?" And I said that's because I don't believe in motivation. Motivation is a door that's locked from the inside. Most people who talk about motivation talk about it as something outside themselves. They think it's something that I have and that I hand to you or give to you. And in a way it's a kind of motivation out of fear. If you guys don't get to work, you're going to be bums, and you'll be a drain on society. And you'll be begging in the streets for money to feed your family, so you had better get to work. Better shape up, you see. That's just society talking.

The only kind of motivation that I understand at all is the kind of motivation that we've talked about all through this book. Which is that motivation which comes from inside you when you see a job that you want to do.

"Well, there's one automatic limit," everybody screams, "to that kind of motivation." "Jess, there's no way of making people do jobs they don't want to do." And the answer is, you're blamed right. There is no way to make somebody do a job they don't want to do. Not in the long run, there isn't. And you say, "Well then, who's going to be the garbage collectors in the world?" And the answer is the guys who are going to be the garbage collectors of the world are the guys who love to collect garbage. And you say. "There ain't no such thing." And I say, there sure is.

Our local garbage collector is Sonny Suhr. He's happy with his job of collecting garbage. And he's got all kinds of funny things written on the sides of his trucks. You know like, "North Dakota Camper" and "Your garbage is our bread and butter." And, "Our business is picking up." When you meet Sonny, this is a guy who doesn't go around hanging his head because he's the lowly garbage collector. He's happy in his work.

And you say, "Yah, well a lot of guys aren't happy collecting garbage." Well I've got news for you. There's a lot of doctors who aren't very happy either. Happiness has got nothing to do with the so called status or size of the profession. It's got something to do with size of the person who's in the profession and the heart of the person who's in that profession. And that's where motivation comes. It comes out of the love for the work.

A columnist I was reading recently claimed that he had never heard of a guy who whistled who got a divorce. So what has whistling got to do with it? Well maybe whistling has got something to do with how we feel inside about ourselves. And how we feel inside about ourselves has got a lot to do with two things: One, who we marry: whether or not we want to marry somebody where we doom ourselves automatically to failure. And then secondly, it's got to do with how we handle whoever we marry: whether or not we give them a half-way chance to be themselves and succeed.

So, you see this view of teaching strikes right at this motivational problem that many people see as a big one in life.

Awhile back I spoke to the high school honor society and told them they should work and study out of love. And I was telling some stories of my own case to illustrate this. Afterwards, a guy came up to me, a faculty member, and said, "Man, you should be talking to our graduate students up at the university. You're talking to the wrong group." And he was really happy about some of the things I'd said.

His wife was standing right beside him and they were parents of an officer in the honor society. And his wife, after the husband had wandered off, looked at me and said, "You don't really believe anyone would study anything out of love, do you?" And I thought, you poor dear. She's been laying the torch to those kids of hers everytime they've come home from school since the time they were in first grade. Beating on them to get good grades. Feeling that no one could ever study anything out of love for it.

Well there just happens to be an awful lot of things that an awful lot of students like. And they like them well enough to do well at them. But particularly, they do so when they are free to set their own pace and to work on things the way they want to work on them. But there's a great misunderstanding of that aspect of learning.

Now, why should this be? I don't know. I think partly, none of you, none of us have been trusted near enough. It is saddening to me. I ask students, "Why do you think there's just one Summerhill? Why is there only one school like that in the whole world?" And it is very simple I think. The answer is there is only one A. S. Neil.

Now why, when A. S. Neil has put forward the examples and ideas that he believes in so strongly and why, when no one in education questions really the validity of these ideas? Some of them say, "Well, I wouldn't want to go quite that far." But nevertheless, there is no massive argument against the set of ideas that Neil has. In fact, there tends to be the opposite, an almost adulation of the ideas Neil stands for. Why then, aren't there more Summerhills? And the answer is there aren't more Summerhills, of course, because a guy like Neil is such a rare animal.

Now, this brings out then what I see as the crucial role and dimension of any leader—and we are all leaders in some way in our homes, our work, or society. But when you look back at the leaders, the people around you, how many of them conveyed any deep belief and trust in you like Neil does in Summerhill? Not very many people in our life do this for us. But to me the miracle is that it is enough for you and for me if one or two people will believe in us and see the majesty in us. And the funny thing is, if one or two people will look into our hearts and really see what is there, it is enough to start us down that path of believing and trusting in ourselves.

And there is a funny way that we've got of knowing that it isn't that one person thinks we're great and the other people think we're horrible. We see that the person who thinks we're great is the only person who really stopped and looked at us. The only person who really saw us as some kind of a legitimate human being with legitimate cares and concerns. And I think this is why we're willing to let, in a sense, a minority view, have a crucial role in our lives. And this is why the parent or the nurse or the boss or the neighbor is so crucial.

Most all of us can look back in our early lives and see the great influence on us of a few people. I had an Aura Kingsley, an Arling Anderson, a Phil Burton, a Howard Longstaff and a wife and kids in my life who really believed in me and thought there was something there, somebody was at home. These are the kind of people who are crucial in our lives. Their belief and lovingness around us is a rare commodity.

Now you may say, "It's a great big impersonal, cruel world and nobody makes a difference." Well you may not make much of a difference in the politics of this country. You may not make much of a difference in the social institutions and mores of this country. But this is one place where, if any one of you have got the guts, you can make just one awful difference. You can walk into a hospital room. You can walk into your business. You can walk into your home. And you can be that one person out of a great many who can believe in people, who can love people, and who can communicate that love and belief to the people around you. They will get the message.

And that one person, you, doing that one thing, can have a decisive effect on, not tens of people, not hundreds of people, but in your lifetime, thousands and even tens of thousands of people. They can be touched by your life if you make it something more meaningful than it's inclined to be if you just let it continue down some of the destructive paths you can follow.

There are, in psychology today, almost two conflicting

viewpoints on dealing with the personal side of teaching to live. And one of them, as near as I can see, is typified by the Alcoholics Anonymous and the Emotions Anonymous approach. That is, the only person that you can attack is yourself. The only story you can tell is yours. The only person you can criticize is yourself.

There is an opposite tendency and an opposite approach to this problem of emotional growth on all of our parts. That's typified by the point of view of the people who say, "Hey, it's good that we should be attacked. You and I should sit down and tell each other, like sorority hell week, 'Hell, Jess, you've got all these hang-ups and it's always bothered me that you have, you know.' Then I tell back to you something equally mean. "I mean it's true, man, it's true. This is honesty we're practicing. Rigorous honesty." Sure it is. Rigorous honesty with the other guy. And you really pound away on each other.

But I find a funny thing about that. I see that, sure you can take those emotional baths. You can really have some really deep, and at the moment, moving experiences in that kind of setting. But the thing that I see about change in you and me and in everybody else is that we don't change until we're ready. My students ask me, "Jess, how fast are we going to move and how fast are we going to change?" And the favorite answer that I have is how the snake sheds its skin. The snake doesn't shed his skin until he's got a full new one grown underneath. And when he's got a full new one underneath, the old one just falls away.

To me, the problem of trying to force change, is we can't do it. You and I aren't going to give up any of the sick games we're playing in life until we get some new games, good ones, of being real with people, of loving people, until we've got some good things coming into our life. And when we have, then we have the strength and are able to give up some of those other games, so that we are able to walk away from them. But our lives are not going to change just because we want them to. Our lives are not going to change because we see some things wrong with them. They're going to change when we have slowly and gradually and steadily rebuilt some fundamental structures. And then the change is just going to sneak up on us. And we're going to recognize one day, "Hey, I lost my old skin," in that one particular area of my life. It just fell away because I didn't need it anymore.

This is the thing that I see that is so wrong-headed about

so many of these opposite views and other ways of looking at change. They see things are coming about because of thinking. And thinking has so little to do with anything in life. It's a wonderful tool when you're trying to navigate across the Pacific. But when you're trying to sail your own little ship around in this puddle of life today, thinking is of very little value to you just by itself. You need feeling, too, and you need a sense of yourself. And out of that comes actions.

There is so much emphasis on the idea if I can see what's wrong, if I can get insight into what's wrong, then things will be different. But they won't be. That insight is not the end. It is just a bare bones beginning. And that insight doesn't mean anything unless you've taken those insights and applied them to your life so that your life gets changed around, and you become different because of being able to do a bunch of things differently. And primarily, of course, these have to do with feeling a lot different.

In some sense, everybody in the whole world feels completely and 100 per cent alone. Sometimes when I'm talking to you in my office, I think I'm talking to the same person over and over again. Because it's so much of a problem of: You feel alone and unworthy inside your skin. Yet within a hundred feet of you is another person who feels exactly the same way, and you could love him or her like a brother or sister if you would but open up and say how it is with you. So the solution to your dilemma is so near at hand, but yet that short distance is the hardest to get across that most of you have ever found any distance in your life to travel.

Also, this business of being yourself as a way of teaching these ideas to others has a frightening side. It isn't very impressive-at-the-moment business. It isn't like, "Wow! I'll perfect some fantastic new surgical technique and go down in history." But there's all kinds of funny things that happen, I find, when I finally start sticking to my own business and tending to what I should do. Yours and my life can smooth out amazingly. And as far as accomplishments go, I think that there is just as much or more accomplishment as there is when we seek accomplishment directly. There's a part of society that seems to say: "Achievement, that's what we've got to have. We've got to have more bank presidents, we've got to have more fancy pants of all different kinds and descriptions." Well, the hell we do.

We don't need any more lame-brained bank presidents, we

don't need any more poor teachers, we don't need any more mechanical nurses than we've already got. What we could use is more good ones. More real good ones. That's what we're talking about. Where you're one of those things because you want to be it. When I talked about goals, I said don't have any of those long-term status-building kinds of goals that are so destructive to you that you follow and go toward without any respect for yourself.

Sure, you have to have goals, I've got to have a goal. I've got to go to lunch, that's a goal. At twelve o'clock, I'm going to go, because if I don't my stomach is going to start complaining violently. Okay, so that's a goal. But I'm not going to have any goal of being some big deal in education or academic life. I'm going to do the things I believe in and the things that I love and let the ends take care of themselves. But this is right at the heart, I think, of this teaching others we need others as a distraction from our terrible sense of inadequacy of who and what *we* are.

Yet, right within us, we've got the most powerful overwhelming tool that God has ever invented. And man has ever seen. And any religion of the five great religions of the world has ever discovered. And that simple, fundamental overwhelming tool that we've got is ourselves. But most of us are in the position of despising that tool. And that shows how little sense of proportion we have when we look at something that is majestic and that is magnificent and despise it. And you all say, "Yah, but you don't know me." And the answer is, "Yes, I do know you, friend, because I know me."

All of the five great religions of the world have said that thing that's inside you is great and you're in the position of saying, "Oh, they're real dumb and I'm smart. They don't know me." The answer is they do know you. And despising yourself is just a convenient, handy way of running away from the world and running away from your own finite and limited place in the world. None of us are going to be gods, ever. We're just common ordinary dumb human beings.

A student of mine was going to teach rock climbing in an Outward Bound school in Ely, Minnesota, this summer. And Jim was saying, "Hey, Jess, I wonder about how I'm going to do as a teacher?" And I said, "Jim, you're going to do great." And he looked at me and said, "Well I've never taught rock climbing before and I'm going to try to have this little school spring quarter where I will try out as a teacher on guys."

I said, "Jim, you've got no problems, because you've got two things going for you. One," I said, "you love rock climbing and you know a great deal about it. The second thing you've got going for you is that you've taken a look at this set of ideas and you've got a halfway decent heart, both toward yourself and toward your students. So you'll be able on the first day of class, to say to them, 'Hey, you guys, you know I'm going to teach you rock climbing. And I know a lot about rock climbing, but I've never taught it to people before. So occasionally, as I go along talking to you here, there are going to be things that I'm not going to explain well, and your job is to bust in quick and ask questions.' "

So Jim's going to explain rock climbing, and somebody's going to ask a question. And what he does right there is what separates the men from the boys. Jim is either going to be able to hear the question and answer it without seeing this as some fantastic frightening threat to his low quality of instruction. So he will answer the question soft and easy. Or, he's going to see that question and hear it as a threat and just knock that kid right out of the saddle and say, "Shut up! If you would listen, you would have heard. I already explained that five minutes ago." And this is the point, right there, that makes the difference between good teachers or poor teachers, good parents or poor parents, good workers or poor workers. I watch the men building our new house. The poor workers are the ones who are too afraid to admit they don't know how to do something so they go ahead and foul things up.

So here again, we find that in teaching these ideas to others and reaching out to them, we've gone full circle. We're right back to the feeling that "I'm just a little dwarf Norwegian worm hiding inside this fancy shell, and I don't dare let anybody see it. Because if I do they'll run away in horror." But I need to understand that there's all kinds of those other semi-dwarf Norwegian worms around too. And that I ain't much, baby—but I'm all I got. So I need to teach by telling my own Norwegian story. It's the only story I know anything about.

NINETEEN

To Be Continued in Our Lives

A woman told me, "I've always been taught that a child is to be seen and not heard. This resulted in my being inferior and inhibited in my behavior." So I told her, "Yes, but what's your excuse today? What can you do for yourself? Get the hell away from it. From where the sun now stands live your own damn life." It reminded me of the woman who was yelling at me recently, "I feel so inferior, I feel like I'm the only person in the world who's no good!" I said, "You dummy." I said, "How can you look around you at all the dumb things other people do and still persist in the delusion you're the only dummy?" "But," she said, "I always thought I was the only one who had all those weird, queer feelings." I realized afterwards that she was just kicking up a cloud of dust, to avoid the problem of coming to grips with her own actions.

The way I likened it is this: It's just like you are on a ship, on an ocean voyage and a tornado comes along and knocks everybody else overboard. So you've come to your senses down there in the hold of the ship. You struggle to the top and look around. Lo and behold you're the only one there and here's this big ocean liner, careening through the water, zig-zagging around. So, what do you do? You find your way to wherever the wheel is and you recognize that thing that's spinning around as the wheel. You grab hold of it and stop it spinning around. You stick a broomstick in it and you look

217

around for something that must be a compass. You're out in
the Atlantic someplace so you figure you'd better get back to
New York or someplace on the coast. Where's that, well, it's
west.

So you turn the ship around until you see a mark on the
compass that goes somewhere near west, whatever it looks
like. You get her headed back west and then you start looking
around for a navigation chart and you start studying navigation like crazy. But you're going to hit somewhere along the
Atlantic coast. Because you know if you're in the Atlantic
and you head west, you're going to hit land, someplace. When
you hit land, you can jump overboard, and swim to shore.

Life is the same way. Sure you feel frightened as you realize you're steering this great big, damned ship. Well, that's
just us. But now either we are in control of that ship or we're
sitting there in the hold pounding our head against the wall
screaming, "Won't somebody come and speak to me? Oh!
Woe is me." That's a beautiful way to go isn't it? "Oh gosh it's
awful that I'm stranded here alone in this ship. Isn't this terrible? Isn't it sad that I am so alone?" No. That person has
never heard my truism, too much philosophy rots the mind.

They're proceeding to let too much philosophy rot their
mind. They're kicking up this storm of questions. This woman
says, "but I have all these questions." You've had all these
questions all your life, and what the hell good have they ever
done you? Not a damn thing. Forget about the damned questions, they're just serving as distractions, from the fact that
you have to get to where in the hell the wheel is and hold it
and then start doing something with it. So I don't give a damn
how you got kicked around. You know we all got kicked
around, in one way or another, through no fault of our parents, through no fault of society really. Because they were the
best parents and the best society that happened to be available
at the moment that the stork dropped us down the chimney.
So, what the hell do we do? From where the sun now stands,
we take whatever resources we have and we go to war with
them. And you say, "Well that isn't enough." And I say,
"Okay, put your head in the sand and forget about it. Let
somebody shoot you in the rear end with a bunch of arrows."

You've got a choice, pick up whatever tools you've got and
go with them. But don't sit around crabbing and complaining
and crying. I don't like the tools I've got to go to war with either sometimes, but they're the best ones I've got. I ain't much,

baby—but I'm all I've got. Right? It seems to me that's all there is to it.

Now, you say, "I'm scared, frightened." So what, so what else is new? So am I. You say, "That's a dumb idea you've got." Name me a better one. You say, "I'm not going to make much progress, I'm not going to be a very good navigator." Who in the hell else is going to run your ship? Will society or your mother or your father's ghost? Hell, no. They'll do a far worse job than you will. Just do what you're supposed to do. But who wants to be doing something he is afraid of doing? Well, that's right. Go out and find the things you can do that are easy for you and do all the things that are easy for you that you can find. Freud says there's two things in the world, to love and to work, so you've got to find some love and you've got to find some work that will give you dignity and self-respect. And that sure as hell doesn't mean things that are mean and distasteful and hard. So you learn to love and you learn to work and the two, they help each other back and forth.

All you can do in life is build your own confidence, like that little guy up in the wheelhouse. You've got the broomstick stuck in the wheel to make it stop spinning. You're headed generally west. You're going through those navigation books like crazy. I sympathize with your plight, I've got the same problem, but I can't get inside your skin. I can't do it for you. I can't help you by doing anything but help myself. If I concentrate on what I'm supposed to be doing, I won't serve as a distraction for you and I won't cause additional trouble for you. The more I am myself, the more you are free to be yourself. All of you have difficulty, all of you have trouble. You say, "Well, you have less troubles than I have." I don't understand that idea. What the hell is less troubles than anybody else? We're both alive.

Many of my students are quite nervous at this point. In fact, a fairly common question is, "Hey Jess, how am I going to make this thing stick? We're sitting here. We've got the support of a whole room full of people who pretty much believe in these ideas. They are pretty willing to use them and go with them as far as they can. What's going to happen two weeks from now, and three weeks from now when this group breaks up and goes to the four winds?"

Someone was asking me this recently. And I said that, in a

way these ideas can be likened to when you were taught to
float. When somebody taught you to float, they held their
hand under you when you floated in the water. And then if
they were wise, they gradually and easily moved their hand
away. And you didn't know it. And it seems to me that this is
one way we can look at taking these ideas and keeping them
going in our life.

There's another way we can look at them. I'll bet you plenty that you will have trouble ever forgetting the idea of acceptance of yourself and acceptance of others. I don't care how
many years it is down the path; you're going to run into some
tough deal with yourself and I just cannot believe that this
concept of acceptance that we have spent so much time on
will be lost to you. And with that idea, you can reconstruct
most of the rest of them. You probably frequently feel alone
and lost. In your aloneness, I think you will find it hard to
forget the idea of, "I've got to take the first step. I've got to go
and be real to somebody or they're not going to be real back."
And if you're having a problem with someone, you're going to
have a hard time forgetting: If there is a problem here, I
caused it.

We've talked of our needs for love from other people.
Some kind of close relationship with them. These ideas are
reinforced by all kinds of other people who are talking about
the same things. The songs, for example, are full of it. I think
you're going to have a tough time forgetting that. Now applying it in your daily life is a little bit different.

Here are a couple of papers I think you might be interested
in. They were written in the middle of my course and typically a lot happens in the last part of the course. But as you can
see, the person who wrote this first paper certainly was a different person than she was, in some ways, at the beginning of
the course. That kind of difference isn't going to disappear
that fast because most of these papers represent not just a
kind of an intellectualization, not just a play back of ideas,
but they're something a little bit deeper than that.

As I see it, the main object in life is to enjoy it to the
fullest. A person should do the things that give him pleasure or merely do as he wants to. A person's actions do
have limits though. These limits are placed on him because of the people he chooses to give his love to. Or one

might say, he places them on himself because of his desire for those he loves to be happy also.

A person derives much of his happiness from the happiness of those who are close to him. The most essential part of a person's life is the people to whom he gives his love and from whom he receives love in return. In my opinion, without people to love and receive love from, life would be empty.

To me, the main objective of this course is to learn how to give love freely and unconditionally. And how to receive the same love from others. This love is so important because it creates a person's happiness. The first step in learning how to love, is to learn to love one's self. A person must accept himself as he is before he can accept others as they are. Once a person loves himself, he can freely give some of this love to others. Or in other words, he can be real.

To be real to others is to accept others as they are and to communicate to them from one's heart. The most amazing thing I find in these ideas is that if a person is real to others and gives his love to them, he automatically receives the same unconditional love back. I see this as the highest compliment there is to human nature. Then from this returned love, one finds more love which he can give to others. This giving and receiving of love can create a never ending chain of happiness.

This never ending chain of happiness is a great thing. But where does it start. It must start within one's self. Most people, for fear of being rebuffed, wait for others to start the chain and consequently miss out on much needed love.

A common feeling is, if he did something for me, then I would do something for him. A person who is truly at peace with himself and loves himself, will have the courage to take the initial step. His philosophy will be, "if I do something for him, then he will do something for me." His objective is not a selfish one concerned with only what he can gain, but merely a realization of his basic need for love from others.

One idea I find especially heartening is that if a person lets himself, there are many people he can love. To every person there is a good side and a bad side. To love a person, one must accept the bad side just as he accepts his own faults, but one must dwell on the good side of a person and give him credit for his good qualities. Too often it is the tendency for people to find fault with others or even to search for it. All these ideas can be reduced to the simple statement, people need to love and be loved. Love is needed before many things can be pursued. Love is needed to attain goals, to learn from others and to make significant changes in one's behavior. Love is needed for happiness.

Now, that was written by a twenty-year-old girl after she had spent five weeks with these ideas. Her words say to me the key ideas. But between the lines, I sense a feeling of a change in behavior.

Now, what are some of the crucial steps that we've gone over? That paper, in a few paragraphs, did a very fine job of saying what it has taken me a whole book to tell you.

Well, we started out talking about the fact that there could be some different kind of life than the one we are leading. And most of you say, "Thank heaven for that!" Because I don't find too many people that are excessively happy with their life. Sometimes we aren't even aware of how we feel.

We're inclined to kind of gloss over our problems a lot of times until it's too late, and then all of a sudden we're brought up real short saying, "Whoa, I was in deep trouble and have been in deep trouble for a long time and didn't even know it."

A student came to my office recently and she said, "Jess, I don't have all those deep problems like I see people having in discussion sections." And I said, "Oh? I don't believe that."

I said, "Tell me about your life." She said she had a boy friend and he and she were fighting a certain amount. And I said, "Well, why?" It turned out they had some problems between them. It turned out that her folks have always been violently opposed to his religion and that this has been a source of friction from the time she started dating.

Okay. Is this a problem between people? Sure it is. It's a sign of the tons of prejudices of one kind or another that we all have. And those prejudices hurt us the worst when we take those prejudices and use them against the people in our own family.

So the point is, all of us have difficulties in our lives. I see proof of this in our small towns. You can see the difficulties people have with life so clearly in a small town because you know so much about so many people. In a typical town in my experience, there are very few exceptionally sweet people who are so much at home with themselves and the world, that they're trouble to no one and they're a help to a great, great many people. Out of a town of five hundred, six hundred or a thousand, there are only a very, very few of these people. To me this is an illustration of just how hard it is to live all these ideas. If I could live the ideas in this book, I would be one of those few. But I have to put myself in with all the rest of the people in that little town. I'm trying but I'm not making it very well, and I can't be lulled to sleep by the fact that these ideas are easy to talk about. They are simple. But they aren't easy. They're terribly hard. There are ten thousand ways that Jess Lair can find to escape from Jess Lair, and not be himself. And there is only one way I can face myself.

I mentioned that the fundamental principle that I see operating here is our need for other people. And this, as I see, is the balance wheel of life. The writer of the paper I quoted pointed it out very nicely. And this is the answer. So many students misunderstand what I'm saying to them as being selfish when I say concentrate on yourself, work on yourself.

You say, "Yah, but there's all those other people out there I've got to help." That's just anger, that's not helping. How can you help others, when you despise yourself? And the people that scream to me most, "I've got to help other people," when I get down to their core, I see and they see, that they do truly despise themselves. This is why they're not looking at themselves. And why they're not willing and able to look at themselves. Because they do so hate and despise the things they see within themselves.

What kind of gifts of love can you carry in a bucket with all those holes in it?

The answer is you cannot help others when you despise yourself. You may be able to loan them five dollars, but if you do so, it will probably be in the kind of poisonous way where you will everlastingly be giving the person the bad eye because they didn't give you back the five dollars. Or they waited too long in giving it back to you. That kind of favor I don't want in my life, and those of you who see your role in life as helping others and who despise yourself, please don't ever help me. I don't think I could stand it.

You need to be willing to go to work on yourself. And as I see it, the balance wheel here is your need for others.

Again, it's like the psychologist with the little rat. Before the rat's going to press his bar, he's going to have to come up with a packet of food pellets. I've never seen a psychologist in the world who's invented some way of getting that rat to press his bar without coming up with the packet of food pellets *first*.

This is the fundamental principle in our lives: If we need other people, we need to find a way to get them. This, of course, is where being real comes in. You can describe it on any of a variety of basis as I've talked about it. Ranging from being real on up to telling it like it is with you in your very deepest heart. That's being real—blazingly so.

I've seen people take and turn on a whole crowd of strangers, just bam! Just like that. By just reaching down into their guts and into their hearts and pulling up something that was there. Now you don't need to be that real regularly, all of the time.

The kind of realness that you need daily, continuously, is rigorous emotional honesty with yourself. I think your anger comes out of your fear, and your fear comes out of your terrible loneliness and your terrible sense of inadequacy.

The minute that you turn and say, I ain't much, baby, but I'm all I got, a lot of that sense of inadequacy goes away because you are able to see that you are no more inadequate than anybody else. And because you are no more inadequate than anybody else, you've got the same tools to work with that anybody else has.

But you've got one great big head start on them in that you know it and you're using your tools because you turned and looked at yourself and the other person hasn't. So much of your fear then, melts away. As the fear melts away, the anger that comes out of it drops away. So the way to handle your anger is not to spew it around the world and get rid of it by blowing your stack every five minutes but the way to get rid of your anger is to get at your fear. So that you can be at peace with yourself, deep down.

When you are around people who are rigorously honest about themselves in the sense of their feelings and their motivations, you are warmed and comforted and reassured and you are calmed down. Your fears go away, and with them, your angers. So rigorous personal honesty, mostly about our own feelings and about our own responses to things is tremendously necessary and yet it is very, very rare.

Then there has to be a desire for change. An awful lot of you have a desire for change. Some of you have not, at this moment at least, seen and felt much of a desire to change. The fact that you've been able to minimize your problems, in a sense, says that your own problems aren't that particularly bad and gnawing at you at the moment. But just give them time, friend, and they will. Cause I've never seen anybody yet that was immune from the problems of life.

Now another way of putting it is there are laws of human relations and those laws are just as fundamental as the laws of physics. If you jump off the top of a building, you're going to fall and you're going to break your leg. One of the things that makes the laws of human relationship tougher to understand, tougher to cope with, tougher to figure out, is that the consequences are usually delayed. We don't get that immediate confirmation of right or wrong.

When we bug somebody, it may be a week later before they bug us back. It's very hard to find out what we did to them. But this is the advantage of some of these other things that we are talking about, these good things. Because there is an immediate response to them. There is an immediate reward or an immediate reaction that tells you, "Yes this is right."

Those of you who have had the experience of being blazingly real have seen, man, that really opens up the door to somebody else. And once you've had that experience, you've seen, yah, there is lawfulness out there. The things that are happening in the world around me are not capricious events. It isn't somebody shooting dice and then dealing me whatever breaks there are without any respect for the things I do. Then you have the comfort of knowing: Not only are you not alone in the world, but the world will treat you about as well as you treat it.

An old alcoholic was telling me about his twenty-five years as an alcoholic and as a wino. The way he put it, "I was a big man in wino circles because I was so good at getting money out of people for a bottle. And in the wino circle, when you can get money for a bottle you are a very big man. I was drinking some kind of off brand stuff. When I would panhandle, I'd ask a guy for a quarter and I'd be breathing right in his face. My breath was so bad, that it practically knocked him over. He'd fish out a dollar just to get rid of me."

That's the way that man lived for a long time. He said,

"They talked about heaven and hell. I don't know about what heaven is or what it might be like, but I know what hell was like cause that's what I was living for twenty-five years." Then he got rid of alcoholism and got sober. And for the first couple of years that he was sober, he said that being sober and thinking as bad as he was was just as bad as being an alcoholic, in fact maybe worse.

In fact, one alcoholic's wife one time said, "You're off the bottle but I wish you were drinking again because you are so cantankerous and so hard to handle." Because the crux of alcoholism is not the bottle but is the stinking thinking that leads to the drinking. And until you get rid of that stinking thinking you're in trouble. "Oh the world is trying to do me in. Oh, woe is me."

This man was talking later about the last twenty years of his life. When he first went dry, he wanted to stay sober and get $10,000 because to him that represented the height of financial security. Well the funny thing is now, he doesn't care about money. He says he doesn't need $10,000 because as long as you've got your thinking right, you don't need any more money than it takes to buy groceries today. The money that it takes to buy groceries tomorrow will take care of itself if you're doing the things that you should be doing. You can make the money that you'll need tomorrow. And if you need an extra thousand dollars or five thousand dollars, all you need to do is just go out and make it. Because you've got the tools all of a sudden to work with.

Now this is how a world that seems completely capricious and unlawful turned into a world of lawfulness. And this man is hanging in there on that kind of thin razor's edge that he has found is the only true way to go.

It's been a funny thing for me. Ten years ago when I went in search of myself I had Grandpa's religion available to me—I had Grandpa's God. But Grandpa's God wasn't able to help me in that process, and it hadn't been in the past because with Grandpa's God, I had managed to get my life all screwed up. No, I don't say there was something wrong with Grandpa's God. That vision of God as frightening and avenging was my own twist. It was my problem not God's or Grandpa's. So I had to get rid of Grandpa's God and get one that worked in my life.

Just as I have told you to make a compassionate break with your parents, it seems to me, that you and I need, too, to look upon our respective religions with compassion. Most of us have some strong negative feelings along this line. But if we can say, "Well, you know, this or that religion and this or that people in that religion did the best they could." They were trying to do something good. If sometimes in our cases, it didn't work out quite as good as they would have liked and you and I would have liked, well that's the breaks of the game, nobody's perfect.

And, when I say Grandpa's God, it doesn't mean you and I need to change to some different God than the one we're with now, it's just a different view of the same God. In the Bible itself are two views—one a vengeful, frightening view of a terrible God, a punishing God. And the other one is a view of a gentle, loving kindly God.

We talked about acceptance of all the different kinds of aspects of our life. Acceptance of our sexuality. A few idiots have misinterpreted what I am saying as, "Oh boy, Jess says that anything goes." Well, if you've gotten this far, you know that I'm saying the exact opposite. The danger is that you can talk yourselves into a lot of things that will be a deep offense to what's in your bones. And the point isn't that anything goes, but very little goes—if anything.

But the answer is we've got a ton of wild feelings and thoughts and problems in this area and we'd better look at them straight, head on and accept them and see them and call them just exactly what they are. Because according to Carl Rogers' statement, the curious paradox is that when I accept myself as I am, then I can change. The paradox is that when we accept all of our sexual feelings just as they are, then they are a lot easier to handle constructively. And they are a lot less likely to be destructive in our life.

I talked to you about acceptance of goals. But many have misunderstood my insistence that we have no goals. You say, "We gotta have goals." And of course we've gotta have goals. I had the goal of being a teacher, and moving to Montana and getting a Ph.D. But I had goals that I was constantly checking against the reality of my life. And I didn't have goals that were destructive to me as a person.

And most of all I did not have those materialistic, status-orientated goals that I see so much in life that just show a complete disrespect for who and what we are. I grant you that a Ph.D. is a status goal and I needed it as an ego patch. But I was able to afford it without making the people in my life pay too high a price for it. It's like a Cadillac. If you need one and can pay cash or handle the payments easily, buy one. But don't buy a Cadillac with your blood or your family's blood.

And furthermore, we've got to watch out that the goals we have, even the short-term ones, don't bind us to ourselves. Because so much of me has been discovered by just letting myself go and letting myself do the things I wanted to do.

This whole area of my teaching that is in this book came about by accident. As a hobby, in a sense, I had been studying these ideas for fifteen years. I started out by reading a couple of books by Reilly on successful human relations. And I'd been studying these things and never really saw their practical application beyond helping me in my own affairs. But the more I studied these ideas, the more I thought about them, the more things that fit into place.

It was almost an accident that I was invited to speak on them. But when I spoke for two and a half days on ideas that I had been sixteen to twenty years in assembling, all of a sudden I found out what it was that was in me. And I didn't even know it was there. Here I was supposed to be some kind of a big shot management consultant. Well, I was a very poor manager of myself because I was not able to look into myself and see truly what was there. And I submit to you that my experience in this thing should be a caution to you. If you say, "I'm going to be this kind of thing or that kind of thing," and if you do that too hard and rigidly, you trap yourself and narrow yourself in and you keep yourself from the kind of growth that is very crucial to you.

I talked about acceptance of our death and grief. Until we can learn to handle grief and our death, we're in trouble. I saw in a quotation in Zen the other day where it said that the goal of Zen is about the same as the goal of Christianity. It is to help us see the spiritual side of life, the non-material side of life, to the point where there is no end to our living. There's a time when we stop breathing, but it's just a smooth calm time and that's it. This is supposed to be a Christian country that believes in Heaven. Yet no country I know of has a more morbid fear of death. I'm scared stiff of dying. It paralyzes me and throws my life out of balance. And I don't handle it very well. And I don't think very many other people I know are able to handle it very well either. Most other people I've seen in society don't. Their behavior in the presence of death is the best sign that they don't handle it very well.

Those are some of the things we've talked about accepting. Those are some of the ways that we can get this rigorous emotional honesty. The idea that I understand the very least is the relationship between acceptance and change. The curious paradox is that when I accept myself as I am, then I can change. It doesn't say how, it doesn't say if we'll change or not. It just says, then I can change. And I know that I don't accept myself completely. I want certain things to change about myself. So I'm not completely accepting and I don't understand this either.

Also, acceptance does not mean approval. I can look at some aspect of my life and say, "Yah I've got this and that kind of wild feelings in this area." It doesn't mean I approve of them. So I don't understand. There are a lot of inconsistencies here and that's not very hard to understand. This life is an infinitely complex thing. And yet we are finite human beings. And I see part of the task of life is to be able to handle that complexity and confusion and face right square into it and take it just that way.

But the thing that I see most of all is that I must do these things. I must get rid of that stinking thinking of yesterday, last year and the years before that. And I must live this way, because if I do not, I will die. Either on my feet or physically. And to me the living death of being dead to the world around me is the worst of all. And this is so hard for me to do that I have to try it five minutes at a time.

One way to put it is that we must be like the little leaf that falls from the tree into the brook. It moves completely with the current. I see that I need to do this with my life so that I am open enough to all that is happening to move with that current. But there is a part of me that fights this idea. I want to put an outboard motor on my little leaf so I can really make progress—whatever that is.

Now that I've had a chance to see how harmful some of that so-called progress is to my life, it is easier for me. Now that I've had a chance to experience the joy and beauty that comes from letting my life go in directions I couldn't possibly have anticipated, it is easier to let go. There is a good phrase to hang onto here—Let go and let God. If the God part is troublesome for you, put it another way and learn to let go and flow with the mainstream of the universe.

Now this all sounds very pat and simple. "It can't be that simple," you say. Well maybe. But there are an awful lot of people I know who live this way and like it a lot better than the way they lived before. "Is it just inside the person?" No. One of the most common comments I hear from students is that the people around them comment on how different they are—how much they have changed. So what we are talking about is something other people can see and feel as well as something you can feel within yourself.

Is there any possibility that this whole new way of living for you or me is just another, more successful form of faking and isn't the real me? Yes, there is that chance because we are finite and can't be certain of ultimate truths. But I know two things. If this is faking it, it sure is a lot more satisfying for me than the old way of faking it. And it's easier on the people around us.

I see my problem as one of intense concentration. How can I live just five minutes at a time so that I can respond to the real situation instead of some stereotyped perception of it. To do this I need to be calm and rested. When I am tired and distracted I make most of my mistakes. So I value my calm.

I have found that a day has only about half as many hours as I used to think it had. So I don't try to do but a few important things each day, and I let the rest go. Only this way can I get those crucial things done well and really be alive to what's going on around me the rest of the day. This way I don't need to throw days away because of being too busy. And most of the time when a problem comes up in my life or a student walks in my office I can truthfully say, "I'm not busy." But part of this is that I don't need being busy any more as a way to run away. I now value its opposite, not being busy, as an important part of my life.

This doesn't mean I don't get as much done. Oddly, I get a lot more and better work done now than I used to. That's nice but it's just a side benefit to the major benefit—the joy of living.

I said earlier that this whole system sounded simple. It is simple. But so is Einstein's formula $E = mc^2$ simple, but I guess it explains an awful lot. Golf is simple too, because what counts is just hitting the ball evenly and smoothly and the shots that go the farthest and straightest are the ones I hit the easiest. So these ideas are simple and they are easy but applying them consistently is the hardest thing there is. It takes intense concentration—five minutes at a time—to do these things this easy, simple way. And it takes great patience with myself so that I can accept all the obvious problems in my life that I don't or can't deal with very well at any given time.

There is one special problem that you will have as a reader of this book. You will not have had the feeling of sitting in a group of people and feeling these ideas grow in the people around you. In that situation, when you have your doubts about what you are feeling being real and being widely shared by all kinds of people, you could simply look at the people around you and feel them feeling the same as you.

You can handle this problem by creating your own groups —your own little centers of realness that will last. As you are more real in your family, the other members of your family can be more real back to you and with each other. And that is something that lasts and can help you day after day. You can do the same thing at work and with your friends. And as you do, you literally remake the world around you.

And in the process you'll realize why the Mona Lisa is smiling. Someone had just told her that people were no damn good. She couldn't help smiling a little as she thought of her own life during the past day and the wonderful things that had happened to her. She realized the person who was telling her people were no good was telling her so much more about himself than he was telling her about the people around him because they were the very same people who were around her.

You can change the whole character of your life. You can change people by coming at them straight so they can come back at you straight and clean. You can stay away from people and situations that are poison for you. You can put yourself continually in situations where it is easy and a joy for you. But only you can direct yourself on this path.

Socrates said an unexamined life isn't worth living. There is some tendency to look down on this examination as being too introspective and self-preoccupied. We think it just isn't manly. A recent *Life* story contrasted the introspective Dustin Hoffman in black and white with a colorful picture of John Wayne, the rugged man of action. I don't see a real contrast.

The examination of our life doesn't need to be done openly and out loud, but it needs to be done and it shows. I am struck that in any group of the roughest, toughest men, there are always a few sensitive ones who play a crucial role in keeping the people in the group happy with each other.

So we are talking about examining our life and then trans-

lating our ideas into deeds that touch the people around us so
they can love us back and keep us alive and happy much of
the time so we can weather the sorrows of life.

While we must always concentrate on ourselves, solve our
own problems, there are many consequences for others in
what we do. We must start by concentrating on being real and
finding our own uniqueness. It's like Bronson, in the television
series "Then Came Bronson," said, "I don't want to conquer
the world, I don't want to save it. I just want to see my part of
it clear." That sounds a little lonely. But it isn't.

Each of us will touch thousands of lives in our life. If we
come at people blindly, oblivious to them because we are
blind to ourselves, we can do great harm. But if we get rid of
a little of our self-blindness and really see the people around
us, we will do less hurt to others and often we will be part of
a great joy with other people. That's the way I'm trying to go
because that's the path the people I love are walking and I
want to go along. And it's where the joy and splendor is and
it's what puts a special excitement in what the next five minutes will bring.

Or, as one of my students put it, "I want to learn to show
my family and friends what they mean to me. Not because I
feel I have to make myself say 'I love you,' but by using all
the things you've brought into focus until it's just natural for
me to let them know by a touch or words that I do love them.
It sounds kind of cold to plan something that ought to be
spontaneous. But if I don't, it will probably never happen."

"And I want, so much, to find real joy by sharing with people, by loving them, because what else is there really?"

Or, as another student said, "Now my eyes have seen what
my heart must feel."

Until we meet again—Salude.

TWENTY

Our Magic Cards

So you can compare your responses to some of the ideas in this book with the responses of my students in class, I've picked out some of the most interesting ones so you could get the feeling of how others react to these ideas. And also they're here for the fun of it.

When I started teaching writing, I was looking for a device to get my students writing more freely. Tom Thiss suggested the idea of each student writing a 3X5 card each day and bringing it to class. I found it was a valuable tool for writing, but I found it was even more crucial to me as a means of letting the class communicate with me freely and privately. So now I use 3X5 cards in all my classes.

The student brings a card to class with some comment, question or feeling written on it. The cards need not be signed and about half of them aren't. The cards are left on the table at the front of the room when the student arrives and since I'm not there when he comes, I don't know who has turned in cards and who hasn't.

At the beginning of class I read all the cards and make any comments that are appropriate. My students and I both like the cards very much. In fact, one student called them our magic cards. They make sure that I always go where my students are. And the cards teach me.

I don't ask that the cards be original and I don't ask that quotations be attributed to their source. Personally, I feel that almost nothing that has been said in the last five hundred years is completely original, and I don't want to snarl up my students in chasing down sources. What I find they do is think up their own words, revise another's words, or use another's words directly to reflect their views or feelings. So what these cards reflect is what my students feel and think rather than always original ways of saying something. And most important for you, these cards show you what people feel and think as they hear and work on these ideas in this book.

Much of what I know, my students have taught me in the privacy of our classrooms. So it is appropriate that you should hear directly from some of them. Here are the cards that I set aside from the general run as being outstanding in some way. I have indicated the class or type of students so you can get some perspective of the writers. Next to my teaching students, I like the freshmen best. They are so fresh.

FRESHMEN

Life is like walking through the snow—every step shows.

You don't know what life is until you give mouth to mouth resuscitation.

Good parents are like turtles—hard on the outside and soft on the inside.

Maturity consists of no longer being taken in by oneself.

Life without love is like a cold kiss.

It does not take much strength to do things but it takes great strength to know what to do.

Security is being held.

The darkest hour in a man's life is when he sits down to plan how he can get money without earning it.

We are fools. What do we care about the world, about life? We were born alive and with a gift. Now we are dead. We do not live. We forgot how or is it that we do not care? The world gives us opportunities but we thrust them away. "Let someone else do it," we say. And so someone else does do it. He is the one that does everything else, too. He is the one of thousands that has lived life. He is the one that struggles, that overcomes, that prays for us, that seeks and finds. Ah yes, he is the one that is alive. And we, we die each day as another chance is left to go untouched. Yes we die and such loathsome fools are we. Such loathsome fools.

No man has done what I have done
No man has seen what I have seen
No man has felt as I have felt
Oh how I see I am alone.

No place to go when all is done
No place to go when all is seen
No place to go when all is felt
Oh now I know I am forever.

Take away all love so that there remains only hate. Take away all peace so that there remains only war. Make man an animal with only the instinctive desire to kill, not for reason but for necessity of nature. Obliteration and destruction ensue, and the world again becomes quiet, engulfed with an unequalled peace and tranquillity, until there once again arises a new force that cannot live with itself.

We cannot tell the precise moment when a friendship is formed. As in filling a vessel drop by drop, there is at last a drop which makes it run over. So in a series of kindnesses . . . there is at least one which makes the heart run over.

In work you find reality and in reality a chance to find yourself. I guess that's why I'm lost.

In the dew of little things, the heart finds its mornings and is refreshed.

If one tries to encompass life, one spreads himself too thin. One must let life encompass him and then take what he needs from it. Thus it is possible to coexist with the system.

What is a friend? I will tell you. It is a person with whom you dare to be yourself.

There isn't much in love but being able to stand another's outside long enough to discover his insides. And any man
and any woman could love each other if they could cope
with the outside long enough.

The ancient sun filters through the branches of ancient trees to
warm the ancient earth. In this world of ancient life,
only my love is new.

"Gee, Mom, Dad is swell. God must be like that."

A friend is one who always is.

Is this life or just confusion?

What you are is your folk's fault. But if you stay that way, it
is your own fault.

The greatest mystery is life.

The nonconformists on campus are starting to look so much
alike I can't tell them apart.

Around and around
I run
In ever widening
Circles
Trying to find
A center
For my life.

Life is too serious to be taken seriously.

The opposite of love is not hate, it is indifference.

There is an appointed time to be born and die but the time between the two is of great importance, use it wisely.

The days are slipping through my fingers no matter how hard
I hold.

Little girls were created for boys to love.
I wonder what is holding the boys up?

The thoughts of a hundred thousand men around me.
If I could comprehend just one.

If a man can only be judged by his enemies, then he himself,
is the best judge.

The presence of death crept up on me like a storm in the night. Before I could grasp the ugly feeling, it was too late. All that is left now is to pick up the broken pieces of life and start again.

The beauty of the glistening snow was lost to me, for the blind feel only the harsh cold.

I am an identity floating through a void called life, seeing all the beauty, glory and majesty; yet it signifies nothing for I have never been loved.

I have taken a tremendous bite of the apple of life and found it to be green—but sweet.

I'll always have to get the last word in—maybe that's why I'm always the loser.

Words of love come from the heart unrehearsed and increase as their meaning is received.

Home is a beautiful wonderful place with warmth, love, and companionship. Someday I'll have my own home—someday.

Remember what you do today will determine what you'll be tomorrow.

The girl I am hides deep in me beneath the woman I claim to be. (Don't tell anyone—Okay?)

I often catch myself looking at the past trying to recapture lost joys rather than trying to find the joys and happiness of the present.

If everyone was put on earth for some purpose, why is it that no one knows what they're doing?

Possibly I have never been
Possibly I shall never be.

Now, the present is the only
Part of time that exists—I am.

My world collapsed today. I turned around and you were gone. The world spins round and round. I just fell off in the pit of reality, never to return. Adios compadre.

Happiness is your girl friend in one hand and a can of beer in the other.

Life is like an unknown path in the woods. One does not know where it leads until he tries it himself.

JUNIORS AND SENIORS

Anyone can wear the mask, few don't.

I have something to expiate; a pettiness.

Life is nothing—to live is a talent few have.

I was born lost, and I take no pleasure in being found.

It always rains on our generation.

My heart doesn't sail, it's pushed and crushed with the pushing.

Fighting for peace is like making love for chastity.

The problem is to consciously live. Take direction instead of drifting with the daily schedules.

Loneliness is being in a roomful of people and not being able to trust any of them.

One may find the faults of others in a few minutes while it takes a lifetime to discover our own.

All things fall and are built again.
And those who build them are gay.

Time
Because it is now
It has its own suspension
Instead of twenty-four hours in a day
There is time
    Time for talking
    Time for silence
    Time for being
    Time for thinking
Yes, and time for eating and sleeping
If I use it wisely
There is more of it.

The singing birds lift my spirits.
Their joyousness gives me courage.

Living right has a lasting kick in it.
Living wrong is a bit of foam on top.

How is it that some people can do just fine when getting
something out of a book for a grade but they don't seem
to have any social awareness of other people and their
feelings. Some of us are wondering if it has anything to
do with concrete and abstract abilities. Memorization
from a book is more concrete. Does interacting with people and having consideration for others really require so
much thinking, or are these activities just so difficult for
lazy people.

If you want something very, very badly, let it go free. If it
comes back to you, it's yours forever. If it doesn't, it was
never yours to begin with.

I heard a very profound statement last night. Unfortunately
I've forgotten it.

Life is to live, so live it.

Hate goes beyond the barriers of race, color and creed. It is
sad that the same thing can't be said about love and
friendship.

Thoughts circle backward down a nervous staircase. In a
scream or a whisper ideas enter and leave, in and out, always, always there are books and words. Education becomes living from page to page.

I looked at you across that narrow yet infinite expanse between us. All the diamonds in the world sparkled in your
eyes. All the roses of spring in your cheeks accented the
smile of your love.
  I died a little.

The world seemed so empty and cold; so did I.

When you are cool, the sun is always shining.

Life is like a gumball machine which emits surprises at the
drop of a coin and a turn of a lever. It is but a game of

chance that everyone plays where no one can win without tasting each ball.

The world is like a woman, always changing, ever restless.
It is constantly seeking an unknown goal,
But will probably never know when it has been attained.
I love you world.

I run until I hurt and then I run until I'm in pain and I keep
running until I'm in agony. And when I'm in agony,
That's when I break records.

Words are only necessary after love has gone.

Prayer doesn't change things.
It changes people and they change things.

Men see the world as a prison.
For youths it is a dark, haunting cell.
Maturity adds a window.

Don't worry about what's ahead.
Go as far as you can.
From there you can see farther.

I am unhappy with my miseries until I see other people's plea-
sures.

Last night I sat and listened. I heard and understood what two
people were saying instead of just realizing they were
talking.

A card should have more thought than the three minute walk
to class, which is all this card has had. However, we go
through life with this short preparation for most of our
actions. Could this be the reason why as individuals and
as a whole, everything seems so messed up?

Nothing gives you more in common quicker than finding out
you dislike the same person.

Love is marvelous. The more you give away. The more you
have.

Happiness is going home for the weekend and seeing your
five-year-old brother break into tears because he is glad
to see you home.

These tears are not tears of hurt, of anger, or of deep sadness, but rather tears of pride.

Reason deceives us often, conscience never.

You can never be satisfied with others until you are satisfied with yourself. Others only mirror your faults.

The University teaches us to save time and waste our lives.

Have you ever felt like a big, white buffalo in a herd of 1,000,000 brown ones?

I woke up this morning and said:
Good morning Self, isn't it going to be a wonderful day.

A marriage of minds last forever.

Silence is a figure of speech which is unanswerable, cold and terribly severe.

Laughter is the song of the angels.

What is more lonely than distrust?

To be or not to be is no longer the question;
The question is: How to be.

It seems that everytime people rebel because they don't believe they have enough freedom, I lose some of my freedom. Why is this so?

I am only one, but I am one.

What a wonderful feeling when liking turns to loving.

After all is said and done, much is said and little done.

What we are is God's gift to us, what we become is our gift to God.

Occasional rebellion at rules and requirements reduces pressures and helps me to accept the rules, requirements and responsibilities of my life.

If you are honest because you think that is the best policy, then your honesty has always been corrupt.

No guts—no glory.

What shadows we are
What shadows we pursue.

Waves of calm wash against
The shores of my soul
From where will come the inevitable storm?
What wreckage will it leave behind
On the beaches of my life?

Isn't life beautiful
Isn't life gay
Isn't life the perfect thing
To pass the time away

The scriptures teach us the best ways of living, the noblest
     ways of suffering, and the most comfortable way of
     dying.

What a nothing man makes of himself
When he allows fate to grind his life away.

How could man have evolved from a species as organized
     as the apes?

He who laughs, lasts.

Today when I awoke, I found I was still waiting for tomor-
     row.

We came only to memorize, not to think or question and how
     very sad it is.

The trouble with life is that it is so daily.

"Good, Moral Guys" commit the same sins as the Pagans.

My hands are free but my mind hesitates.

In hope, in faith, I'll love again. The fool I am, I'll always
     pick another wild flower and watch it wilt in my hand.

Laughter bars beautifully.

We need a world in which it is safe to be human.

Every man has his own eyes to choose the world with.

The greatest thing man can create is himself.

Life is a hereditary disease.

Love is a brick wall put up piece by piece, each brick building and strengthening the total wall.

Santa is a hippie.

Love consists in this: That two *solitudes* protect and touch and greet each other.

The most important thing a father can do for his children is love their mother.

Live all the days of your life.

By increasing our capacity to expect the best of others—to offer them our trust—we can enrich our own lives immeasurably.

Why do college children marry?

I see myself as you must see me! I've known what I'm like for a long time, but I've refused to admit it.

My heart knows what my mind still seeks to learn.

We choose our joys and sorrows long before we experience them.

Manliness is not all swagger and swearing and mountain climbing. Manliness is also tenderness, gentleness, consideration. You men think you can decide on who is a man, when only a woman can really know.

A closed mind is a closed heart.

The child in me is crying but I cannot help,
For I know not where he is hurt.

There is but one time—the love time—and all life begins in this season that is so different in each of us.

Is there a greater fault than being conscious of the other person's faults?

Security is when I'm very much in love with somebody extraordinary who loves me back.

What you are when you aren't trying is what you really are.

What is hell? I maintain that it is the suffering of not being able to love.

Joy is not in things, it is in us.

You can love me and I can accept it.
You can hate me and I can accept it.
But I cannot accept indifference.

I learn how much there is to learn.
People in a hurry can neither grow nor decay;
They are preserved in a state of perpetual puerility.

Just imagine: When you were my age, I was just born.

When people are free to do as they please,
They usually imitate each other.

Identity is a gift man confers on another.

Why me God?

The beauty of life is nothing but this,
That each should act in conformity with *his* nature and *his* business.

If you were another person, would you like to be a friend of yours?

I am me, or am I?

Love is not sentimental or gushy. Love is always just, and, in its justice, it is on occasion, tough.

The life you once lived can be found only in the life you now express.

I feel you should play each day man-to-man and set up short-term goals only when they complement your previous accomplishments in that direction.

While there may be one part of us that is seventeen, twenty-two, or forty years old, there may be another part of us which has not yet been born. (Or let us hope there is.)

No problem is so big or so complicated that it can't be run away from.

We are afraid to die, yet are afraid to live.

There is one man who has the right to dominate my life. Who
    is that man? Me!

I'm not as good as I hope to be,
I'm better than I used to be,
And I'm not as bad as I was.

Why didn't somebody tell us what kind of game we were
    playing or how to play it before they gave us life?

Life is the greatest unsolved puzzle in the world.

NURSES—ALL ADULTS

I shall pass this way but once.

Love cures all—if it's true love.

Comfortable to hear being yourself is good (acceptable).
    Much preferred to games. Letting future take its own
    way takes lots of worry out of life.

To accept ourselves as we are sometimes hurts.
Confidence, trust, mutual understanding is really caring.
I am my own worst enemy.

Still water runs deep
                        wide
                            long

There am I
        desperate
                struggling
                        darkness
                            drowning

Suddenly there
            is a hand

And then
        light
            sunshine
                gladness
                    love

How can you overcome the feeling of distrust once you have
    been deceived?

My mind feels like it has been stuffed full of ideas, not all new, but now I don't feel guilty about having them. I did before.

GRADUATE STUDENTS

I feel selfish when I do some things that I enjoy doing.

We were told last week to go out and tell three people that we love them. What is love?

People often don't realize that being able to take love and happiness is as difficult as learning to give it.

I think writing can be harder than just saying what you feel because I know this will be read. What I say is not always really heard.

At the bottom of most fears will be found an over-active mind and an under-active body. We generate fears while we sit. We overcome them by action.

Praise is like sunlight to the warm human spirit; we cannot flower and grow without it. And yet, while most of us are only too ready to apply to others the cold wind of criticism, we are somehow reluctant to give our fellows the warm sunshine of praise.

TEACHERS-TO-BE

The process of controlling behavior has an outstanding characteristic: When it's effective you can't tell who is controlling who.

Education is to live each day in wide-eyed wonder and open ears.

How can somebody love you so much, and yet other people walk by you, as if you don't even exist?

Why can't parents of today understand us?

There is reciprocity in the mother-child relationship. If the mother has no love or trust, neither will the child.
The same is true of the teacher-student relationship. Treat the student like a cheater and he will know what you are.

He can land on the moon but he can't stop war.

He can transplant hearts but he can't fill his own with love.

He can explain love to anyone but he can't stop hating the guy next door.

No riddle, no absurdity—simply man.

When a student learns when and how to reinforce himself, he becomes independent. The teacher has succeeded.

Whatever character or role we play and whatever the scene or setting, the success of the play "Life" like any other play, depends on the picking up of cues.

As a mirror reflects our facial or physical features, the eyes of others will either reflect the warmth or coolness we emit.

Mama tried!

Did you ever wake up in the morning and wonder if that was really you last night?

Everyone is emotionally crippled and we have to rise above this disability.

Our experiences in life are usually forecast by our expectations.

What frightens me is life leaking through my fingers.

Benevolence is a form of hatred.

A bird does not sing because he has an answer . . . he sings because he has a song.

My mind is like a sponge—it absorbs until it feels like collapsing, but it never spills any of its contents. And it perturbs me because I can't communicate with anyone—yet I feel like I am learning. I've heard that learning comes in spurts and plateaus. Could I be at the plateau level now? All these penetrating things are on my mind but while awaiting some semblance of order, they can in no way be communicated with anyone else. (Am I crazy?)

The trouble with being open-minded is that your brains may fall out.

Children are not things to be molded;
But are people to be unfolded.

Life is what living makes it.

Happiness is knowing someone cares.

The real you is somebody else. I want to find that somebody.

I feel like a fly in a nudist colony. I know what to do but I don't know where to start.

Crowding a life does not always enrich it.

When I act differently with different people, does it mean I'm a phony and don't act myself all the time?

Conform to the things that aren't important to you and don't conform to the things that are important to you.

All life is an experiment.

A teacher creates human personalities—in all students with whom he interacts—including himself.

For what's been done to us, are we normal?

There is no misery in not being loved;
Only in not loving.

The beautiful people—those who show love.

People who prefer the finer things in life—prefer people.

Men are ticking with fresh ideas—packed with good news for women.

The tragedy of life is what dies inside a man while he lives.

Human life is unsafe at any speed—and therein lies much of its fascination.

The more you take out of your bucket and put in someone else's, the more you will have in your bucket.

I keep my hands empty for the sake of what I have had in them.

If the happier a person is, the less he eats, then I may die of starvation.

I think it is true that we begin to understand a subject when we begin to teach and practice it. What we have read and learned does not seem to really come alive until we believe it enough to dare act upon it. I never before realized how important action is to development.

There is an old wheeze that love is what makes the world go round. It isn't true. Love keeps it populated. Change is what makes the world go.

Can hate be a defense mechanism?

I would like to thank the guy who spoke up yesterday. He said, "The biggest compliment a woman could give a man was that she wanted to have his child." I had said that once to my husband shortly before we were married. It had impressed him then and he even mentioned it several times later. But, we had really taken what you call wrong turns since then. That simple statement brought back memories of a lot of forgotten things I'd overlooked. I guarantee my husband's life will be easier for a day or two to come. Thank you.

Empathy—your pain in my heart.

Fat. Yep, that's my name. Because of it I can't: wear cute clothes, feel comfortable with people, dance, date, or be attractive. Oh, it was such a convenient excuse for anything that went wrong. Okay. I will accept myself as I am and not use fat as an excuse—already I feel better. Now for five minutes at a time I will try to eat foods that are not fattening. For once I feel I have found an answer.

The law of self-preservation is "me first." Who will and can deny that? You professor??????????????

A clean mind is one that cannot be shocked. To be shocked is to show you that you have repressions that make you interested in what shocks you.

One thing that makes it so hard to accept ourselves is that we are conditioned from the beginning to be so concerned with public opinion. Fear that a lot of people will think you're weird if you're yourself, keeps a lot of people from facing themselves, let alone accept it.

My father was never a very friendly man. He loved people and helped many when they were in need, but he never was one to talk.

A few years back he became very ill and went to the hospital. I could see the will to live leave him. Too many times he felt he had been cut down by people. Many flowers, notes, and cards came but I don't think he ever really saw them.

There is a point where a man loses the will to live and then cannot be helped by flowery words of cheer.

Change? Why I'm like the fellow in the song they sing: "I don't hardly know where I are."

The subject of touching has really been bugging me. I don't object to someone putting a hand on my shoulder or an arm around my neck. But I become fighting mad if someone slaps me on the back or brushes the hair off my face. Since my feelings are so strong, it is difficult to do this. Even my teenage children object to me touching them, but I am trying to work through this and help them chip away their covering.

Can't you "over love" someone? Won't they feel pampered and picked at? People also want to be left alone.

You want me to change and grow. I decided to try it so instead of walking in the house after class and plopping myself down quietly as I normally do, I greeted my wife and my kids with a smile and a kiss. You know, it didn't hurt a bit.

What a dilemma! I have spent years learning how to exist—peacefully—and now you tell me I must revert back to the hell of living. Help me—I'll try.

"Our lives are formed by those who love us and by those who refuse to love us."
I think this really pertains to parental love.

I have always been taught as a child to be seen and not heard. This has resulted in my being inferior and inhibited in my behavior. What can I do for myself. Maybe I could overcome some fears by doing that which I fear, but who wants to do something he is afraid of doing?

You have said, "Do what you want to do." Much of the time I have made myself do what I didn't want to do because it seemed like I would grow from the experience. Looking back I would not give up those experiences. They helped me find and have confidence in myself. Is this wrong in your mind?

Greatness. No matter how large or small the tasks, I am not going to try and make them great. But maybe as I become myself and the tasks are done as I feel them, only this way they may be great, or perhaps interesting.

Thank you for teaching me what I wanted to learn.

Books I Use

Berne, Eric, M.D. *Games People Play*. New York: Grove Press, Inc., 1964. $1.25 in paper. The first fifty pages and the last twenty are loaded with ideas. Read some of the games, too.

Gibran, Kahlil. *The Prophet*. New York: Alfred A. Knopf, Inc., 1923. This book I have used for twenty-four years. It says in a few pages what I have needed many years to start to learn.

Hastings, Donald W., M.D. *Impotence and Frigidity*. Boston: Little Brown and Company, 1963. This book is the only one I've found with a common-sense approach to intercourse. The key findings of the Masters-Johnson studies are included. The book calms you down.

Holland and Skinner. *The Analysis of Behavior*. New York: McGraw-Hill, Inc. $5.95 in paper. A programmed textbook on reinforcement psychology that will make you a more knowledgeable and humane controller of the behavior around you. Anyone with a high school education can learn from this book in ten hours a ton of psychology that has immense applications to everyday living.

Kazantzakis, Nikos. *Zorba The Greek*. New York: Ballantine Books, Inc., 1952. 75¢. Contains Zorba's view on sin and women. Shows a man with a heart and a mind trying to teach something to a college-professor type.

Masters and Johnson. *Human Sexual Inadequacy*. Boston: Little, Brown and Company, 1970. $12.50. This book shows that many sexual problems can be quickly solved by teaching the partners about sex and how to communicate with each other sexually. But, to me, it also demonstrates a deeper point. There must be a reasonably good heart between two people and toward themselves before sex can be much more than just a successful physical act. A powerful book and all the husbands and wives I know could benefit from reading it.

May, Rollo, Ph.D. *Man's Search for Himself*. New York: W. W. Norton & Company, Inc., 1953. 95¢ in paper. May analyzes the roots of the problems of our times and tells us how to free ourselves so we can use our past and ourselves more constructively.

Mink. *The Behavior Change Process*. New York: Harper & Row, 1968. About $2.00. A shorter version of the ideas in Holland and Skinner. You can get a lot of psychology in two or three hours.

Neil, A. S. *Freedom—Not License*. New York: Hart Publishing

Co. $1.65 in paper. A good answer to the question of the difference between freedom and permissiveness.

————. *Summerhill: A Radical Approach to Child Rearing*. New York: Hart Publishing Co., 1964. $1.95 in paper. This book explains the idea of freedom applied to formal education.

Reilly, William J. *Successful Human Relations*. New York: Harper & Row, 1952.

————. *How To Make Your Living in Four Hours a Day—Without Feeling Guilty About It*. New York: Harper & Row, 1955. Either of these two books give you details on Reilly's system of human relations and work. The second book is out of print but is in many libraries.

Reps, Paul. *Zen Flesh, Zen Bones*. New York: Doubleday Anchor Books. $1.45 in paper. It has a wonderful introduction that explains that Zen is not a sect but a habit of self-searching through meditation. The stories are just a few sentences each but hit like a hammer.

Rogers, Carl, Ph.D. *On Becoming A Person*. Boston: Houghton Mifflin Company, 1961. This book gives Rogers' views on the process of psychotherapy and the role of the therapist.

Roth, Philip. *Portnoy's Complaint*. New York: Bantam Books, Inc., 1970. $1.50 in paper. This is the only book I have ever seen that tells some of the wild feelings of boys and the boys in men have about sex. It helps my male students see their sexual feelings clearer. And it helps my female students, especially the married ones, see why their husbands act, feel and need as they do.

Snitzer, Herb. *Living at Summerhill*. New York: Collier Books, 1964. $1.95 in paper. Many wonderful pictures and has conversations from the school's meetings.

Van Doren, Carl. *Benjamin Franklin*. World Publishing Company. A fine biography of a man of many parts who was an amazingly effective practicing psychologist. I don't see any man since his time who has exceeded him in this respect.

ABOUT THE AUTHOR

Leaving a career as marketing and management consultant, Jesse Lair received a Ph.D. in Psychology from the University of Minnesota and then moved his family to Montana, where he is doing what he likes best—teaching—in the school of education at the state university. He privately issued the original version of this book for his students but as it went on to win wide readership and high praise, he rewrote and expanded it to the present form. He is also the author of *"Hey God, What Should I Do Now?"*